Canadian Literature

Canadian Literature

Faye Hammill

Edinburgh University Press

© Faye Hammill, 2007

Edinburgh University Press Ltd
22 George Square, Edinburgh

Typeset in Ehrhardt
by Servis Filmsetting Ltd, Manchester, and
printed and bound by CPI Group (UK) Ltd
Croydon, CR0 4YY

A CIP record for this book is available from the British Library

ISBN 978 0 7486 2161 3 (hardback)
ISBN 978 0 7486 2162 0 (paperback)

The right of Faye Hammill
to be identified as author of this work
has been asserted in accordance with
the Copyright, Designs and Patents Act 1988.

Contents

Series Preface

The study of English literature in the early twenty-first century is host to an exhilarating range of critical approaches, theories and historical perspectives. 'English' ranges from traditional modes of study such as Shakespeare and Romanticism to popular interest in national and area literatures such as the United States, Ireland and the Caribbean. The subject also spans a diverse array of genres from tragedy to cyberpunk, incorporates such hybrid fields of study as Asian American literature, Black British literature, creative writing and literary adaptations, and remains eclectic in its methodology.

Such diversity is cause for both celebration and consternation. English is varied enough to promise enrichment and enjoyment for all kinds of readers and to challenge preconceptions about what the study of literature might involve. But how are readers to navigate their way through such literary and cultural diversity? And how are students to make sense of the various literary categories and periodisations, such as modernism and the Renaissance, or the proliferating theories of literature, from feminism and marxism to queer theory and eco-criticism? The Edinburgh Critical Guides to Literature series reflects the challenges and pluralities of English today, but at the same time it offers readers clear and accessible routes through the texts, contexts, genres, historical periods and debates within the subject.

Martin Halliwell and Andy Mousley

Acknowledgements

I am grateful, first of all, to the editors of this series, particularly Professor Martin Halliwell, for much wise advice, and also to Jackie Jones at Edinburgh University Press, for assistance and encouragement. James Dale managed the publication process with great professionalism.

I am also very grateful to Professor Coral Ann Howells for her wonderful support and advice in relation to this particular project, and also during the course of my earlier research in the field. For invaluable comments on draft sections, I would like to thank Dr Susan Billingham, Professor Michael Burgess, Dr Louise Harrington, Professor Jonathan Percy, Dr Verena Klein, Meichuen Wang, and especially Emma Smith and Professor Ged Martin. For suggestions about material to include, I would like to thank the two anonymous readers of my book proposal, as well as Dr Laura Moss. This book contains several ideas originally suggested to me when I was a student, by Dr Chris Gittings and Dr Danielle Fuller, and I appreciate our ongoing conversations.

None of the sections in this book is reprinted from another source, although certain short passages are adapted from my earlier publications. Two paragraphs on each of *The Journals of Susanna Moodie* and *Wilderness Tips* are adapted from *Literary Culture and Female Authorship in Canada, 1760–2000* (Amsterdam and New York: Rodopi, 2003). Two paragraphs on *Wild Geese* are taken from 'The Sensations of the 1920s: Martha Ostenso's *Wild Geese* and

Mazo de la Roche's *Jalna*', in *Studies in Canadian Literature*, 28: 2 (2003), 66–89. Several sentences in the introduction are adapted from 'British-Canadian Literary Relations' in *Britain and the Americas: Culture, Politics, and History: A Multidisciplinary Encyclopedia*, ed. Will Kaufman and Heidi Slettedahl Macpherson (Santa Barbara: ABC-Clio, 2005), pp. 535–40.

   I am grateful to Cardiff University for research support and for a period of study leave, and to the AHRC for a research leave award to enable the completion of this book.

Arts & Humanities
Research Council

Abbreviations

Abbreviations used in the Chronology and Glossary are as follows:

Canadian provinces and territories

AB	Alberta
BC	British Columbia
MB	Manitoba
NB	New Brunswick
NL	Newfoundland and Labrador
NWT	Northwest Territories
NS	Nova Scotia
NU	Nunavut
ON	Ontario
PEI	Prince Edward Island
QC	Quebec
SK	Saskatchewan
YT	Yukon

Other abbreviations

BNA	British North America
CBC	Canadian Broadcasting Corporation

Note on spelling

The English names for Quebec, Montreal and so on are used instead of the French forms (Québec, Montréal), except when they occur as part of a quoted phrase in French or the name of a French organisation.

Chronology

Items marked with an asterisk are defined in more detail in the Glossary. Standard abbreviations are used for Canadian provinces (see Abbreviations), but 'Newfoundland' is not abbreviated in the table until 1949, when it became a province of Canada.

Date	Historical Events	Literary Events
11000 BC	Evidence of human habitation in Canada (Yukon); humans probably present much earlier	
9000 BC	Permanent fishing settlements on northwest coast	
1000 BC	Evidence of agriculture, Atlantic regions	
800 BC	Dorset culture, Hudson Strait	
300 AD	Prairie village culture	
985	First European sighting of Canada	
1000	Viking settlement in Newfoundland; Thule culture begins to supersede Dorset	
1390-1450	*Iroquois Confederacy founded	
1497	Giovanni Caboto sails under English flag from Bristol to Newfoundland	

Date	Historical Events	Literary Events
1524	Giovanni da Verrazzano, sailing under French flag, names the northeastern coastal region of North America *'New France'	
1534	Jacques Cartier sails from St Malo to the Gulf of St Lawrence	
1556	First map of New France	
1576-8	Martin Frobisher's Arctic expeditions; by now Thule has developed into Inuit	Earliest extant writing about Canada (exploration accounts)
1583	Newfoundland claimed as England's first overseas colony	
1604	Settlement in French colony of *Acadia	
1605	Samuel de Champlain founds Port-Royal, Acadia	
1606	First performance of a play in Canada (*Le Théâtre de Neptune*, in Port-Royal)	
1608	Champlain founds Quebec	
1610	Henry Hudson sails from London to Hudson and James bays	First letters sent from *Jesuit mission in Acadia
1632		*Jesuit Relations* first published (annually to 1673)
1642	Ville Marie (Montreal) founded	
1649	Iroquois destroy Huronia; deaths of missionaries Brébeuf and Lalemant	
1670	Founding of *Hudson's Bay Company	
1689-97	King William's War: first of four intercolonial wars (or French and Indian Wars) between France and	

Date	Historical Events	Literary Events
	Britain over North American territories	
1690-2		Henry Kelsey keeps journal of Saskatchewan expedition (published 1749)
1697	France gains control of Newfoundland	
1713	Treaty of Utrecht: France cedes Newfoundland, most of Acadia and captured territories in Hudson's Bay to Britain	
1736		John Gyles's 'Indian' captivity narrative, *Memoirs of Odd Adventures*, published
1749	Halifax founded by the British as chief town of NS	
1751		First printing press (Halifax)
1752		First newspaper (*Halifax Gazette*)
1755-62	Expulsion of Acadians	
1756-63	*Seven Years' War (or fourth intercolonial war)	
1759	Battle of the Plains of Abraham: British under Wolfe defeat French under Montcalm, but both generals die	
1763	Treaty of Paris cedes remainder of New France to Britain	
1763-4	Last major Native resistance to westward expansion of colonies: Ottawa chief Pontiac and allied forces drive British out of Great Lakes forts	

Date	Historical Events	Literary Events
1769	Island of St John (later PEI) separated from NS and given its own colonial government	France Brooke, *The History of Emily Montague*
1774	Quebec Act instates Roman Catholic religious freedom and French civil law, partly to prevent French from joining American revolutionaries	
1776-83	American Revolution: c. 40,000 United Empire Loyalists migrate to Maritimes and Canada	
1783	Peace treaties outline border between US and BNA to Lake of the Woods (extended to Rockies 1818)	
1784	NB separated from NS and established as a province; Scottish immigration increases due to Highland clearances (which last until 1854)	James Cook, *A Voyage to the Pacific Ocean*; many other anglophone travel accounts published 1790s onwards
1789		First literary periodical (*Nova Scotia Magazine*)
1791	Constitutional Act divides province of Quebec into *Upper Canada and Lower Canada	Elizabeth Simcoe, wife of first lieutenant-governor of Upper Canada, begins journal (to 1796; published 1911)
1792	Captain George Vancouver and Spanish navigators Valdés and Galiano chart Pacific coast	
1798		George Vancouver, *A Voyage of Discovery*
1812-14	*War of 1812	
1815	Wave of immigration from Europe following Napoleonic Wars	

Date	Historical Events	Literary Events
1821		Thomas McCulloch's 'Letters of Mephibosheth Stepsure' begin appearing in *Acadian Recorder*
1824		Julia Beckwith Hart, *St Ursula's Convent*
1825		Oliver Goldsmith, *The Rising Village*
1829	Death of last of Beothuks in Newfoundland	Methodist Book Room (later Ryerson Press) established, Toronto
1831		Peter Jones (Kahkewaquonaby), central figure in earliest Native literary coterie, makes speaking tour of Britain
1832		John Richardson, *Wacousta*
1836		Catharine Parr Traill, *The Backwoods of Canada*; Thomas Chandler Haliburton, *The Clockmaker*
1837-8	*Rebellions against colonial government	
1838		*Literary Garland* established (to 1851); Anna Jameson, *Winter Studies and Summer Rambles in Canada*
1839	Lord Durham's report on BNA investigates causes of rebellions, and recommends uniting the Canadas under a self-governing legislature	
1841	Act of Union	
1844		Toronto *Globe* established

Date	Historical Events	Literary Events
1845	Last sighting of Franklin's second expedition in Baffin Bay. Its disappearance sparks 42 further Arctic expeditions (1847-79)	
1847	Mass Irish immigration begins, following potato famine	
1848	NS becomes first BNA colony with responsible government	Royal Lyceum Theatre opens in Toronto
1849	Vancouver Island established as Crown colony; anti-French riots cost Montreal its status as Canada's capital	
1852		Susanna Moodie, *Roughing It in the Bush*
1854	Reciprocity Treaty (trade agreement between BNA and US)	
1856	Grand Trunk Railway links Montreal and Toronto	Charles Sangster, *The St Lawrence and the Saguenay*
1857	Ottawa chosen as capital of Province of Canada by Queen Victoria	Charles Heavysege, *Saul*
1858	Crown colony of British Columbia established; Fraser River gold rush	Thomas D'Arcy McGee, *Canadian Ballads*
1864		Rosanna Leprohon, *Antoinette de Mirecourt*
1866	BC and Vancouver Island united; Fenian raid from USA on Niagara peninsula	
1867	BNA Act: *Confederation creates Dominion of Canada, with four provinces (NB, NS, ON, QC); John A. Macdonald becomes first Prime Minister (to 1873)	
1868	Canada First (nationalist group) founded	Charles Mair, *Dreamland*

Date	Historical Events	Literary Events
1870	Hudson's Bay Company territories transferred to dominion as North-West Territories, with Manitoba created as a separate province (following Métis Red River Rebellion led by Louis *Riel)	
1871	BC joins Confederation; prairie land treaties signed with First Nations 1871-7	
1873	North-West Mounted Police established (renamed Royal Canadian Mounted Police 1920); PEI joins Confederation	
1876	Indian Act establishes rights of Aboriginals but turns them into wards of state; Intercolonial Railway links NS and NB to QC and ON	Toronto Women's Literary Club established
1877		William Kirby, *The Golden Dog: A Legend of Quebec*
1879	Macdonald introduces 'National Policy' of tariff protection and western development	
1880		Charles G. D. Roberts, *Orion*
1884	Native *potlatch ceremony prohibited	Isabella Valancy Crawford, *Malcolm's Katie*
1885	Chinese Immigration Act imposes head tax; *Canadian Pacific Railway completed; Riel's Northwest Rebellion fails	
1887		*Saturday Night* magazine established (to 2001)
1888		James de Mille, *A Strange*

Date	Historical Events	Literary Events
		Manuscript Found in a Copper Cylinder
1895		Pauline Johnson, *The White Wampum*
1896	Wilfrid Laurier becomes first francophone PM (to 1911)	Gilbert Parker, *The Seats of the Mighty*
1897	Klondike gold rush	Ralph Connor, *Black Rock* (serialised)
1898	Yukon Territory formed, to maintain order during gold rush	Ernest Thompson Seton, *Wild Animals I Have Known*
1899	Canadian troops dispatched to Boer War (opposed by most French Canadians)	
1901	Marconi receives transatlantic wireless message (St John's)	University of Toronto Press established
1904		Sara Jeannette Duncan, *The Imperialist*
1905	Saskatchewan and Alberta (previously part of NWT) created as provinces	
1907	First air flight in Canada	Robert Service, *Songs of a Sourdough*
1908	Canada claims Arctic archipelago	Nellie McClung, *Sowing Seeds in Danny*; L. M. Montgomery, *Anne of Green Gables*
1912	Boundaries of MB, ON and QC extended northward	Stephen Leacock, *Sunshine Sketches of a Little Town*
1916	First female suffrage bills (Prairie Provinces)	
1917	Halifax explosion: cargo of chemicals exploding in harbour	

Date	Historical Events	Literary Events
	kills 1,500 and injures 9,000; Conscription Crisis alienates many, especially francophones, from government	
1919	Winnipeg general strike; national strike wave	*Canadian Bookman* established
1920	Group of Seven officially formed	*Canadian Forum* established
1921	William Lyon Mackenzie King, Canada's longest-serving PM, elected	Canadian Authors' Association established
1923	Chinese Exclusion Act prevents immigration (revoked 1947)	Laura Goodman Salverson, *The Viking Heart*; E. J. Pratt, *Newfoundland Verse*
1925	United Church of Canada combines Presbyterians, Methodists and Congregationalists	F. P. Grove, *Settlers of the Marsh*; Martha Ostenso, *Wild Geese*
1926		Robert Stead, *Grain*
1927		Mazo de la Roche, *Jalna*
1928		Morley Callaghan, *Strange Fugitive*; Frank Parker Day, *Rockbound*
1929	Persons Case overturns legal definition of 'person' as male, allowing women to participate in all aspects of public life	Raymond Knister, *White Narcissus*
1931	Statute of Westminster recognises dominions (including Canada and Newfoundland) as fully self-governing	
1932	Canadian Radio Broadcasting Corporation established (becomes CBC in 1936)	
1934		Grey Owl (Archie Belaney), *Pilgrims of the Wild*

Date	Historical Events	Literary Events
1935	RCMP stop March to Ottawa of unemployed from western Canada	
1936		Governor General's Literary Awards established; A. J. M. Smith et al., *New Provinces*
1939	King George VI is first reigning monarch to tour Canada; Canada enters WWII	Irene Baird, *Waste Heritage*; Howard O'Hagan, *Tay John*
1940	Mackenzie King commits Canada to continental defence strategy dominated by US	A. M. Klein, *Hath Not a Jew*
1941		Emily Carr, *Klee Wyck*; Hugh MacLennan, *Barometer Rising*; Sinclair Ross, *As for Me and My House*
1942	Internment of Japanese Canadians; conscription plebiscite (all but QC accept)	Earle Birney, *David and Other Poems*; Thomas Raddall, *His Majesty's Yankees*
1943		E. K. Brown, *On Canadian Poetry*
1944		Dorothy Livesay, *Day and Night*
1945	Russian espionage in Canada exposed	Irving Layton, *Here and Now*; F. R. Scott, *Overture*; Miriam Waddington, *Green World*
1946	Massive postwar immigration from Europe	Louis Dudek, *East of the City*; P. K. Page, *As Ten As Twenty*; Raymond Souster, *When We Are Young*
1947	Canadian citizenship comes into effect; title 'dominion' dropped; provincial voting	Paul Hiebert, *Sarah Binks*; Malcolm Lowry, *Under the Volcano*;

Date	Historical Events	Literary Events
	rights given to all Canadians except Aboriginals and Japanese	W. O. Mitchell, *Who Has Seen the Wind*
1948	Repeal of act making race a grounds for exclusion from federal franchise	
1949	NL enters Confederation; NATO established largely thanks to Canadian diplomacy	Hugh Garner, *Storm Below*; James Reaney, *The Red Heart*
1951	Indian Act amended, permitting potlatch and sun dance but restricting entitlement to Indian status	Massey Report on the arts and sciences; Anne Wilkinson, *Counterpoint to Sleep*
1952	Vincent Massey becomes first Canadian-born governor general; first CBC TV station launched	Ernest Buckler, *The Mountain and the Valley*
1953		National Library of Canada established; Stratford Shakespeare Festival established (ON)
1954		Ethel Wilson, *Swamp Angel*
1956		Mavis Gallant, *The Other Paris*; Adele Wiseman, *The Sacrifice*
1957		Canada Council (arts funding) established; Jay Macpherson, *The Boatman*
1958		Norman Levine, *Canada Made Me*
1959	St Lawrence Seaway (ship canal system from Montreal to Great Lakes) opened	*Canadian Literature* and *Tish* established; Mordecai Richler, *The Apprenticeship of Duddy Kravitz*; Sheila Watson, *The Double Hook*

Date	Historical Events	Literary Events
1960	*Status Indians acquire federal voting rights; start of *Quiet Revolution in Quebec	Margaret Avison, *Winter Sun*; Eli Mandel, *Fuseli Poems*; Brian Moore, *The Luck of Ginger Coffey*; Farley Mowat, *Ordeal by Ice*
1962	Trans-Canada Highway opened	John Newlove, *Grave Sirs*; Rudy Wiebe, *Peace Shall Destroy Many*
1964		Margaret Laurence, *The Stone Angel*; Gwendolyn MacEwen, *The Rising Fire*; Jane Rule, *Desert of the Heart*
1965	Adoption of maple leaf flag	A. L. Purdy, *Cariboo Horses*; Northrop Frye, 'Conclusion' to *The Literary History of Canada*
1966		Margaret Atwood, *The Circle Game*; Leonard Cohen, *Beautiful Losers*; Robert Kroetsch, *The Words of My Roaring*
1967	Expo 67 (Montreal)	House of Anansi Press established; bpNichol, *JOURNEYING & the return*; Scott Symons, *Combat Journal for Place D'Armes*
1968	Pierre Trudeau elected PM (to 1979; 1980-4); Parti Québécois formed to demand independence	bill bissett, *awake in th red desert* [sic]; Dennis Lee, *Civil Elegies*; Alice Munro, *Dance of the Happy Shades*
1969	Official Languages Act makes French and English equal throughout government	Graeme Gibson, *Five Legs*

Date	Historical Events	Literary Events
1970	*October Crisis (QC); Royal Commission on Status of Women reports on gender discrimination in industry; 'Canadian content' broadcasting rules tightened	Robertson Davies, *Fifth Business*; John Glassco, *Memoirs of Montparnasse*; Audrey Thomas, *Mrs Blood*; Michael Ondaatje, *The Collected Works of Billy the Kid*
1971	Official multiculturalism policy implemented; Department of the Environment established	
1973	Calder Case: Supreme Court of Canada recognises that Aboriginal titles to land could exist in common law	Maria Campbell, *Halfbreed*; Gary Geddes, *Letter of the Master of Horse*
1975		Lee Maracle, *Bobbi Lee: Indian Rebel*
1976	Death penalty abolished	Marian Engel, *Bear*; Jack Hodgins, *Spit Delaney's Island*; Alistair MacLeod, *The Lost Salt Gift of Blood*
1977	French is made the only official language in QC	Timothy Findley, *The Wars*
1978		Joan Barfoot, *Abra*; Aritha van Herk, *Judith*; Rita Joe, *Poems of Rita Joe*
1980	QC votes against separation in referendum; 'O Canada' (1880) adopted as national anthem	George Bowering, *Burning Water*; Kristjana Gunnars, *Settlement Poems*
1981	International Council for Canadian Studies established	Joy Kogawa, *Obasan*
1982	Patriation of the Constitution (severs constitutional and legislative ties with Britain)	Joan Clark, *From a High Thin Wire*; Guy Vanderhaeghe, *Man Descending*
1983		Beatrice Culleton Mosionier, *In Search of*

Date	Historical Events	Literary Events
		April Raintree; Susan Swan, *The Biggest Modern Woman of the World*
1984	Jeanne Sauvé becomes first female governor-general	William Gibson, *Neuromancer*
1985		Jeannette Armstrong, *Slash*; Fred Wah, *Waiting for Saskatchewan*
1986		Janice Kulyk Keefer, *The Paris-Napoli Express*; Jane Urquhart, *The Whirlpool*
1987	Canada-US Free Trade Agreement announced (disputed, but effective from 1989)	
1988	Canadian Multiculturalism Act; redress for Japanese-Canadians	Tomson Highway, *The Rez Sisters* (first performed 1986); Daphne Marlatt, *Ana Historic*
1990	Meech Lake Accord (amendments designed to make the Canadian Constitution acceptable to QC) fails to be ratified	George Elliott Clarke, *Whylah Falls*; SKY Lee, *Disappearing Moon Café*; Daniel David Moses, *Coyote City*; Nino Ricci, *Lives of the Saints*; Djanet Sears, *Afrika Solo*
1991		Douglas Coupland, *Generation X*; Rohinton Mistry, *Such A Long Journey*; Monique Mojica, *Princess Pocahontas and the Blue Spots* (first performed 1989)
1992	Charlottetown Accord (more extensive constitutional amendments) defeated by national referendum	Sandra Birdsell, *The Chrome Suite*; Elizabeth Hay, *The Only Snow in Havana*

Date	Historical Events	Literary Events
1993	Kim Campbell becomes first female PM	Carol Shields, *The Stone Diaries*
1994	North American Free Trade Agreement implemented	Hiromi Goto, *Chorus of Mushrooms*; M. G. Vassanji, *The Book of Secrets*
1995	Second Quebec sovereignty referendum narrowly defeated	
1996		Ann-Marie Macdonald, *Fall on Your Knees*; Anne Michaels, *Fugitive Pieces*; Shani Mootoo, *Cereus Blooms at Night*; Anita Rau Badami, *Tamarind Mem*
1997		Dionne Brand, *Land to Light On*; Robert Majzels, *City of Forgetting*
1998	Worst ice storm on record	Wayne Johnston, *The Colony of Unrequited Dreams*
1999	Nunavut (previously part of NWT) established as a territory, populated and partly owned by Inuit	Wayde Compton, *49th Parallel Psalm*; Camilla Gibb, *Mouthing the Words*
2001	Quebec City Summit on free trade targeted by anti-globalisation protests	Yann Martel, *Life of Pi*; Richard B. Wright, *Clara Callan*
2002	Canada signs Kyoto Accord on environment	George Bowering becomes Canada's first poet laureate; Austin Clarke, *The Polished Hoe*; Katherine Govier, *Creation*
2003	SARS (Severe Acute Respiratory Syndrome) outbreak in Toronto; first legal same-sex marriage (ON)	Frances Itani, *Deafening*

Date	Historical Events	Literary Events
2004	Sponsorship scandal uncovered (misuse since 1996 of public funds intended for government advertising in QC)	Wayson Choy, *All That Matters*; Miriam Toews, *A Complicated Kindness*
2005		David Bergen, *The Time in Between*; Lisa Moore, *Alligator*
2006	Arrest of 15 terrorists, allegedly planning attack on Ottawa Parliament and banks	

Introduction

So.
    In the beginning, there was nothing. Just the water.
    Coyote was there, but Coyote was asleep. That Coyote was
    asleep and that Coyote was dreaming. When that Coyote
    dreams, anything can happen.
    I can tell you that.
                    Thomas King, *Green Grass Running Water*[1]

'Coyote' is one of the names of the trickster figure in Native
Canadian mythology, and in Thomas King's 1993 novel *Green Grass
Running Water*, the ambiguously gendered Coyote is creative and
powerful, but also mischievous and prone to blunders. One of
Coyote's dreams is about a dog, but the dream gets loose, reverses
its name, and proclaims itself GOD; subsequently, GOD's attempt to
rename and reclassify everything in Canada according to a
Christian worldview is counteracted by a group of shape-shifting
Indigenous deities. In the carnivalesque world of King's novel, the
trickster continually disrupts efforts to establish fixed identities
based on nationality or race, sexuality or gender, religion or social
class. Such disruption can be seen as part of a larger, transnational
postmodern project, which – in basic terms – discredits the coherent, knowable subject which was largely taken for granted in earlier
periods. In the specific context of Canada, the question of national
identity becomes particularly compelling, since the general difficulty

of defining a nation is compounded by the striking diversity of Canada's populations and natural landscapes.

Like many other Canadian fictions, *Green Grass Running Water* evokes aspects of Canada's history, mythology and culture but resists the notion of a single, definable national identity, enacting this resistance through parody and allegory as well as through representations of identity as provisional and performative. Indeed, performance, reinvention, imposture and play are explored in a whole range of Canadian texts, from John Richardson's *Wacousta* (1832), which centres on a British aristocrat masquerading as an 'Indian' chief, to Tomson Highway's *The Rez Sisters*, in which Nanabush, another trickster figure, appears at different times as a seagull and a bingo master. Tricksters and impostors such as these mock the earnest quest for the Canadian identity which has generated so much critical and literary discourse. As Margaret Atwood remarks in her book *Strange Things: The Malevolent North in Canadian Literature* (1995):

> A great deal has been made, from time to time, of the search for 'the Canadian identity'; sometimes we are told that this item is simply something we have mislaid, like the car keys, and might find down behind the sofa if we are only diligent enough, whereas at other times we have been told that the object in question doesn't really exist and we are pursuing a phantom. Sometimes we are told that although we don't have one of these 'identities', we ought to, because other countries do.[2]

The question of 'Canadian identity', vexed though it is, cannot be ignored here, since this book seeks to distinguish Canadian literature from other national literatures, even while acknowledging that the boundaries are permeable. In *Strange Things*, Atwood suggests a useful approach, noting that when we look for national identities, what we see is: 'on first sight, a collection of clichéd images – that is, images that have been repeated so often and absorbed so fully that they are instantly recognized'.[3] These, she argues, relate to 'fact or historical reality of some sort', and artists and writers can 'make variations on them, explore them more deeply, utilise their imaginative power . . . or turn them inside out'.[4] Also, Canadian literature from all periods is shaped by Canada's particular social and physical landscapes, and by its history, and this book will pay attention to these contexts in order to explore what makes this body of literature distinctive.

There is at present no critical overview of anglophone Canadian literature in print. This is surprising, given that it is a well-established and fast-growing subject for study and research in countries around the world. There is an urgent need for a book which synthesises and updates existing accounts of Canadian literary history while also offering new close readings of key texts, reflecting on the contours of the subject, and explaining the relevance of different theoretical approaches. Canadian literary studies has changed rapidly in recent years, partly because scholars have embraced new theoretical or interdisciplinary approaches, and partly because the national literary canon has been expanded in two directions. Firstly, scholars and educators are increasingly attending to the divergent literary inscriptions of Canada in the work of different ethnic, regional or linguistic groups, focusing in particular on writing by ethnic minority authors and Native Canadians, but also analysing the construction of whiteness as a dominant category. Secondly, researchers have begun to recover the work of neglected nineteenth- and early twentieth-century writers, many of whom have been passed over because they wrote in popular genres or published in ephemeral formats such as magazines. Another very significant change is the marked increase, since about 1990, of the status of the most widely read Canadian authors on the international cultural scene: the phenomenon of the literary superstar has changed the way Canadian literature is perceived, both at home and abroad.

This introduction contains four parts. The first provides a very concise historical account of English-Canadian literature, and the second reflects on the processes of constructing a national canon. The next section considers the special place of Native writers in Canadian literary studies and comments on the different terms which may describe them (such as Native, First Nations, Indigenous and Aboriginal), while the final part explains the structure and purposes of the book.

HISTORICAL SYNOPSIS OF CANADIAN LITERATURE IN ENGLISH

Canada's involved history of colonisation, immigration and federation complicates accounts of its literary production, and the term 'Canadian literature in English' must be carefully defined. It generally refers to all anglophone literary writing produced in what is now Canada, including the work of immigrant writers and certain temporary residents, as well as literature from regions which in the past were politically separate from Canada, such as Newfoundland. The larger category of 'Canadian literature' incorporates writing in French and in the languages of Aboriginal or diasporic groups, as well as English translations of such texts, but such material falls outside the remit of this book because the Edinburgh Critical Guides series is devoted to anglophone literatures. While some survey studies treat francophone literature as a subdivision of Canadian literature as a whole, this book, in explicitly focusing on English-Canadian writing, acknowledges that the rich, diverse and fascinating literature of French-speaking Canada should be the subject of a separate critical guide.

The English and French literatures of Canada are widely held to have developed along fairly independent trajectories, although, of course, mutual influence is discernible. But while the national literature can be subdivided according to language, its history cannot. The history of France's New World colonies, as well as the more recent development of the province of Quebec, is very relevant to students of English-language literature, as my discussions of authors such as Frances Brooke, John Glassco, Leonard Cohen and E. J. Pratt demonstrate. And French and English are not, of course, the only languages of Canada. In terms of official languages (those with privileged legal status), Canada comprises one francophone province (Quebec), one bilingual (New Brunswick) and eight anglophone (Alberta, British Columbia, Manitoba, Newfoundland and Labrador, Nova Scotia, Ontario, Prince Edward Island and Saskatchewan), together with three territories. In political terms, territories have more limited rights and competences than provinces. The Yukon is a bilingual territory, while in the Northwest Territories and Nunavut, English, French and also some Aboriginal languages are official. In terms of spoken language, the situation is much more complex: Aboriginal languages are very numerous (see discussion below), and owing to immigration from Asia, Scandinavia and elsewhere, the population of Canada also includes many other language communities. The histories of all these groups are very much intertwined, as the Chronology makes clear, and some knowledge of Canada's complex linguistic situation is important for students of its literature.

An approximate division into periods is necessary to most literary historical narratives, and in the case of Canada, it is convenient to think in terms of the country's political evolution, since its major shifts coincide with certain noticeable developments in the broad patterns of the national literary canon. The following account, therefore, surveys the dominant forms of literary output in each of four periods. The first section focuses on the earlier colonial era, when France and Britain fought for dominance over the territories which would become Canada, and the second section on the nineteenth century, when Canada was controlled by Britain and received tides of emigration from Europe. Writers in these two periods were largely dependent on European aesthetic conventions, although some began to experiment with form and genre in their attempts to engage with North American subject matter. Confederation, in 1867, marks the start of a new phase of self-determination in Canadian history and literature, while the 1951 Massey Report into the arts in Canada, which launched the era of cultural nationalism, may be taken as the next landmark. During the second half of the twentieth century, Canadian literary production became extremely prolific and diverse, so that in a survey of this limited length it is possible to pick out only a small selection of the major authors and themes. The Chronology provides a more comprehensive list of names, but even this represents only a proportion of Canada's extensive modern canon.

Earlier colonial era: to 1815

Canadian literary history starts with the narratives of explorers, missionaries and fur-traders in the early seventeenth century; the majority of this writing is in French. Important anglophone exploration narratives, recounting the voyages of men such as George Vancouver, James Cook and Alexander Mackenzie, did not begin to appear until the 1780s. English Canada's earliest imaginative literature was written in mid-eighteenth century Nova Scotia by English, Scottish and Irish emigrants and colonial officials, and their essays, journals and Augustan verse reveal a desire both to maintain British traditions and to value local culture. Canada's first printing press was brought to Halifax in 1751, and other presses gradually followed: in Quebec (1764), Saint John (1783), Montreal (1785), Charlottetown (1787) and Niagara (1793), as literary production became established in those areas.

The first novel written in, and about, Canada is *The History of Emily Montague* (1769), the work of an Englishwoman, Frances Brooke, who spent five years in the town of Quebec during the period following the fall of New France to the British. Brooke uses the imported form of the novel of sentiment, but she was the first author to exploit the topicality, novelty and exoticism of New World subject matter for a British audience. Later novels by visiting British authors included John Galt's *Bogle Corbet; or, The Emigrants* (1831), Frederick Marryat's *The Settlers in Canada* (1844) and R. M. Ballantyne's *Snowflakes and Sunbeams; or, The Young Fur Traders* (1856).

During the American Revolution of the 1770s and 1780s, thousands of United Empire Loyalists came north to what remained of British North America. The northward migration included Dutch, German and Iroquois peoples, but it was the English Loyalists who came to exert the most influence in literary and cultural terms. This increase in the educated population enabled the establishment of periodicals, beginning with the *Nova Scotia Magazine and Comprehensive Review of Literature, Politics and News* in 1789; while the new magazines initially relied mainly on reprints from foreign journals, they also published some locally produced fiction and poetry. During this period several Canadian residents brought out volumes of verse, either in London or with the new colonial presses. The poetry of the 1780s and 1790s reveals the colonial desire to be part of a universal cultural reality, which was perceived to be expressed most adequately in European – and especially English – literature. Some poets described the society and scenery of British

North America, but within the framework of inherited literary forms and ideologies.

Emigration and settlement: 1815–1867

During the earlier nineteenth century, the United Empire Loyalists were joined by other settlers of English descent, many of them former officers now unemployed or on half-pay following the end of the Napoleonic Wars. The sons of impoverished genteel families also came to Canada, either in official capacities or in order to take up land grants, while English parishes often sent paupers across the Atlantic. Scottish families and communities had been voluntarily moving to Upper Canada from the 1750s onwards, and in the later eighteenth and early nineteenth centuries, many more were forced to emigrate by the famines and Highland clearances. But the largest wave of immigrants came from Ireland, as a result of the potato famine of the late 1840s.

Poets in Canada were becoming more interested in the particularity of colonial experience, and literary subjects could be found in local legends and history, the culture of Native Canadians, or the experience of emigration and settlement. This growing attention to the immediate environment did not, however, disrupt the prevailing emotional and cultural attachment to Great Britain. It was affirmed in the War of 1812, when United Empire Loyalists and other migrants from America joined British garrisons, Irish and Scottish immigrants, Native Canadian followers of Tecumseh, and French-Canadian *habitants* (or peasants) to repel the invasion from the United States. The anti-American feeling shared by these various groups strengthened the bond between Britain and its remaining North American colonies, and this was clearly visible in much of the literature produced in Canada.

Oliver Goldsmith, great-nephew of the author of *The Vicar of Wakefield* (1766), was the first Canadian-born writer to publish a volume of verse, an epic of settlement entitled *The Rising Village* (1825). The earliest novels by authors born in Canada were Julia Beckwith Hart's *St Ursula's Convent* (1824) and Richardson's *Wacousta* (1832). *Wacousta* has been a particularly influential text: a Gothic romance, it is structured by the opposition between garrison and wilderness which was later identified as a central Canadian literary preoccupation. Richardson was among several White writers who drew on the legends and tales of Native Canadians which had been recorded by European anthropologists and folklorists, and in this same period, the efforts of Victorian missionaries led to the development of literary creativity in English among Indigenous Canadians. The first Indigenous literary coterie was formed by young Ojibwa men who had been educated by Methodists in the 1820s. They included Peter Jones (Kahkewaquonaby), George Copway, Henry Steinhauer and others, and they became known nationally and internationally through their public readings, orations and lectures, delivered wearing Native dress.

Among first-generation settler authors, two of the best known are Catharine Parr Traill and her sister Susanna Moodie, who emigrated from England with their husbands in 1832. In their various semi-autobiographical texts, notably Traill's *The Backwoods of Canada* (1836) and Moodie's *Roughing It in the Bush* (1852), the two writers significantly modify inherited literary forms in order to capture colonial experience. Although they never returned to Britain and tried to adapt to the new environment, both sisters also clung tenaciously to their English identity and resisted the incursions of American culture. Other writers, by contrast, began to define the Canadian character in terms of its positioning between Britain and America, and its distinction from both; among them was the Nova Scotian Thomas Haliburton. He started publishing periodical sketches featuring his comic American hero Sam Slick in 1835, and they were collected in volume form as *The Clockmaker* (1836). Although the book was intended to make Nova Scotians realise that they were exploited by both America and Britain, it achieved wide sales in both countries and became the first best-seller by a Canadian.

Confederation and the earlier twentieth century: 1867–1950

Following the confederation of Canada as a dominion (that is, a self-governing territory within the British Empire), the imperialist movement began to advocate a strengthened empire in order to counteract the influence of America. Similar ideals were held by

'Canada First', a political, intellectual and literary grouping whose founders included the poet Charles Mair. He and his contemporaries, including Isabella Valancy Crawford and the Confederation Poets (Charles G. D. Roberts, Archibald Lampman, Bliss Carman and Duncan Campbell Scott), attempted to treat the universal human themes of western literature while using local settings and history to add a specifically Canadian dimension. During the 1890s, they called for the establishment of an association for Canadian authors and a national literary magazine, but it would be more than twenty-five years before these things took place.

The 1890s also saw the emergence of Canada's most famous Native writer, the poet E. Pauline Johnson (Tekahionwake), whose work reveals a dynamic between the oral culture she inherited from her Mohawk father and the English literary heritage bequeathed by her White mother. She also draws on the tradition of writing and performance established by the Ojibwa coterie of the 1820s and 1830s; like Peter Jones and his colleagues, Johnson used her oratorical skills to mediate between White and Indigenous cultures, and her popularity was established through her compelling public readings.

Sara Jeannette Duncan, in her important novel *The Imperialist* (1904), analysed the society and political culture of a small Ontario town, as well as exploring imperial politics more broadly. Duncan was rare among her compatriots in that her firm allegiance to British culture did not preclude her admiration for American writers, especially William Dean Howells and Henry James. Like them, she was a committed realist, whereas a majority of Canadian novelists and novel-readers favoured idealistic, often didactic fiction, and deplored the influence of realism and naturalism. L. M. Montgomery's *Anne of Green Gables* (1908) was a much more representative novel for this period than *The Imperialist*. The story of the orphan Anne, set in an idyllic Prince Edward Island village, rapidly gained enormous audiences, and has remained popular ever since. Montgomery was, however, viewed with some contempt by the largely male Canadian literary establishment; she had achieved the international recognition which they had hoped for, but *Anne* by no means fitted their concept of what the Great Canadian Novel should be.

In the 1920s the popularity of idealistic romances, family sagas and animal stories continued, and authors such as Montgomery, Nellie McClung, Marshall Saunders and Mazo de la Roche were among the best-known literary names. But it was during this decade that the realistic novel finally began to gain attention; early examples of novels using realist techniques (in combination with some romance elements) include Frederick Philip Grove's *Settlers of the Marsh* (1925), Martha Ostenso's *Wild Geese* (1925) and Robert Stead's *Grain* (1926). These novels are all set on the prairies; indeed, during this period it was regional writing, in both idealist and realist forms, which flourished in Canada. Literary modernism, which tended to encourage an internationalist aesthetic, had a rather limited effect on Canadian fiction (although there were a few exceptions, notably Morley Callaghan, who was intermittently attracted to modernist forms). In poetry, by contrast, modernism was an important – if somewhat belated – influence. During the interwar years, a group of anglophone Montreal poets, most prominent among them F. R. Scott and A. J. M. Smith, founded and edited several periodicals which published modernist writing along with articles attacking the mediocrity of more traditional Canadian verse. A further group of modernist poets, including Dorothy Livesay, Louis Dudek, Irving Layton and Raymond Knister, came to prominence during the 1940s and 1950s. Several other important Canadian writers also emerged during these decades, notably Robertson Davies, Mordecai Richler, P. K. Page and James Reaney, and the scene was set for the dramatic flowering of Canadian literature in the second half of the twentieth century.

Cultural nationalism and multiculturalism: 1951 to present

The Massey Commission, officially titled the Royal Commission on National Development in the Arts, Letters and Sciences, reported in 1951. It considered how the arts, research, broadcasting and conservation could be used to foster a sense of national identity, and concluded that Canada was culturally threatened by the United States. The report recommended the creation of government-sponsored institutions and funding bodies, and as a result, the National Library of Canada was established in 1953 and the Canada

Council for the Arts in 1957. Other literary institutions which date back to the 1950s include the Shakespeare Festival in Stratford, Ontario, McClelland and Stewart's New Canadian Library series of classic titles, and the academic journal *Canadian Literature*.

The volume of new writing in all genres grew rapidly in the succeeding decades. Canadian novelists, in particular, began to achieve a high profile abroad; among them Davies, Richler, Margaret Laurence, Mavis Gallant, Alice Munro, Margaret Atwood and Norman Levine. The literary concerns of these authors and their peers are multiple and diverse, but it may be noted that the traditional Canadian preoccupation with wilderness was beginning to evolve into a concern with environmental issues; that gender politics were becoming very prominent; and that interest in the relationship with Britain had largely been superseded by anxieties about the power of the US over Canada's economy and culture.

The 1960s and 1970s were strongly marked by cultural nationalism, and the ideals of Canada First recurred in new forms. Literary critics produced survey studies of the national literature and celebrated works which they thought displayed typically Canadian preoccupations, an approach known as thematic criticism (see Chapter 2). The government promoted Canadian culture by establishing prizes and fellowships for artists and writers, and also encouraged Canadian studies abroad.

Over the course of the twentieth century, Canada became increasingly autonomous in almost all policy matters, but it was not until 1982 that the constitution was patriated (transferred from Westminster to Ottawa). This meant that Canada had finally ended its effective political subordination to Britain, even though it retained Queen Elizabeth II as head of state. Canadian politicians and intellectuals were now rather less concerned with their country's level of independence, becoming preoccupied instead with the cultural diversity of their society. In 1971 Canada had become the first country to implement an official policy of multiculturalism, largely in response to tensions between anglophone and francophone citizens, and in 1988 a fresh piece of legislation emphasised the multiracial, multilingual nature of Canadian society and sought to foster appreciation of minority cultures (see Chapter 1). Educators, critics and canon-makers increasingly recognised the significance of ethnic minority and Native Canadian writers, although there was still a danger that such writers would be exoticised, or interpreted according to White paradigms.

Migration, exile and diasporic experience are the subjects of a substantial proportion of late twentieth- and twenty-first-century Canadian texts, especially in the important genre of life writing. Also notable is the burgeoning of the postmodern historical novel (see Chapter 4), and in many such texts, a fascination with Canada's history coexists with a scepticism about the whole project of writing national histories. Many of the best-known contemporary novelists are also poets (Anne Michaels, Robert Kroetsch, Dionne Brand and many more), while numerous experimental writers blur the boundaries between poetry and fiction or history or autobiography (Daphne Marlatt, George Elliott Clarke, Michael Ondaatje and others). Canadian drama is also flourishing, and among the most successful playwrights are Timothy Findley, Tomson Highway, Ann-Marie Macdonald, John Mighton and Richard Greenblatt. The plays of the bilingual author Robert Lepage have been performed around the world, and his productions of Shakespeare, also presented internationally, have evoked both high praise and intense critical debate.

The production and reception of contemporary writing in Canada has been greatly influenced by three related phenomena: the rise of literary celebrity, the proliferation of book prizes and the advent of mass reading events. Authors including Atwood, Ondaatje, Alice Munro and Yann Martel have become international stars, and are now at the centre of intense debates about literary value, popularity and the economics of culture. Such debates have been further stimulated by the enormous success of projects such as 'Canada Reads' and other mass reading events, which exploit the appeal of celebrity authors in order to stimulate book sales and encourage communal reading and discussion of Canadian books (see Conclusion).

CANON-MAKING AND LITERARY HISTORY IN CANADA

I have, so far, offered three different 'histories' of Canadian literature. The first appears in the Contents: the set of texts for discussion constitutes a highly selective sampling of the national literature, while the chapter titles collectively propose one way of conceptualising the Canadian canon according to prominent themes. The second version of Canadian literary history appears in the right-hand column of the Chronology, which lists either the best-known publication or the first major book by each of around 150 authors. The third history of Canadian literature is in narrative form, just above. These three histories can, and should, be interrogated by other readers, since my inclusions, exclusions and generalisations are open to challenge from those with different reading experiences or political viewpoints. Literary histories ought to be negotiated and debated, rather than considered as fixed. In any case, no book – however thick – which takes the whole of Canadian literature in English as its subject can ever be comprehensive; an introductory book such as this can offer only a representative sample of Canadian texts and pick out some of the most significant themes and critical approaches, although of course the definition of what is 'representative' or 'significant' is itself a matter for debate.

My choices of texts and topics have been determined in various ways, and in reflecting briefly on them here, I am also drawing attention to the selectivity, subjectivity and ideological bias of every account of a national literature. The elements of individuality, political investment and value judgement are, though, precisely what makes literary histories interesting to read, and allows them to enter into dialogue with each other. The corpus of texts discussed or mentioned in this book results, of course, from my own reading experience, and I have naturally given emphasis to authors I enjoy, because literary study can become unproductive if it takes no account of the pleasures of reading. But this does not mean that the table of contents represents my personal canon, since the set of primary texts I have read was itself largely determined by the choices of educators, librarians, editors, publishers and critics. As an undergraduate student, most of the Canadian books I read were picked by my tutor; as a doctoral researcher, I was influenced in the choice of material for my thesis by discussion with supervisors, media coverage of particular authors, the availability of library books, the choices made by anthologists, the arguments of published critics, and my own ethnic, gender and class identity. Now, as a lecturer, I can teach seminars only on books which are available for sale in the UK, and substitutions frequently have to be made when texts go out of print. Indeed, the teaching canon of Canadian literature is very much determined by publishers, whose own choices are often directed by the variable costs of reprinting different texts. The influence exerted among publishers, critics, teachers and students is, however, multidirectional: for example, the reactions of my classes to the books we study may lead me to change the reading list in subsequent years, while the lists fixed on by academics and schoolteachers can affect publishers' decisions about which texts to keep in print. Also, the selection of writers for discussion in the chapters which follow was derived, in part, from comparing Canadian literature syllabuses at different universities, because if I want people to buy my book, I need to write about authors they are likely to be studying or teaching.

My choice of books and authors, then, is inevitably both idiosyncratic and also subject to scholarly trends and market forces. But there is also the question of the structure of this book, and of the account of Canadian literary history given above. These are strongly influenced by previous literary histories and by canon-making documents in the form of survey studies, chronological tables, encyclopedias, reading lists, reprint series of 'classic' texts, teaching syllabuses and conference programmes. Literary historians must inevitably impose a coherent structure and a sense of orderly progression on the disorderly, shifting set of texts which compose a national literature, and in developing these somewhat artificial structures, it is difficult to escape the influence of previous literary historical narratives, or to see beyond the concept of nation which those narratives enshrine.

Most histories of Canadian literature, for example, would start a new chapter at 1867: it seems self-evident that the moment when the nation – symbolically at least – came into being must have had an effect on the creative arts. This impulse is strengthened by the fact that the best-remembered anglophone poets from this era have been labelled 'the Confederation Poets'. Yet the choice of 1867 actually encodes particular assumptions about the meaning of Canada as nation, and these are not shared by all Canadians. Indeed, competing forms of nationalism exist within Canada, since several populations there can be identified as 'stateless nations'; that is, they define themselves as nations, even though their territories are not officially nation states. The most obvious examples are the Inuit, the First Nations (both collectively and individually) and Quebec nationalists. In Quebec two referenda have so far been held on the question of separating from the Confederation, and there have also been separatist movements in the Maritimes and Western Canada. Canada is, in addition, home to significant populations with dual or complex national or ethnic identification: the Métis (those of mixed White and Native ancestry); Chinese Canadians; Ukrainian Canadians; African Canadians; Icelandic Canadians and so on. These various groups might not identify the 'Canada' which came into being in 1867 as their nation at all.

Accordingly, E. D. Blodgett in *Five-Part Invention: A History of Literary History in Canada* interprets Canadian literary histories as a set of texts that articulate the separate yet interrelated perspectives of five groups within the Canadian population: anglophones, francophones, First Nations, Inuit and immigrant ethnic communities. He argues that: 'those truths that appear perfectly valid for histories conceived as the articulation of a specific group or even two groups with designedly shared preoccupations lose much of their validity when examined from a larger perspective'.[5] Blodgett's project is to read these histories as literary texts, outlining their 'plots' and value systems. He explains:

> Literary history . . . is governed by profound metanarrative designs. It has a didactic purpose that is aimed at constructing an idea of a nation, and it does so by giving it a certain form in both time and space. It requires clarity of origin and precise delimitation. As history, it constructs a past by selecting texts (canonization) and commemorating events so that the nation may be imaginatively shaped . . . into a kind of central protagonist that is born, grows, and reaches a certain maturity.[6]

The academic reading of literature is still carried out largely within national frameworks, and the grand-narrative style of literary history retains a strong influence. These patterns of reading and criticism were, though, challenged in the later twentieth century, because they tended to assume a direct relationship between literature and the nation state. Therefore, when reading literary histories, survey studies, or even reference books and chronological tables, it is important to remain aware of the various and competing ideas of nation which inform them.

In a specifically Canadian context, canon-making has always posed a range of particular challenges, owing to the country's shifting political structures, and the ethnic and linguistic diversity and complicated migrations of its populations. The difficulty of determining which authors and works count as Canadian is considerable, because many literary texts about Canada have been written by foreign explorers and travellers, or by recent immigrants, temporary visitors or Canadian-born expatriates. This is particularly noticeable in earlier periods, but even today many of Canada's celebrity writers, such as Yann Martel, Michael Ondaatje, Carol Shields, Rohinton Mistry or Dionne Brand, were born and brought up in other countries.

Projects to expand or challenge the Canadian canon are generally made in the name of one or more relatively excluded groups of authors. These might be Indigenous, francophone, Black, ethnic minority or expatriate writers, or perhaps women, gay writers, working-class writers, popular novelists or those from regions distant from the traditional cultural centre of Ontario. Apollo O. Amoko comments that in recent years critics have 'focused on ways in which literary narratives constructed from perspectives outside or marginal to the discourses of official nationalism – what are referred to as 'minority discourses' – may provide opportunities for contesting the exclusionary social narratives of national consolidation'.[7] W. H. New, however, in the second edition of *A History of Canadian Literature*, notes the dangers of commitment to minority positions, writing of the late twentieth-century political and literary climate: 'Perhaps inevitably, some claims upon the validity of the margin became competitive – as though whoever was most disenfranchised was most worthy'.[8] Finally, though, New endorses the value of engagement with competing codes of identity:

> Some writers made of their chosen category not so much a place of refuge as a place of resonance. In these instances, the

category labels may articulate a position of origin, but they do not restrict or contain the literary experience or the insight into human behaviour.[9]

Certain recent narratives of Canada's literary development are affected by a critical tendency to privilege the contemporary and reject writers whose ideological outlooks or aesthetic preferences jar with modern sensibilities. It is true that the post-1960 period provides particularly rich possibilities for literary study; nevertheless it is crucial for students to engage with Canada's cultural past, as contemporary writers do themselves. Therefore, this book, while weighted towards contemporary literature (as are most university syllabuses), also discusses a selection of earlier texts written from a variety of ideological positions.

INDIGENOUS CANADIANS

The question of Indigenous literature in Canada requires particular consideration because pre-contact Indigenous culture was oral in nature, yet the term 'literature' implies a written text. The work of many contemporary Native Canadian writers draws on oral and storytelling traditions, adapting English or the written forms of Native languages in order to evoke and express orality. Penny van Toorn, in a valuable essay on Aboriginal writing in Canada, argues that: 'Far from automatically extinguishing oral traditions, writing can potentially sit beside them'.[10] She also points out, however, that until relatively recently:

the predominant belief among anthropologists, mission societies, media theorists, and government policy makers was that oral and literate cultures are successive, mutually exclusive stages in a single, unavoidable path of cultural evolution. This belief justified assimilationist policies, which were considered merely a means of hastening the inevitable 'progress' of 'primitive' Aboriginal peoples into the 'modern' world . . . Aboriginal peoples in Canada today are . . . living with the legacies of such ideas, having seen their cultures threatened or destroyed by missionaries who prohibited traditional languages and ceremonies, and by welfare and residential school systems that obstructed cultural transmission by separating children from their families. Erroneous as it was, the idea that cultures evolved from orality to literacy became a self-fulfilling prophecy because it was enforced through government policies.[11]

These 'legacies' are explored in detail by many Native authors, among them Daniel David Moses, Thomas King, Lenore Keeshig-Tobias, Tomson Highway and Lee Maracle. The ways in which Native Canadian cultures were threatened can be explored through study of, firstly, colonialist texts and historical fictions (examples discussed in this book include Brooke's *The History of Emily Montague* and Pratt's *Brébeuf and his Brethren*), and, secondly, more recent texts which examine relationships between White and First Nations Canadians (such as Laurence's *The Diviners* or Cohen's *Beautiful Losers*).

A note on terminology may be helpful here. The words 'Indian', 'Eskimo' and 'halfbreed' are used by characters in many Canadian literary texts, but these terms should be avoided in essays, since they perpetuate colonial racial hierarchies. 'Eskimo' is considered insulting, since it is popularly believed to derive from a word meaning 'eater of raw meat', and the term 'Inuit' (Inuk in the singular) is preferred. 'Inuit' simply means people, and refers to eight tribal groupings in Alaska, Greenland and the Arctic regions of northern Canada, who speak common or related languages. Likewise, 'halfbreed' is unsuitable, as it is suggestive of animal husbandry, and 'Métis' should be substituted. Strictly speaking, this term refers to those of mixed French-Canadian and Aboriginal descent, although it is often also used (with or without the accent) to designate Canadians of mixed White and Aboriginal ancestry in general. Lastly, 'Indian' embodies a famous error of identification: Columbus's belief that he had discovered a route to India. Although this designation is still widely used by Aboriginal and non-Aboriginal North Americans, it can lead to confusion. There is much debate about the political and legal implications of the alternative terms Native Canadian, Aboriginal, Indigenous and First

Nations, and each is considered objectionable by certain groups and individuals.[12] As I am not in a position to endorse or reject any of these, I use them interchangeably. It should be noted, though, that the Inuit and Métis are culturally distinct from the rest of Canada's Native peoples, and the terms 'Indian' and 'First Nations' usually exclude such people, while 'Aboriginal' and 'Indigenous' include all Native groups.

The peoples labelled 'Indian' by colonists did not understand themselves as a collectivity, but as distinct tribal groupings. These peoples may, in some cases, share a good deal in terms of cultural heritage, and today they certainly share many experiences and problems arising from their being treated as a homogeneous population by White Canadians. Many aspects of social practice, language and cultural tradition, however, remain specific to particular groups. It is impossible to specify how many different named peoples were present when European colonisers first arrived, or how many exist today, because over time numerous groups have migrated, subdivided, merged or formed into confederacies and nations, while others – such as the Beothuk of Newfoundland – were obliterated by colonisers. Olive Dickason estimates that Canada should be considered as having fifty-eight 'founding nations', rather than the two which are officially acknowledged (that is, the English and French).[13] *The Canadian Encyclopedia* contains entries for more than ninety Aboriginal groupings, but some of these refer to confederacies (in historical terms) or consolidated kinship groups, while others refer to their component tribes and bands (that is, clans or families). Some peoples are listed twice under different names because they self-identify using terms from their own language, while being known outside their communities by another name: for example, the Siksika (commonly known as Blackfoot), Innu (formerly referred to as Montagnais and Naskapi) and Anishnabek (known also as Ojibwa, Chippewa and Salteaux).

One way to think of Indigenous groupings is by the division into eleven language families. None of these is spoken in Canada alone; most cross the border with the United States or extend into Greenland (a Danish territory). The Native peoples of North America view such political boundaries as White political constructs, and would, of course, have crossed freely in the pre-contact era. Eskimo-Aleut (or Eskimoan) languages extend the furthest: across the Arctic regions from Alaska to Greenland. The Iroquoian language family is the only one which belongs exclusively to eastern Canada (to the south of Quebec and Ontario), while Algonkian languages stretch from the prairies to Ontario, primarily to the north of these areas in the subarctic or boreal forest region. Athapaskan languages predominate across what are now the Northwest and Yukon Territories, the British Columbian interior and the northern prairie provinces. Siouan is spoken in southern Saskatchewan and Manitoba. The other language families are found only in British Columbia – these are Kutenai, Salishan, Tsimshian, Tlingit, Haida and Wakashan. Some of the languages in these groups have now been lost, but more than fifty distinct languages are still spoken today; the precise number depends on the definitions of 'language' and 'dialect' which are adopted. Those with the largest number of speakers are Inuktit, an Eskimoan language, and Cree, an Algonkian language. It is estimated that up to 93 per cent of the pre-Columbian population of the Americas may have been obliterated by important diseases in the sixteenth century, while today, First Nations, Inuit and Métis peoples together make up just 4 per cent of Canada's population. This rapid survey cannot do any kind of justice to the complex histories, cultures and languages of Canada's Aboriginal populations, but it will at least serve to make some of the names familiar to readers.

ABOUT THIS BOOK

This book is primarily intended for undergraduate students and lecturers planning courses in Canadian literature. Its main purpose is to provide an introduction to the subject and to suggest ways of studying key literary texts and combining them in essays or teaching programmes. It also seeks to stimulate discussion by raising broad questions about methods of reading Canadian literature, as well as more specific questions about particular authors, texts and genres. In addition, the book provides a framework for learning and teaching in the form of factual sections, discussion questions and guides to resources. For postgraduate students, the value of the book will be somewhat different: it offers introductions to texts, authors and aspects of literary history which may be unfamiliar; brings together in one volume a range of essential and up-to-date reference material; and surveys the possible future of Canadian literature as a field of study and research.

The main body of the book comprises four themed chapters, each containing a general introduction to the topic followed by concise close readings of five key texts. The first chapter, 'Ethnicity, Race, Colonisation', concentrates on representations of Native Canadians, migrant identities and hybridity, and explores colonial and modern literary inscriptions of the encounter between White and Indigenous peoples. Authors considered as case studies are Frances Brooke, Pauline Johnson, Michael Ondaatje, Thomas King and Tomson Highway. Chapter 2, 'Wilderness, Cities, Regions', takes as its starting point a classic Canadian wilderness narrative, Richardson's *Wacousta*, assessing its legacy to later writers. The relationship between wilderness and garrison, and later between forest or prairie and urban settlements, has always been considered a central preoccupation of Canadian literature, and in recent decades this theme has been revisited and parodied in a range of self-conscious, postmodern fictions. The chapter also examines the literary construction of Canada by region. Authors discussed are L. M. Montgomery, Ethel Wilson, Robertson Davies, Carol Shields, Margaret Atwood and Alice Munro.

The third chapter introduces a less expected topic, but one which may also be seen as fundamental to Canadian literature: 'Desire'. The Canadian poetics of landscape is intimately bound up with the body and with longing, while the impulse to explore the country's history may also become entwined with the erotic. The chapter examines these interrelationships, and also addresses homosexual desire, recently acknowledged as an important strand in Canadian literature. Authors chosen for this topic are Martha Ostenso, Leonard Cohen, John Glassco, Anne Michaels and Dionne Brand. The last chapter, 'Histories and Stories', considers the fascination with history evident in Canadian literature from the early nineteenth century onwards. It begins with the well-established genre of the historical long poem, before moving on to discuss the proliferation of postmodern texts which problematise the relation between history and literature. The chapter also analyses intertextual relations between colonial and postcolonial literature. Authors discussed are E. J. Pratt, Margaret Laurence, Margaret Atwood, Joy Kogawa and Daphne Marlatt. The Conclusion to the book surveys the recent development of Canadian literary studies, as well as considering the increasing significance of literary stars, prizes, mass reading events and book clubs.

As well as representing significant themes in Canadian literary texts, the topics chosen for the different chapters also map loosely onto particular theoretical approaches. Therefore, Chapter 1 explores postcolonial reading strategies, Chapter 2 discusses theories of space and place, Chapter 3 includes an introduction to the theorisation of desire, and the final chapter considers postmodern perspectives on the relationship between literature and history. Detail about specific literary and historical contexts is also provided where appropriate, to assist students in producing nuanced and historically aware readings of their own. Although some of the books I have chosen for close reading fit naturally with one of the four topics, many of them could equally well have been placed in a different section. Daphne Marlatt's *Ana Historic*, for example, could have been allocated to the chapter on desire, or the one on wilderness and cities, and if it had been, my reading would have emphasised her perspectives on lesbian love or on forest and urban landscapes, rather than her exploration of history. The rich, complex texts introduced here offer far more material for discussion than can be indicated in my short account of each one, and while the case studies seek to offer fresh perspectives on each text, they also – and more importantly – suggest possible directions for students' reading and discussion. The chapters do include conclusions and summary points, but their primary purpose is not to present definitive readings but to open up the texts for further analysis.

The main text of the book is framed by supplementary material designed to assist interpretation and suggest new reading possibilities. The Chronology provides an overview of Canadian literary history and of Canada's cultural development and evolving political structures. The Student Resources section includes questions for discussion on each of the twenty texts (which indicate additional approaches beyond those suggested in the chapters); a list of alternative primary texts for each of the four chapter topics; and an annotated selection of electronic resources. The Glossary explains historical, literary and cultural concepts which are central to Canadian studies, and defines terms which may be unfamiliar to those coming to the subject for the first time. Finally, the Guide to Further Reading provides a list of the most relevant and up-to-date books and articles, subdivided according to the topics covered in this study.

NOTES

1. Thomas King, *Green Grass Running Water* (Toronto: HarperCollins, [1993] 1994), p. 1.
2. Margaret Atwood, *Strange Things: The Malevolent North in Canadian Literature* (Oxford: Clarendon Press, 1995), p. 7.
3. Ibid., p. 8.
4. Ibid., p. 2.
5. E. D. Blodgett, *Five-Part Invention: A History of Literary History in Canada* (Toronto: University of Toronto Press, 2003), p. 4.
6. Ibid., p. 10.
7. Apollo O. Amoko, 'Resilient ImagiNations: *No-No Boy*, *Obasan* and the Limits of Minority Discourse', *Mosaic: A Journal for the Interdisciplinary Study of Literature*, 33: 3 (2000), 35–55 (p. 35).
8. W. H. New, *A History of Canadian Literature*, 2nd edn (Montreal and Kingston: McGill-Queen's University Press, 2003), p. 322.
9. Ibid.
10. Penny van Toorn, 'Aboriginal Writing', in *The Cambridge Companion to Canadian Literature*, ed. Eva-Marie Kröller (Cambridge: Cambridge University Press, 2004), pp. 22–48 (p. 24).
11. Ibid.

12. See ibid., p. 45n; Olive Dickason, *Canada's First Nations: A History of Founding Peoples from Earliest Times*, 3rd edn (Don Mills, ON: Oxford University Press, 2002), pp. xiv–xv.

13. Dickason, *Canada's First Nations*, p. x.

CHAPTER I

Ethnicity, Race, Colonisation

Everything in front of us is virgin land. From the beginning
of time, the grass along this stretch of prairie has not been cut.
About a mile east is a spot which was once an Indian buffalo
jump, a high steep cliff where the buffalo were stampeded and
fell to their deaths. All the bones are still there, some sticking
right out of the side of a fresh landslide.
Uncle could be Chief Sitting Bull squatting here. He has the
same prairie-baked skin, the deep brown furrows like dry river
beds creasing his cheeks. All he needs is a feather headdress,
and he would be perfect for a picture postcard – 'Indian Chief
from Canadian Prairie' – souvenir of Alberta, made in Japan.

Joy Kogawa, *Obasan*[1]

Racial and ethnic identity and the history of colonisation are among
the most intriguing, yet complex, subjects of Canadian writing. Joy
Kogawa captures some of this complexity in this passage from her
1981 novel about the Canadian government's persecution of its citizens of Japanese origin during the Second World War. At first
adopting the vocabulary of the White coloniser, the narrator,
Naomi, refers to 'virgin land', meaning land which has been neither
cultivated nor subdivided according to White systems of ownership, and to 'Indians', the name which colonists used for the
Indigenous peoples of the Americas. But this apparent alignment
with a colonising perspective is immediately subverted by Naomi's

association of her own ethnic group, Japanese-Canadians, with Indigenous peoples, who have likewise been treated unjustly by White Canada. Also, the image of the buffalo being stampeded over the cliff is only superficially a comment on 'Indian' practices; metaphorically, it anticipates Kogawa's story of Japanese-Canadians being herded into detention and labour camps, where many of them died. Lastly, Kogawa disrupts the signifying practices of White cultures by mocking undifferentiated and exoticised views of racial others. Naomi imagines her uncle turned into a commodity, and the postcard she envisages is doubly inauthentic: not only does it not represent an 'Indian', but it is not even made in Canada. And yet for Naomi, the recollection of Uncle sitting on the prairie becomes quite literally a 'souvenir of Alberta, made in Japan', because 'souvenir' is the French word for memory, and Uncle was born in Japan.

This, then, is a slippery piece of writing: its perspective is difficult to establish, and its use of metaphor complicates, rather than clarifies, the relationships among Canada's different ethnic and racial groups. The same is true of the other texts which will be discussed in this chapter, and, indeed, of much Canadian writing which addresses race, diaspora, hybridity and colonial encounter. Bringing together in one chapter the work of Indigenous or part-Indigenous writers such as Tomson Highway, Thomas King and Pauline Johnson with books by a Japanese-Canadian author and an English visitor to Canada (Frances Brooke) is an awkward project, and the comparison of work from the eighteenth, nineteenth and twentieth centuries poses a further challenge. Yet such a diverse selection of material can at least gesture towards the multiplicity of literary perspectives on ethnic and racial identity, migration and empire which are available in Canadian literature. This multiplicity is largely a result of Canada's intricate history of colonisation, internal migration and immigration from around the world, aspects of which will emerge in the close readings included in this chapter.

The first close reading is of the earliest novel about Canada to be published in any language, Brooke's *The History of Emily Montague* (1769), which explores the interactions between English colonists, French-Canadians and Huron peoples in post-conquest Quebec. The second author chosen for discussion, Canada's most famous

Native writer, E. Pauline Johnson/Tekahionwake, also focuses on Native – White encounter, and her poems dramatise a range of points of view on Native issues and colonisation. Joy Kogawa's *Obasan* is next examined, while the fourth and fifth sections concentrate on two of the best-known contemporary First Nations texts, Tomson Highway's *The Rez Sisters* (first performed 1986) and Thomas King's *Green Grass Running Water* (1993). These authors use comic techniques both to celebrate First Nations culture and also to critique the erosion of that culture through White policies of assimilation. Other chapters in this book discuss literary representations of Black, Jewish, eastern European and Scandinavian diasporas (see sections on Brand, Michaels, Ondaatje and Ostenso), and these texts offer a further range of points of view on Canada's multicultural society.

Multiculturalism forms an important context to Canadian literary study. It means, in policy terms, an approach to the management of ethnically diverse societies which emphasises tolerance of difference and mutual respect among ethnic groups. In 1971 Canada became the first country to implement an official multiculturalism policy, following the recommendation of the Royal Commission on Bilingualism and Biculturalism, which reported in 1969. The commission was set up in 1963 in response to ongoing tensions between francophone and anglophone cultures in the majority White population, but the evidence submitted to its hearings related to other ethnicities as well, and the wording of the policy which was finally implemented referred to 'bilingualism and multiculturalism'. The substitution of 'multicultural' for 'bicultural' was, however, mainly driven by White Canadians who were not from anglophone or francophone cultures, such as those of Scandinavian or eastern European origin. Critics of the policy argued that it was colour-blind, and did not address the more pressing problems of racism. But while the royal commission may have taken insufficient account of Black, Asian or Native Canadians; more recent debates on multiculturalism focus primarily on these groups.

In 1988 the Act for the Preservation and Enhancement of Multiculturalism in Canada was passed. It emphasises the racial diversity of Canadian society, and its objectives include fostering appreciation of minority cultures and preserving languages other than English and French. Proponents of multiculturalism have constructed a narrative of progressive nationhood in which Canada increasingly recognises the rights of every component of its 'mosaic' society (this image, evoking unique parts fitting together into a coherent whole, is preferred to the American 'melting pot'). One of the dangers of this approach, though, is that it presents racial discrimination as a thing of the past, denying its persistence in modern-day Canada. Multiculturalism has also been criticised, in Canada and worldwide, for being a divisive force which reduces national unity and encourages ghettoisation and stereotyping; for tacitly consenting to the discrimination against women which occurs in some minority cultures; and for propounding a concept of human identity as wholly determined by race or ethnicity. Yet despite these various critiques of multiculturalism, its core values of respect and tolerance are, on the whole, widely accepted in Canada.

The Canadian preoccupation with categories of identity, together with its complex history of conquest, settlement and colonisation, irresistibly invite a reading of its literature in post-colonial terms, even as these factors make such reading projects awkward and challenging. Postcolonial theories, which are largely concerned with power relationships and resistance, alterity and hybridity, history and language, are very relevant to Canadian literature, but the conjunction of Canada and the postcolonial immediately raises some rather vexed issues. Since Canada was formerly part of the British Empire, and parts of it were also previously French colonial possessions, it may arguably be thought of as a postcolonial country. The view that the legacy of empire, or 'the colonial mentality', continued to influence, and, indeed, to restrict or damage Canadian culture well into the twentieth century has been articulated by many historians and literary critics, most famously by Northrop Frye in his conclusion to *The Literary History of Canada* (1965) and Margaret Atwood in *Survival: A Thematic Guide to Canadian Literature* (1972). These critics argue that Canada's art, literature and cultural institutions were, at least until the earlier twentieth century, derived mainly from European models, but that gradually the influence of Britain and France was exceeded by that of the United States, to the extent that Canada has been economically and culturally colonised by the US. (According to this view, French Canadians are doubly colonised, by both English-Canada and America.) Caught between two powerful and longer-established cultures, Canada has, critics contend, faced particular challenges in evolving towards independent nationhood. As Frye puts it: 'Canada became a colony in the mercantilist sense, treated by others less like a society than as a place to look for things. French, English, Americans plunged into it to carry off its supplies'. He adds: 'It is not much wonder if Canada developed with the bewilderment of a neglected child, preoccupied with trying to define its own identity'.[2]

More recently, however, the view of Canada's White population as colonised has been strongly challenged, and White Canadians have been recast as colonisers of Indigenous peoples. These peoples have had their land seized, their populations severely reduced or even obliterated, and their cultural practices, beliefs and languages attacked and eroded, whether in the name of religion, education, economics or social assimilation. Yet despite this compelling, and frequently horrific, dimension of colonial interaction in Canadian space, Canada is still generally omitted from discussions of the politics, history and literature of postcolonial countries. A majority of books in the burgeoning field of postcolonial studies concentrate entirely on Africa, Asia, the Caribbean and Latin America, and do not engage with settler colonies in North America or Australasia. The most recent example is the *Cambridge Companion to Postcolonial Literary Studies* (2004), edited by Neil Lazarus, which – valuable though it is – does not even list Canada in the index, and mentions Australia and New Zealand only once each, in passing.

In her editor's introduction to *Is Canada Postcolonial? Unsettling Canadian Literature* (2003), Laura Moss explains:

There has long been a debate over the legitimacy and utility of studying the literary culture of a nation like Canada in the same terms as the Anglophone literature of the most conventionally accepted postcolonial contexts of India, Trinidad, and South Africa, for example. A clear divide in the postcolonial paradigm is often perceived between the 'invader-settler' nations of Australia, New Zealand, and Canada, where the process of colonization was predominantly one of immigration and settlement, and those parts of the world where colonization was more predominantly a process of displacement, impoverishment, sublimination, and even annihilation. However, too sharp a division may obscure the terrible consequences of colonialism for the Indigenous peoples in the territories settled, as it might overlook the complexity of cultural and political reconstruction in territories exploited under the economic and political imperatives of empire.[3]

At the same time, as Moss cautions, the model of Canada as a White settler colony with an invaded Indigenous population is also too simplistic, not least because 'it places Native populations in a constant state of opposition rather than separation' and 'freezes First Nations writers in a historical role'.[4] In addition, this model fails to acknowledge Canada's ethnic diversity – not all Canadian writers are descended from either 'those who settled or those who invaded' – and nor does it 'allow room for resistance or opposition to the very real threat of American cultural imperialism'.[5]

As long as these caveats are borne in mind, postcolonial theories and strategies of reading can be very productive when applied in a Canadian context, as the varied and intriguing essays in Moss's collection, together with numerous other books on the subject, amply demonstrate (see Guide to Further Reading). It is wise, though, to pay attention not only to what is shared across the spectrum of postcolonies, but also to the ways in which they differ, and local specificities of history, geography, demographics, politics and culture need to be taken into account in order to produce nuanced readings of Canadian texts in a postcolonial context. Also, postcolonial models are relevant in different ways to the literature of different periods or ethnic groups. Applying postcolonial reading strategies to an eighteenth- or nineteenth-century text by a White visitor to Canada will probably produce a broadly oppositional interpretation: that is, one which seeks to uncover ideologies and assumptions which the text takes for granted or perhaps conceals. Applying similar strategies to a novel written in the 1990s by a Native Canadian will usually lead to a reading which is largely sympathetic, and consonant with the political orientation of the novel itself. But it is not always this simple: depending on your perspective, it is of course possible to discern resistance to colonial stereotyping in an eighteenth-century text, or indeed to read a Native-authored work oppositionally, arguing for its complicity with imperialist ideologies.

Many questions and issues might be explored when reading Canadian literature 'postcolonially'. For example, a study of literary representations of ethnic minorities might consider how far their histories and cultures are normalised and/or constructed as exotic, perhaps comparing texts by members and non-members of the minority group. Another focus could be the forms of resistance to colonial ways of seeing which are encoded in authors' use of dialect and new Englishes, or allegory and symbolism. For texts exploring Canada's past, the question of how far such narratives can work to decolonise the historical imagination is a pertinent one. In relation to contemporary writing, an issue gaining increasing critical attention is the interaction between the politically committed project of the postcolonial and the supposedly apolitical one of postmodernism. Questions such as these inform several of the close readings in this book, and a fuller list of questions for postcolonial reading is provided in the Student Resources.

The perspective of a literary text on questions of race cannot, of course, be 'read off' directly from the identity of its author. Some texts by White authors evince racist attitudes towards Black, Asian or Native Canadians, others reject such attitudes. Many texts by Aboriginal or mixed-race authors resist colonial stereotypes of the 'savage', but some – especially those from earlier periods – partially reinscribe them. The literary text may dramatise conflicts between different attitudes to racial issues without explicitly endorsing any of them, and it is also important to be aware of the disruptive potential of strategies such as parody, mimicry and satire, which have been extensively discussed by major postcolonial critics such as Gayatri Spivak and Frantz Fanon. Dee Horne offers a helpful summary of these ideas in a Canadian context:

> Mimicry can be a major problem for postcolonial writers who write in European languages. In adopting the language,

discourse, and mode of production of the colonizer/settler, the colonized writer can be trapped in a 'Manichean world' of subject/object, us/them, superior/inferior, civilized/savage wherein the settler is perceived as the 'original' – the master that must be slavishly imitated.

There is, however, a peculiar twist to this mimetic process. In imposing the language of the dominant culture on the colonized, the settler provides the colonized with the means to subvert what Homi Bhahba terms the 'rules of recognition' – the construction of the native as other – from within the discourse of the dominant culture . . . What I will call the *creative hybrid text* does not merely reverse the Manichean opposition; it deconstructs it . . . The First Nations writer infiltrates the dominant discourse by appearing to conform with it, but all the while critiquing it. This critique often alienates settler readers. The First Nations writer can use colonial hybridity to create a new form, new rules of recognition, which the settler needs to learn to comprehend the text.[6]

Mimicry and hybrid narrative modes, then, can be highly effective in resisting colonial discourses, but also place stringent demands on readers. Parodic, carnivalesque texts such as Thomas King's *Green Grass Running Water* (1993), for example, may be comic, entertaining and easy to read, but are often difficult to interpret and politically provocative. Horne's concept of the creative hybrid text is not only useful for reading contemporary authors such as King or Highway, but is also very relevant to an earlier writer such as Pauline Johnson, who inscribed her own racial and cultural hybridity in her texts and also performed it during public readings by changing from a Native costume to formal Victorian dress. Creative hybridity is not a strategy limited to First Nations artists: it is also used effectively by Canadians from other historically colonised groups. For example, Black authors such as Austin Clarke, Dionne Brand and George Elliott Clarke deploy non-standard English to evoke the voices of their communities and to resist White linguistic and cultural norms (see Chapter 3), an approach which is also used by numerous Indigenous authors.

FRANCES BROOKE, *THE HISTORY OF EMILY MONTAGUE* (1769)

The History of Emily Montague is often referred to as the first Canadian novel. It contains the earliest fictional account of life in Quebec under British rule and of the encounter between English colonists and Native peoples. *Emily Montague* is also the first female-authored text about Canada; all the earlier extant writings were by male explorers and fur traders. Frances Brooke (1723-89), an Englishwoman, lived in Canada for five years. She travelled to Quebec in 1763, after the Treaty of Paris (see Glossary, under Seven Years' War) had ceded the colony of New France to Britain, to join her husband, who was chaplain to the British garrison. She already had several plays, translations and essays to her name, together with a successful novel, *The History of Lady Julia Mandeville* (1763). But it is *Emily Montague* for which she is remembered, since the book became 'required reading for early British travellers to Canada',[7] and was later canonised as a Canadian classic.

Frances Brooke's subject, the social life of post-conquest Quebec, was returned to by many authors in the succeeding century. Novelists and poets such as Rosanna Leprohon, Gilbert Parker and William Kirby, writing in English, or Philippe-Joseph Aubert de Gaspé, Octave Crémazie and Laure Conan, in French, sought to recapture the period of the Seven Years' War, the feudal *ancien régime*, and the culture and folklore of the French *habitants*. But Brooke's novel is of special value, since she wrote about the ethnically mixed society of late eighteenth-century Canada from the perspective of a participant, and although her main characters are almost all English, she engages in detail with the social practices of the French-Canadians and the Huron. Following the defeat of their tribes by the Iroquois Confederacy in 1649, some of the scattered Huron peoples had settled in Loretteville, near Quebec City, and several of Brooke's characters interact with Huron people (see Glossary on Huron and Iroquois).

The History of Emily Montague is part travel narrative, part love story. The sentimental heroine, Emily Montague, is engaged to Sir George Clayton, a match arranged by her uncle since her father is presumed dead. Following an unexpected acquisition of wealth and consequence, Sir George reveals a concupiscence and arrogance which repel his fiancée. At the same time, she and Colonel Edward Rivers fall in love. Emily breaks her engagement, but at first refuses to marry Rivers because their income would be so small that they would have to remain in Canada in order to live comfortably. Further difficulties arise when an attractive French-Canadian widow, Madame des Roches, also falls in love with Rivers. Eventually, Emily and Rivers do become engaged, and return to England, where Emily's father reappears and bestows a large fortune on the couple. In two parallel developments, Emily's more lively friend Arabella marries an Irish captain, Fitzgerald, while Rivers's sister Lucy, left behind in London, marries her brother's best friend, Temple, formerly a rake.

Emily Montague is an epistolary novel. The principal letter-writers are Arabella (arguably the novel's true heroine) and Rivers, who both write in a witty, light-hearted vein, while Arabella's father, Sir William Fermor, sends home detailed and earnest accounts of the colony. The other English characters contribute occasional letters. While many eighteenth-century novels were made up of a small number of letters by just one or two characters, containing lengthy confessions or retrospections, Brooke's text is composed of 228 letters by 11 characters, creating an unusual multi-voiced, conversational structure. This is particularly notice-able in the notes sent locally, which are often answered the same day. A question of especial relevance here (and one on which critics differ) is whether this structure is used to facilitate a genuine dia-logue on the question of race, or whether the differing views expressed are finally contained within an overarching colonialist ideology.

Many of the opinions which Brooke's characters express about the Huron and the French-Canadians would be labelled racist or prejudiced in today's terminology. In the eighteenth century, though, it was normal for the English to privilege whiteness and also to assert their own superiority over other European nations, whom they considered to belong to different races from themselves. While we would distinguish racial difference (such as that between White and Aboriginal inhabitants of Canada) from ethnic or national difference (such as that between French and English colonists), writers in Brooke's era habitually used the term 'race' in both cases. The English characters in *Emily Montague* take a pseudo-anthropological approach to the Huron and to the French-Canadians of all classes, enquiring into their habits and seeking to explain these unfamiliar groups to correspondents at home. Arabella remarks: 'The French ladies . . . seem born without the smallest portion of curiosity, or any idea of the pleasures of the imagination, or indeed any pleasure but that of being admired'.[8] She characterises the *habitants* in equally sweeping terms, writing to Lucy: 'I have been rambling about among the peasants, and asking them a thousand questions', and remarking that they are 'proud', 'idle' and 'useless' (p. 50). Her father considers them 'brave, hardy, alert in the field, but lazy and inactive at home' (p. 119). This hostility is not surprising. Britain had been engaged in a series of lengthy military conflicts with France, and while the Seven Years' War was over, the contest for imperial supremacy was ongoing. As Cecily Devereux argues, Brooke's novel constructs Canada as a space where 'Britishness could be defined in opposition to its French other' and where 'the righteousness of British imperialism could be performed through the government of a group of people who were seen to be both a major imperial contestant and a regressive, "uncivilized" underclass'.[9]

The novel does portray one French-Canadian character sympathetically, the wealthy landowner Madame Des Roches. But while she is romantic, generous and intelligent, she also, as Dermot McCarthy notes, 'incorporates all the modes of alterity – race, sex, religion, and landscape – that represent the Other in Brooke's novel'. McCarthy adds: 'her rejection should be understood in terms of the rejection of a future life in the colony by Brooke's principals'.[10] For all her attractions, Madame Des Roches is subordinated to the idealised, and very English, Emily by the logic of the plot. Similarly, although both Arabella and Rivers fantasise about establishing a permanent 'coterie' or community of friendship in Quebec (p. 97), the novel ends by reasserting the value of family and of England. The concluding section returns Rivers to his mother and sister, Emily to her father, and all the principal characters to an Eden located in Rutland, where – appropriately – they take up gardening.

William Fermor writes of the peasants: 'they resemble the savages, whose manners they seem strongly to have imbibed' (p. 119). In thus aligning the French and Indigenous inhabitants of Canada, Fermor positions both as colonial subjects of Britain, suggesting that they are equally in need of a civilising influence. He recommends that both communities be persuaded to learn English 'manners', as well as 'the mild genius of our religion and laws, and that spirit of industry, enterprize, and commerce, to which we owe all our greatness' (p. 189). Fermor's is not, however, the dominant voice in the novel, and his views are juxtaposed with the more ambivalent responses of his daughter and Colonel Rivers who, unlike Fermor, experience personal interaction with Huron people. Arabella even shares a picnic with some squaws, an unusual proceeding for a woman of her class. She refers to 'my good sisters the squaws', a designation which is generous by eighteenth-century standards – many other English writers equated Aboriginals with animals. Yet the phrase is somewhat patronising, as is her comment that 'they danced, sung, shook me by the hand, and grew so very fond of me, that I began to be afraid I should not easily get rid of them' (p. 41).

The History of Emily Montague is rare among novels of its period in its detailed attention to the Native peoples of North America, but some of Brooke's observations are not so much designed to shed light on Huron society as to criticise British ideologies of gender.[11] One sequence of letters, positioned so that they comment implicitly on one another, intersperses Arabella's remarks on Aboriginal marriage conventions with reports on the progress of Emily's amours. Arabella admires the Huron men for allowing their wives total freedom of movement, but then recoils on discovering that the parents apparently 'marry their children without ever consulting their inclinations' (p. 46). The interspersed letters relate the attempts of Emily's relatives to force her to marry the tiresome Sir George, so that the section as a whole suggests an element of savagery in both European and Huron societies. A second comparison relates to female political power. Rivers writes:

The sex we have so unjustly excluded from power in Europe have a great share in the Huron government; the chief is chose by the matrons . . . In the truest sense of the word, we are the savages who so impolitely deprive you of the common rights of citizenship . . . By the way, I don't think you are obliged in conscience to obey laws you have had no share in making; your plea would certainly be at least as good as that of the Americans. (p. 27)

Despite its flippant tone, this last assertion is particularly subversive, not only in its perspective on Britain's increasingly troubled relation to its New World colonies but also in its very progressive attitude to female suffrage.

Brooke's commentary on religion also seems to cut both ways, which is perhaps surprising for the wife of a clergyman. Rivers says of the Huron:

I have already observed, that they retain most of their antient [sic] superstitions. I should particularize their belief in dreams, of which folly even repeated disappointments cannot cure them . . . As I happened to smile at the recital a savage was making of a prophetic dream, . . . 'You Europeans', said he, 'are the most unreasonable people in the world; you laugh at our belief in dreams, and yet expect us to believe things a thousand times more incredible.' (p. 29)

Passages such as these somewhat undermine William Fermor's unexamined assumption that the British have nothing to learn from Aboriginal peoples, and should strive to remake them in their own image.

Except through brief quotations of their words, the perspective of the Huron themselves is not elucidated. 'To read a Canadian text postcolonially', writes Laura Moss, 'is to read Quebec in Frances Brooke's *The History of Emily Montague* as a synecdoche of a hybrid nation', and to wonder why the Huron 'have no representative voices in this polyphonic narrative'.[12] It might be added that French-Canadians have no voice either. All the letters are written by English characters, and Madame Des Roches's speeches are merely reported or paraphrased (and sometimes altered) by Emily or Arabella, so that the threat she poses is contained.[13] Inevitably (given the ideology of her period), Brooke privileges the English perspective, but she does also point out some of its flaws. The novel thus goes some way towards challenging images of the Hurons as 'savage' and the French as degenerate, which were already stereotypes at the time of writing. Yet in other ways it reinforces those stereotypes and transmits them to later generations. Attention to Brooke's novel reveals the value of considering colonial literature from a postcolonial point of view, not only in order to illuminate the colonial texts themselves, but to improve our understanding of what came later.

TEKAHIONWAKE/E. PAULINE JOHNSON, SELECTED POETRY

Emily Pauline Johnson (1861-1913), also known by her chosen Mohawk name, Tekahionwake, was the child of an unusual mixed marriage. While many relationships between White men and Aboriginal women took place in colonial Canada, the opposite situation was rare. Johnson's mother was an Englishwoman of good family; her father was a Mohawk chief (the Mohawk Nation was part of the Iroquois Confederacy). The couple's home, Chiefswood, was a mansion on the Six Nations Reserve near Brantford, in Canada West (now southern Ontario). Following the death of her father in 1884 and the loss of Chiefswood, Pauline Johnson started publishing poems in magazines in order to earn a living. In 1892 she began giving stage recitals, and their increasing popularity soon made her a celebrity. Her first poetry collection, *The White Wampum* (1895), was well received by critics, but the second, *Canadian Born* (1903), was much less successful, and Johnson increasingly turned to prose writing, publishing fiction, essays and retellings of Indigenous legends. She moved to Vancouver in 1909.

Johnson's poetry is varied in both form and content, and her influences range from English Romanticism to the oral legends of the Iroquois. Her primary subjects are nature, romantic love and Native experience, and she also wrote patriotic verses. While some individual poems adopt clear-cut positions on the subjects of empire, nationalism or Aboriginal issues, her work as a whole explores a broad spectrum of political views, and no single text should be taken as representative of her opinions. The speakers of her poems and stories are, of course, rhetorical constructs, not to be directly identified with Johnson herself, and while this is obvious in her dramatic monologues, it is also true of her lyric poetry.

As the editors of Johnson's *Collected Poems and Selected Prose* comment, her frequent use of first-person narrators suggests 'the presence of listeners', and evokes the storytelling traditions of the First Nations.[14] Many of her verses and stories originated in legends told to her by her Mohawk community, and later by the Squamish people who welcomed her in Vancouver. She does not, though, construct storytelling as an exclusively Native practice; 'Wolverine' (1893), for example, is narrated by a trapper, who begins: 'Yes, sir, it's quite a story, though you won't believe it's true',[15] clearly positioning himself as storyteller, and revealing the presence of a narratee. Other examples of narrative poems in White dialects include 'The Lumberman's Christmas' (1888) and 'Beyond the Blue' (1890).

It is Johnson's poems on First Nations subjects, however, which have generated the most interest among audiences and critics, although they represent only a limited proportion of her output. They are complex, both individually and collectively, in their attitudes to the relationship between White and Aboriginal Canadians, and their perspectives shift according to current circumstances. Early poems tend to promote reconciliation; in '"Brant": A Memorial Ode' (1886), for example, the speaker advises Indigenous peoples to:

> love the land where waves the Union Jack.
> What though that home no longer ours! To-day
> The Six Red Nations have their Canada,
> And rest we here, no cause for us to rise
> To seek protection under other skies. (p. 21)

But Johnson went on to write dramatic poems about conflict and vengeance among different Native groups. Following the Northwest Rebellion (see under 'Riel rebellions' in the Glossary) of 1884-5, in which Métis and First Nations peoples protested against the land policies of the Dominion and were opposed by government forces, race relations in Canada degenerated, and Johnson became more explicit in her poetic condemnation of injustice against Aboriginals. In later years, however, she tended to choose prose forms when exploring such questions. As Gerson and Strong-Boag note: 'Her few later Indian poems, like the earliest, seem to reincorporate First Nations into normalizing Euro-Canadian conventions, albeit with subtle reminders of difference'.[16]

Examples of poems dramatising conflicts between Indigenous peoples are 'Ojistoh' (1895), about a Mohawk wife taken captive by Huron; 'The Avenger' (1892), about bloody rivalries between Cherokee and Iroquois; and 'As Red Men Die' (1890). The latter evinces admiration for the bravery of an Iroquois captive, forced to choose between slavery or death by walking on red-hot coals: 'loyal to his race, / He bends to death – but *never* to disgrace' (p. 69). The poem celebrates the eventual victory of the Iroquois over their Huron enemies, achieving dramatic effect by contrasting the captive's imprisonment in the present moment with the narrator's knowledge of the outcome of the wars: 'He knoweth not that this same jeering band / Will bite the dust – will lick the Mohawk's hand' (p. 69). But while the logic of the poem as a whole privileges Johnson's own 'invincible' (p. 69) Mohawk community at the expense of the Huron, some lines express revulsion for both groups' violent practices: 'His death will be avenged with hideous hate / By Iroquois, swift to annihilate / His vile, detested captors' (p. 68).

In a related manoeuvre, 'A Cry from an Indian Wife' (1885), published during the Northwest Rebellion, is clearly on the side of the Indigenous peoples in their conflicts with White colonisers, yet also laments the deaths of young soldiers and warriors from both races. Like several of Johnson's poems, it offers a specifically female perspective on battle: the narrator combines vigorous support for the 'Indian' cause with a passionate conjugal devotion and regret for the necessity of war and bloodshed. In other poems, the theme of conflict is displaced and female desire becomes central. 'Wave-Won' (1892) is one of several pieces centring on lovers sailing in a canoe which have an erotic intensity unusual for a woman writer of this period. The couple in 'Wave-Won' are 'in delirium' with 'maddened hearts', but though the man has a 'god-like head', he in fact adopts the passive position, lying supine while the speaker, her 'arm as strong as steel', paddles over the rapids (p. 86). In 'The Idlers' (1890), the female perspective emerges through the eroticisation of the male body: the beloved's 'arm superb is lying, brown and bare' and his clothes fall 'well aside', revealing his 'muscle' (p. 61).

Another point of view which Pauline Johnson repeatedly adopts is that of a Christian. Her frequent invocation of Christian ideology and iconographies does, to a certain extent, align her with the White side of her heritage, yet the vitality of Christian belief among First Nations Canadians in the nineteenth century should not be under-estimated. This religion had, of course, been forcibly imposed on many of them, or on their forebears (see Chapter 4), but during Johnson's lifetime, Christianity was an important part of the culture and heritage of many Indigenous and Métis groups, and Native leadership was increasingly common within church – and especially Catholic – communities. Among Johnson's most explic-itly religious poems is 'A Request' (1886), which asks for more mis-sionaries to save 'Indian souls' (p. 23), while 'Easter Lilies' (1886), 'Easter' (1888), 'Christmastide' (1889), 'The Seventh Day' (1891) and 'Brier' (1893) reflect on particular festivals and saints. In other poems, however, Christian practices are questioned by First Nations speakers. In 'The Cattle Thief' (1894), for example, the outraged daughter of a Cree man shouts at the White settlers who murdered him: 'How have you paid us for our game? how paid us for our land? / By a *book*, to save our souls from the sins *you* brought in your other hand' (p. 99). In speaking as a Christian, Johnson was speaking for a significant minority of Native Canadians, while also offering points of contact and a sense of communality of belief to non-Native readers. But as always, she resists identification with a singular viewpoint, and poems such as 'The Cattle Thief' offer no comfortable reading position for White audiences.

A significant amount of critical writing on Johnson focuses on her negotiation of her mixed-race identity. While her parents raised their children to respect both sides of their heritage, they were never fully integrated into either Anglo-Canadian or Iroquois society, and the legacy of this upbringing is evident in Johnson's poetry and in her public presence. At readings, she would begin in a buckskin costume (partly copied from a drawing of Longfellow's mythic Minnehaha), displaying on her body various symbols of 'Indian' culture, such as feathers, necklaces made of animal teeth and claws, wampum belts, moccasins and a hunting knife. After the interval, she would return in Victorian evening dress. As Mary Elizabeth Leighton comments: 'Audiences read her performances as illustrative of the "vanishing" [of Native culture]. They were reluctant, however, to concede that her evening gown was as much a costume as her Native outfit'.[17]

If overly straightforward biographical readings can be avoided, the interplay between Pauline Johnson's texts, performances and life experiences opens up productive lines of critical inquiry. Marilyn J. Rose argues:

> To read Pauline Johnson in a postcolonial context is to recognise the many-layered resistance which marks her public presence . . . [She] refuse[d] to be some/thing, some (one) properly classifiable thing – a Victorian lady, a Native voice, an incipient feminist, a thespian, a Canadian patriot, or anything else . . . By generating and cultivating competing identities, and by refusing to be simply categorised in any direction, Johnson was constructing herself as a . . . veritable 'field of identities' which tacitly posits Canadian identity as multivocal and hence contestative of classical, imperial and univocal notions of nationalism.[18]

It is illuminating, therefore, to read Johnson's work in relation to the critical and biographical texts which surround it, and to consider how far her 'competing identities' originate with Johnson herself, and in what ways critics have collaborated in constructing her as a feminist or patriot or Native spokesperson. Rose's admirably self-aware critical stance prevents her from fixing Johnson into any one of these roles, yet the vision of her as 'multivocal' and 'contestative' is itself a role. It is a further reinvention of Johnson, consonant with postmodern approaches to identity and with the 1990s and twenty-first-century emphasis on the racial and cultural complexity of the Canadian population. Although the

Canadian literary establishment in the middle decades of the twentieth century rejected Johnson because her work diverged so far from modernist aesthetic and internationalist ideals, she has now been fully reinstated in the national literary canon, and is among Canada's most highly-regarded Native authors.

JOY KOGAWA, *OBASAN* (1981)

Like Pauline Johnson, Joy Kogawa is a writer who continually negotiates a dual identity: that is, her identity as a Canadian-born person of Japanese ancestry. Kogawa was born in Vancouver in 1935, and she and her family and community were persecuted and interned during the Second World War. In the 1960s Kogawa became known as a poet, and the first of her four collections, *The Splintered Moon*, appeared in 1967. Her first novel, *Obasan*, was awarded several prestigious prizes, and in 1982 Kogawa published a sequel to it, *Itsuka*, which focuses on the campaign for redress for Japanese-Canadians. She is also the author of a children's book, *Naomi's Road* (1986), and has published two Japanese versions of this text.

Obasan is narrated by Naomi Nakane, a Sansei, or third-generation Japanese-Canadian. The narrative present takes place in 1972, when Naomi is thirty-six, and her retrospection returns to the period of her childhood during the war. She begins her story on the day her great-uncle dies. Uncle and his wife, Obasan (the Japanese word for aunt), brought Naomi and her brother, Stephen, up because they had been separated from their parents. Their father was forced to join a work gang, while their mother and grandmother became trapped in Japan by wartime travel restrictions, and never returned to Canada. White British Columbians had long seen the cohesive Asian-Canadian communities in the province as an economic and racial threat. This led, in 1923, to a law banning most Chinese from immigrating to Canada, while eighteen years later, following Japan's bombing of Pearl Harbor in 1941, the provincial authorities seized the opportunity to demand the removal of Canadians of Japanese origin from coastal areas. In the novel, Obasan, Uncle and the children are sent to a deserted mining town in the interior of the province, and though their father joins them, he soon dies of tuberculosis. At the end of the war, Japanese-Canadians were not permitted to return to BC, and Naomi's family, in an 'exile from our place of exile' (p. 197), are sent to Lethbridge, Alberta to work on a beet farm, suffering great hardship. In 1949 permission was finally given for Japanese-Canadians to return to the west coast, but their property had been sold off and their communities destroyed. Many evacuated people remained where they were, and in *Obasan*, Naomi's family stays permanently in Alberta.

At the end of the novel Naomi discovers that her mother, grandmother and other relations were in Nagasaki on 9 August 1945, when the atom bomb was dropped. The letter describing their sufferings, written by the grandmother, who survived, is extremely disturbing, and was deliberately kept from Naomi and Stephen. It is eventually shown them by their mother's sister Emily, who works tirelessly to uncover the injustices suffered by Japanese-Canadians and to assert their rights. In the earlier parts of the narrative, Naomi resents being forced to recall her painful memories, but her argument that they should 'turn the page and move on' (p. 42) is fiercely resisted by her Aunt Emily, who tells her: 'You have to remember . . . You are your history. If you cut any of it off you're an amputee' (pp. 49–50). In response to this demand, and in response also to the recurrent nightmares in which her repressed memories surface and the voices of her dead relatives haunt her, Naomi begins to reconstruct her own wartime experiences and those of other families she knew. She also incorporates into her narrative the lengthy diary which Emily kept during the war, so that the text becomes a collaborative act of remembering. This remembering and recovery is done by women, and the ancestral lines which the text explores are primarily those of female relationship (mothers, aunts, daughters). There is not space to explore this here, but the novel is a fertile site for feminist interpretation as well as for readings focusing on race.

By the end of the novel Naomi has confronted her past and, having discovered what happened to her family, she is able to finish the mourning process. In a poetic concluding section, she lays the ancestors to rest while also memorialising them:

This body of grief is not fit for human habitation. Let there be flesh. The song of mourning is not a lifelong song.

Mother, father, my relatives, my ancestors, we have come to the forest tonight . . . We have turned and returned to your arms as you turn to earth and form the forest floor . . . our serving hands serve you still.

My loved ones, rest in your world of stone. (p. 246)

But this lyrical final chapter is not quite the end of the novel. On the last pages, an extract from a memorandum sent to the House and Senate of Canada appears. Coral Ann Howells comments:

this is a novel which betrays the deep divisions of much revisionist historical fiction in its double ending, where the narrative of female subjectivity is supplemented by harsh documentary realism in the form of a 1946 Memorandum condemning government policy on Japanese Canadians, reminding readers in 1981 that the past was not settled.[19]

It was not until September 1988 that Prime Minister Brian Mulroney announced a redress settlement, following extensive campaigning by the National Association of Japanese Canadians. The settlement included payments to all surviving evacuees, the clearing of criminal records related to violations of the War Measures Act, a reinstatement of citizenship to those who had been 'repatriated' to Japan, and contributions to community and race relations funds. Negotiations for redress for Chinese-Canadians are still ongoing.

In Kogawa's novel, on a trip back to the area of BC where they were confined during the war, Naomi and her family 'looked for the evidence of our having been in Bayfarm, in Lemon Creek', which was a camp 'carved out of the wilderness'. But they find that: 'Not a mark was left. All our huts had been removed long before and the forest had returned to take over the clearings' (p. 177). 'Wilderness', which is White Canada's dominant cultural myth (see Chapter 2), has been invoked to erase the history of a minority group within the country. Joy Kogawa was the first Canadian writer to reinscribe that history through fiction, yet her novel suggests that Japanese-Canadians were sometimes complicit with the obliteration of their history, whether because of fear of reprisals or a desire to leave behind a painful past and integrate themselves. This 'forgetting' is imaged in the figure of Obasan, whose memory has become faulty as she ages: 'Everything is forgetfulness. The time of forgetting is now come' (p. 30), she says. She makes this comment after misplacing a parcel from Aunt Emily containing papers relating to the internments and dispersals. Therefore, her remark implicitly applies to the way that Canadians, and even Japanese-Canadians themselves, have deliberately forgotten the persecution of the 1940s.

Naomi notes that for her aunt, 'the injustice done to us in the past was still a live issue' (p. 34), not realising that her own narrative has already demonstrated the continuing presence of racism in Canada. The government's postwar dispersal policy was designed, as Emily points out, 'to make sure we'd never be visible again' (p. 34), and it has succeeded: people of Japanese origin seem so unfamiliar in Alberta that Naomi's pupils cannot, or will not, pronounce her name properly, while their parents tell her she looks too young to be a teacher, and seem 'surprised' by her 'oriental face' (p. 6). Naomi is continually asked where she is from: 'People who meet me assume I'm a foreigner' (p. 7), she says, but at this point, she seems resigned to this, and does not share her aunt's fierce anger. In the face of the institutionalised racism which her people have suffered in Canada, Emily refuses to retreat into her Japanese identity, choosing instead to affirm her Canadian citizenship, which she constructs as compatible with her Japanese heritage. In some of her private papers, the sentence 'I am Canadian' is 'underlined and circled in red . . . so hard the paper was torn' (p. 39), and when Naomi suggests that her own childhood nourishment of westernised food and traditional Japanese stories represented culture clash, Emily disagrees, saying that the Japanese stories are also Canadian stories because: 'Everything a Canadian does is Canadian' (p. 57).

Naomi eventually accepts this outlook, but recognises that it is available only to the second and third generations, such as Emily and herself, and cannot be shared by Obasan's generation (the Issei), who did not grow up in Canada. Near the end of the narrative, she writes:

Where do any of us come from in this cold country? Oh Canada, whether it is admitted or not, we come from you, we

come from you . . . We grow where we are not seen, we flour-
ish where we are not heard . . . We come from Canada, this
land that is like every land, filled with the wise, the fearful, the
compassionate, the corrupt.

Obasan, however, does not come from this clamorous
climate. She does not dance to the multi-cultural piper's tune
or respond to the racist's slur. She remains in a silent territory,
defined by her serving hands. (p. 226)

This passage reveals a scepticism about the official multiculturalism
which was so strongly emphasised by the government under Prime
Minister Trudeau. He held office almost continually from 1968 to
1984, and as Apollo O. Amoko argues: 'Coming about ten years into
Trudeau's multiculturalist pedagogy, Kogawa's minority text dis-
turbs, through its belatedness, the progressivist, continuist narratives of Canadian nationalism'.[20] *Obasan* reminds Canadians in
1981 that justice has still not been done to Japanese-Canadians, that
racism persists; but it also raises larger questions about the way
nations are discursively constructed.

Naomi's perspective on this subject changes over the course of
her narrative. Towards the end, she returns to the point about being
always treated as a foreigner, but now expresses herself much more
angrily. When the owner of the farm on which her family had previously been forced to labour visits to condole with Obasan on the
loss of her husband, he says 'It was a terrible business what we did
to our Japanese', and Naomi reflects:

Ah, here we go again. 'Our Indians'. 'Our Japanese'. 'A terrible business'. It's like being offered a pair of crutches while
I'm striding down the street. The comments are so incessant
and always so well-intentioned. 'How long have you been in
this country? Do you like our country? You speak such good
English. Do you run a café? My daughter has a darling
Japanese friend. Have you ever been back to Japan?' (p. 225)

Whether deliberately or not, all these comments function to
exclude visible minorities from full participation in the Canadian
nation. In connecting Asian diasporic communities and Indigenous

Canadians, in terms of their shared experiences of racism and dis-possession, *Obasan* implicitly suggests that the writing produced by these peoples might usefully be compared.

TOMSON HIGHWAY, *THE REZ SISTERS* (1988)

Tomson Highway (b. 1951) is of Cree descent, and grew up in northern Manitoba. At six, he was sent to a Catholic boarding school and began learning English. He later studied in Winnipeg, trained as a concert pianist in England and took a music degree at the University of Western Ontario. After seven years working at Native cultural and friendship centres, Highway began his career as a playwright. His early work, including *Aria* (first performed 1987) and *New Song . . . New Dance* (first performed 1988), was produced on reserves and in Native community centres. In 1986 *The Rez Sisters* won an award for the best new play of the year in Toronto, and played in Canada's major cities on a sell-out tour. It was pub-lished two years later. His next play was *Dry Lips Oughta Move to Kapuskasing* (1989), and he then wrote a novel, *Kiss of the Fur Queen* (1998), which was very well received, and a musical play, *Rose* (first performed 2000). Highway is among the best-known contemporary Aboriginal authors in Canada, and his work is widely performed, read and studied.

The Rez Sisters is set on a reserve with a mixture of Cree and Ojibway inhabitants. It is on Manitoulin Island in Lake Huron, a place with historical resonance since it was once at the centre of a controversy: in 1836 Sir Frances Bond Head attempted to segre-gate Aboriginal inhabitants of Upper Canada from Whites by inducing Aboriginals to settle on the island, but he was opposed by an influential British pressure group, the Aborigines' Protection Society. The characters in Highway's play are: Pelajia Patchnose and her sister Philomena Moosetail; their three half-sisters, Marie-Adele Starblanket, Annie Cook and Emily Dictionary; the sister-in-law of all five, Veronique St Pierre; and her adopted daughter, Zhaboonigan Peterson. The final character is Nanabush, a trickster. The seven women engage in fundraising activities in order to travel together to Toronto to attend THE BIGGEST BINGO IN THE WORLD.

The name of this is always given in full and in capital letters, and is repeated over and over, giving the effect of an advertising slogan while simultaneously suggesting that the bingo represents something beyond itself. The possibility of winning allows the women to indulge in a range of fantasies, and the bingo thus comes to stand for their ultimate desires.

The Rez Sisters is dedicated to the author's mother, 'a Rez Sister from way back'.[21] Her name, Pelagie Philomene Highway, is even borrowed for the names of two of the characters, a gesture which explicitly links the play to the personal experience of the author and his family. Preceding the first-edition published text of the play is an extended biographical sketch of Highway, unattributed and possibly written by him, which emphasises his ex-centric positioning in relation to Canada's urban centres and dominant White culture:

> Tomson Highway was born on his father's trap-line on a remote island on Maria Lake away up in northern Manitoba, where it meets the borders of Saskatchewan and the Northwest Territories. Maria Lake is about 100 miles north of the reserve Tomson belongs to – Brochet, Manitoba – which is located 76 miles, as the crow flies, northwest of the mining town of Lynn Lake, Man, northern end of the CN rail line. He was born in a tent, like all his brothers and sisters, in the middle of a snowbank on December 6, 1951, not ten feet from the dog-sled in which they travelled in those days. (p. vi)

This passage could be read as authenticating Highway's Cree heritage and knowledge of traditional Native lifestyles, or it could be seen as an attempt to market him in terms of the exotic. The insistence on his identification with the 'north' (the word appears five times, and is reinforced by images of snow and dog sleds) might tap into White audiences' fascination with the mythology of the Canadian wilderness (see Chapter 2), although the play itself contains only remembered traces of such things. Similarly, in the narrative of Highway's life, wilderness experience is confined to his early childhood: 'For the first six years of his life he lived an exquisitely beautiful nomadic lifestyle among the lakes and forests of remote northwestern Manitoba, trapping in winter, fishing in summer' (p. vii). This idyll is contrasted with the unhappiness which followed: 'During these years at school Tomson was able to visit home for only two months every summer. Then he was sent to Churchill High School in Winnipeg where he lived in a series of white foster homes' (p. vii). This is a clear criticism of Canada's policies of education and 'integration' which eroded the cultures and communities of the First Nations and caused extremely serious social problems.

The Rez Sisters engages with such problems by disclosing a series of painful events in the past lives of the women, each one a result either of White cruelty or of the social deprivation caused by government intervention. It transpires that Zhaboonigan was raped by two White boys with a screwdriver; Pelajia lives alone because her husband and sons can only find work a hundred miles away; Emily left the reservation to get married, but suffered domestic violence and then drug problems, and is now pregnant by an abusive Cree man; Marie-Adele has an alcoholic and depressive husband; and Philomena became pregnant by her White boss, unaware that he was married, and was forced to give the child up for adoption.

The deprivation and discontent on the reservation make Highway's characters restless. But rather than longing nostalgically for a past era of wilderness living, most of them fantasise about escape to the city. Sitting on the roof of her 'little two-bedroom welfare house' (p. 2) in the first scene, Pelajia says:

> From here, I can see half of Manitoulin Island on a clear day . . . I can see the seagulls circling over Marie-Adele Starblanket's white picket fence. Boats on the North Channel . . . the mill at Espanola, a hundred miles away . . . and that's with just a bit of squinting. See? If I had binoculars, I could see the superstack in Sudbury. And if I were Superwoman, I could see the CN Tower in Toronto . . . Philomena. I wanna go to Toronto. (p. 2)

This litany of Espanola, Sudbury, Toronto – a series of increasingly large, increasingly distant towns – is repeated numerous times in the play, and is emblematic of a desire for a mythologised modernity, identified with an urban locale and material luxuries. Most of the sisters play bingo in order to win the price of various consumer products – a new stove, a mink coat, Patsy Cline records, even a pedestal toilet. Only Marie-Adele imagines using her possible winnings to buy 'an island', with 'lots of trees – great big bushy ones – and lots and lots of sweetgrass' (p. 36). She alone desires a lifestyle more akin to the traditional Aboriginal existence, in a wholly natural environment. It is significant that, in Pelajia's rooftop panorama, it is Marie-Adele's house which is associated with the seagulls, since a seagull is one of the guises which Nanabush adopts in the play, and among all the seven women, only Marie-Adele and Zhaboonigan are aware of Nanabush's presence. One of the stage directions states that Nanabush and the two women 'play "games" with each other. Only [they] can see the spirit inside the bird and can sort of (though not quite) recognize him for who he is' (p. 18).

The trickster, as Highway remarks in a note at the start of the play, is 'as pivotal and important a figure in the Native world as Christ is in the realm of Christian mythology'. He lists the trickster's different names: '"Weesageechak" in Cree, "Nanabush" in Ojibway, "Raven" in others, "Coyote" in still others' (p. xii). Additional regional variants include 'Old Man' and 'Glooscap', and when these names are rendered in English, their spelling varies widely – 'Nanabush' may be spelt as 'Nanabozho', for example, or 'Weesageechak' as 'Wisakedjak'. Highway also remarks in his prefatory note: 'Some say that "Nanabush" left this continent when the whiteman came. We believe he is still here among us – albeit a little the worse for wear and tear – having assumed new guises' (p. xii). In the play, Pelajia laments that Nanabush has been forgotten (p. 6), and hopes he will 'come back to us' (p. 59), whereas Marie-Adele and Zhaboonigan (who is labelled 'mentally disabled' but in fact is perceptive in unusual ways) are conscious that he remains near them. Played by a male dancer, Nanabush is revealed to the reader only through stage directions since he is almost silent during the play, except towards the end when he adopts the guise of the bingo master, and thus becomes associated with the women's deepest desires. At times mocking, at times violent, at times romantic, Nanabush is always rather inscrutable, and so retains a crucial element of mystery and magic.

Towards the end, Nanabush appears as a black bird heralding death; he 'escorts Marie-Adele into the spirit world' (p. 104) and she addresses him in Cree, recognising that he belongs to the world of Native mythology. The text of the play, although primarily in English, also contains a number of speeches in Cree and Ojibway, most of them uttered by Marie-Adele, and this captures the code-switching of multilingual communities. For readers of the published text, translations are provided, but a performance of the play would be experienced differently by speakers and non-speakers of the two Native languages. At the same time, the play's accessibility to non-Indigenous audiences, and to speakers of Indigenous languages other than Highway's own, has enabled it to be more widely performed and read. As Thomas King has remarked, 'as Native storytellers have become bilingual . . . they have created both a more pan-Native as well as a non-Native audience'.[22]

THOMAS KING, *GREEN GRASS RUNNING WATER* (1993)

Green Grass Running Water has numerous affinities to *The Rez Sisters* – it, too, is partly set on a reservation (in this case a Blackfoot reservation in Alberta), and once again, the figure of the trickster is central. Like Highway, King uses techniques of fantasy and the surreal, and includes occasional words and phrases in Native languages. Thomas King, born in California in 1943, is of Cherokee, Greek and German descent, and has spent substantial time with Alberta Blackfoot communities, with whom he feels at home. He completed his PhD in English and American studies in 1986, and has taught Native studies and creative writing at several North American universities. King's comic scripts for CBC radio, *The Dead Dog Café*, were broadcast during the 1990s. His publications include a volume of short stories, *One Good Story, That One* (1993), and the novels *Medicine River* (1989), *Truth and Bright Water* (1999), and *DreadfulWater Shows Up* (2002, published under a pseudonym), as well as *Green Grass Running Water*, which is one of the most widely read and discussed novels by a First Nations author.

Green Grass Running Water is a complex and multi-layered text. In the frame story, an anonymous narrator and Coyote, a trickster figure of uncertain gender, tell a series of creation stories, juxta-posing Christian and Native versions. Within this frame is a narra-tive which is more realist in form (though incorporating some 'magical' elements), concerning a group of Blackfoot characters. They include Alberta Frank, a university lecturer; her two lovers Charlie Looking Bear, a successful lawyer, and his cousin Lionel, a TV salesman; Lionel's sister Latisha, owner of the Dead Dog Café; their uncle Eli Stand Alone, a retired professor; and his sister Norma. It is significant that all these characters are related. In 1990 King titled an anthology of Native writing *All My Relations*, and comments in his introduction that this phrase not only emphasises family relationships, but 'also reminds us of the extended relation-ship we share with all human beings'. He adds: 'the relationship that Native people see goes further, the web of kinship extending to the animals, to the birds, . . . to all the animate and inanimate forms that can be seen or imagined'.[23] This explains the reproach which the First Nations characters sometimes give the White figures in *Green Grass Running Water*: 'You are acting as though you have no relations'.[24]

Non-Blackfoot characters in the novel include Eli's wife, Karen, who fetishes racial otherness; Lionel's rather racist employer, Bill Bursum; and the American Dr Joseph Hovaugh (a name deriving from 'Jehovah'), who is authoritarian yet ultimately ineffectual. The novel's other main characters are four old Indians. Coyote and the old Indians belong primarily to the frame story, but sometimes jump into the modern story and interact (visibly or invisibly) with the characters. The Indians at times take the names Lone Ranger, Ishmael, Robinson Crusoe and Hawkeye. At other points they assume the guises of women from Native mythology: First Woman, Changing Woman, Thought Woman and Old Woman. According to the Indigenous belief system which King draws on, First Woman represents a Navaho goddess whose words created the fifth world on which the emergent people, humans, live. Changing Woman, another Navaho goddess, was impregnated by the sun and gave birth to human beings, while Thought Woman is a Pueblo deity whose characteristic is that whatever she thinks about appears. Old Woman is an archetypal adviser to the sun, who knows everything.

But the western figures in the book cannot accept Aboriginal self-determination, and seek to reclassify the old Indians according to their own ideologies. In one of the narrator's stories, when Old Woman encounters Young Man Walking on Water, he tries to cast her as a witness to one of his miracles, even though he fails to perform the miracle (calming the storm) and she has to do it for him. In another story, Thought Woman meets 'A. A. Gabriel, Heavenly Host', whose business card sings a parodic version of the national anthem: 'O Canada! / Our home and native land!' becomes 'Hosanna da, our home on Natives' land' (p. 270). Gabriel asks Thought Woman, whom he addresses as Mary, to sign a 'Virgin Verification Form' (p. 270). King's conflation of colonialist and Christian ideology in this episode points to their inextricable inter-connection in the history of empire.

In the modern part of King's story, the White characters, like the crazy figures in the creation narratives, try to understand Indigenous religions in relation to Christianity: Latisha's school-mate asks her 'if the Sun Dance was like going to church' (p. 369), but does not listen to Latisha's answer, instead detailing Catholic practice to her. The non-Native characters attempt to impose identities drawn from White culture on the Blackfoot characters. Karen is excited by Eli's otherness; during lovemaking she describes him in terms borrowed from westerns – 'You're my Mystic Warrior' (p. 164). Eli, it transpires, is himself susceptible to the lure of western novels, though before beginning one, he 'looked around the room to make sure he was alone' (p. 160), which sug-gests he is ashamed of his complicity in the exoticisation and stereotyping of 'Indians'.

After the deaths of his wife and his mother, Eli begins to under-stand the possibilities for resistance to racist stereotyping and injus-tices against Aboriginals. He returns to the reservation, moves into his family home, and obtains an injunction to prevent it being demolished to allow a newly built dam to go into operation, which in turn would allow lakefront developments on Native land. Sifton, a White agent from the company which owns the dam, repeatedly argues with Eli, and their conversations dramatise debates con-nected with the legality and costs of the land treaties (see Glossary) which the Canadian government made with First Nations people. In their set-piece disputes, Eli also indicts racist emphases on cultural 'authenticity'. Sifton says: 'you guys aren't real Indians anyway. I mean, you drive cars, watch television, go to hockey games. Look at you. You're a university professor'. Eli responds: 'That's my profession. Being Indian isn't a profession' (p. 141). While Sifton assumes that 'Indians' give up all Aboriginal claims when they adopt westernised lifestyles, Eli points to the way First Nations people have adapted to modern conditions while retaining their cultural heritages, and demands respect for those heritages.

Eventually Sifton's dam bursts, because an earthquake throws three cars into it. The cars are, mysteriously, 'sailing' on the lake: a 'Nissan, a Pinto, and a Karmann-Ghia' (p. 407), they represent the ships from Columbus's expedition, the Nina, the Pinta and the Santa-Maria, which crossed the Atlantic exactly 500 years before King's novel was published. The cars are controlled by Coyote, who also causes the earthquake which destroys them, thus enacting a seizure of power from the colonists. At the same time, Coyote subverts Christian metanarratives by creating an immaculate conception, intervening to make Alberta pregnant because she longs for a child but does not wish to commit herself to either Charlie or Lionel. Coyote's power and that of the Native goddesses far outstrips that of the 'Christian' GOD, who features in the interspersed creation stories but has no influence outside them. GOD tries to assume authority over the Navaho deities:

> So that GOD jumps into that garden, and that GOD runs around yelling, Bad business! Bad business! That's what he yells . . .
> Who are you? says First Woman.
> I'm GOD, says GOD. And I am almost as good as Coyote.
> Funny, says First Woman. You remind me of a dog.
> And just so we keep things straight, says that GOD, this is my world and this is my garden.
> Your garden, says First Woman. You must be dreaming. And that one takes a big bite of one of those nice red apples.
> Don't eat my nice red apples, says that GOD . . . All this stuff is mine. I made it.
> News to me, says First Woman. But there's plenty of good stuff here. We can share it. (p. 69)

In this passage, Christianity is reduced to the status of a dream, while the conflict between Christian and Native belief systems is rendered in terms of different attitudes to ownership. First Woman decides to leave the garden with Ahdamn (whose name has become a curse), but GOD, in a futile attempt to reinterpret events in order to assert his own possession of the land, shouts, 'You can't leave because I'm kicking you out' (p. 69).

Certain levels of meanings in King's text are not available to all readers. For example, the Cherokee syllabics placed at the start of each section of the book stand for red, blue, black, white, north, south, east and west. For those familiar with the Cherokee language and culture, the syllabics represent 'the four sacred directions of the earth and the cycle of life',[25] thus giving additional meaning to the circular patterns of the narratives within the novel. Despite his inclusion of this kind of material, King has said of *Green Grass, Running Water* that it is, 'more than his previous work, directed at non-Native readers, reflecting the need to engage those readers in a mutual decolonisation'.[26] The comedy of the novel, and its absorbing, accessible narratives, have ensured its appeal to a wide audience, and by addressing White readers, King seeks to challenge their potentially stereotyped and undifferentiated understandings of 'Indian' cultures.

CONCLUSION

In Canada, writes Margery Fee, 'Anglo-Canadians are seen as without ethnicity, as possessed of a "Canadian" ethnicity (generally depicted as not much different from no ethnicity at all), or as possessing the national high culture'. She adds that ethnic minorities, on the other hand, 'are permitted to have broken English, colourful costumes, exotic dances, and unusual food. Their writing, categorized as "ethnic writing", is instantly devalued as both less than national and therefore, less than literature'.[27] The set of texts taken to be constitutive of the 'national' literature of Canada has changed rapidly over recent years, and the teaching canon is no longer composed exclusively of White writers. Yet, as Fee points out, the attempt to redress the balance by incorporating Indigenous and ethnic minority writers into the 'national' literature raises many new problems. The very term 'ethnic' can signal devaluation, or, indeed, a fetishising of the exotic, while issues of appropriation arise when critics, writers and teachers from dominant ethnic groups seek to interpret or draw on materials from minority cultures. As Métis writer Lee Maracle puts it:

> If you conjure a character based on your in-fort stereotypes and trash my world, that's bad writing – racist literature and I will take you on for it. If I tell you a story and you write it down and collect the royal coinage from this story, that's stealing – appropriation of culture. But if you imagine a character who is from my world, attempting to deconstruct the attitudes of yours, while you may not be stealing, you still leave yourself open to criticism unless you do it well.[28]

Perhaps the best approach for students and critics of Canadian literature is to be conscious at all times of who is speaking. In terms of literary narrative, this entails making careful distinctions between the narrator, the various characters or speakers, and the historical author, so that particular opinions, linguistic choices or uses of imagery can be accurately attributed. Images surrounding race and ethnicity can never be detached from the cultures in which they originated; the stereotype of the noble savage, for example, says more about the Romantic ideology of the White writers and artists who propagated it than it does about the Native peoples of North America. An awareness of perspective is particularly important for the interpretation of multivocal, parodic or hybrid texts, in which clashes between different points of view are dramatised and irony is used to destabilise accepted ideas. While these strategies are commonly associated with postmodern writing, they may also be found in earlier Canadian literature, as the texts discussed in this chapter reveal.

• In many Canadian texts, multiple narrators and shifts in perspective are used to dramatise conflicting views on ethnic and racial questions, and the text as a whole may retreat from adopting a fixed position on such questions.

- An awareness of audience can add subtlety to readings of Canadian writing on race. This is especially relevant to books which simultaneously address White and Indigenous readers, and to those which incorporate words in languages other than English, or which seek to render oral culture in written form.
- Much twentieth-century Canadian writing about race and ethnicity needs to be read in relation to the government policies (especially on 'Indian' affairs and multiculturalism) which have shaped the modern political climate.
- Similarly, earlier Canadian texts are illuminated by an understanding of historical context, and particularly of the relationship between the colonial or Dominion administrations and the diverse populations they governed.
- Questions of race and ethnicity often intersect with questions of gender in Canadian literature, because literary explorations of both race and gender tend to centre on differences of perspective and on power relations.

NOTES

1. Joy Kogawa, *Obasan* (Harmondsworth: Penguin, [1981] 1983), p. 2. All subsequent references in the text are to this edition.
2. Northrop Frye, 'Conclusion' in *Literary History of Canada*, ed. Carl F. Klinck (Toronto: University of Toronto Press, 1965), pp. 821–49 (p. 339).
3. Laura Moss, 'Is Canada Postcolonial? Introducing the Question', in *Is Canada Postcolonial? Unsettling Canadian Literature*, ed. Laura Moss (Waterloo, ON: Wilfrid Laurier University Press, 2003), pp. 1–23 (p. 2).
4. Ibid., p. 11.
5. Ibid., p. 12.
6. Dee Horne, 'To Know the Difference: Mimicry, Satire, and Thomas King's *Green Grass Running Water*', *Essays on Canadian Writing*, 56 (1995), 255–73 (pp. 255–6).
7. Lorraine McMullen, *An Odd Attempt in a Woman: The Literary Life of Frances Brooke* (Vancouver: University of British Columbia Press, 1983), p. 115.

8. Frances Brooke, *The History of Emily Montague*, ed. Laura Moss (Ottawa: Tecumseh, [1769] 2001), p. 40. All subsequent references in the text are to this edition.

9. Cecily Devereux, '"One firm body": "Britishness and Otherness" in *The History of Emily Montague*', in Brooke, *History of Emily Montague*, pp. 459–76 (p. 464).

10. Dermot McCarthy, 'Sisters under the Mink: The Correspondent Fear in *The History of Emily Montague*', *Essays on Canadian Writing*, 51–2 (1993–4), 340–57 (p. 345).

11. See Faye Hammill, 'Inspiration and Erudition: Literary Creativity in *The History of Emily Montague*', in Brooke, *History of Emily Montague*, pp. 437–50.

12. Moss, 'Is Canada Postcolonial?', p. 4.

13. See McCarthy, 'Sisters', pp. 347–50.

14. Carole Gerson and Veronica Strong-Boag, 'Introduction' in E. Pauline Johnson/Tekahionwake, *Collected Poems and Selected Prose*, ed. C. Gerson and V. Strong-Boag (Toronto: University of Toronto Press, 2002), pp. xi–xliv (p. xxx).

15. Johnson/Tekahionwake, *Collected Poems and Selected Prose*, p. 91. All subsequent references in the text are to this edition.

16. Gerson and Strong-Boag, 'Introduction', pp. xxxiii–xxxiv.

17. Mary Elizabeth Leighton, 'Performing Pauline Johnson: Representations of "the Indian Poetess" in the Periodical Press, 1892–95', *Essays on Canadian Writing*, 65 (1998), 141–64 (p. 149).

18. Marilyn J. Rose, 'Pauline Johnson: New World Poet', *British Journal of Canadian Studies*, 12: 2 (1997), 298–307 (p. 305).

19. Coral Ann Howells, 'Writing by Women', in *The Cambridge Companion to Canadian Literature*, ed. Eva-Marie Kröller (Cambridge: Cambridge University Press, 2004), pp. 194–215 (pp. 204–5).

20. Apollo O. Amoko, 'Resilient ImagiNations: *No-No Boy*, *Obasan* and the Limits of Minority Discourse', *Mosaic: A Journal for the Interdisciplinary Study of Literature*, 33: 3, 35–55 (p. 49).

21. Tomson Highway, *The Rez Sisters* (Calgary, AB: Fifth House, 1988), p. v. All subsequent references in the text are to this edition.

22. Thomas King, 'Introduction' in *All My Relations: An Anthology of Contemporary Canadian Native Fiction*, ed. Thomas King (Toronto: McClelland and Stewart, 1990), pp. ix–xvi (p. ix).
23. Ibid.
24. Thomas King, *Green Grass Running Water* (Toronto: HarperCollins, [1993] 1994), p. 351. All subsequent references in the text are to this edition.
25. Arnold E. Davidson, Priscilla L. Walton and Jennifer Andrews, *Border Crossings: Thomas King's Cultural Inversions* (Toronto: University of Toronto Press, 2003), p. 47.
26. Herb Wyile, '"Trust Tonto": Thomas King's Subversive Fictions and the Politics of Cultural Literacy', *Canadian Literature*, 161–2 (1999), 105–24 (p. 118).
27. Margery Fee, 'What Use Is Ethnicity to Aboriginal Peoples in Canada?' (1995), repr. in *Unhomely States: Theorizing English-Canadian Postcolonialism*, ed. Cynthia Sugars (Peterborough, ON: Broadview, 2004), pp. 267–76 (p. 270).
28. Lee Maracle, 'The Post-Colonial Imagination' (1992), repr. in Sugars, *Unhomely States*, pp. 204–8 (p. 208).

CHAPTER 2

Wilderness, Cities, Regions

> While I was still in the process of giving these lectures, I was
> interviewed by a young man from Canada . . . who was con-
> cerned about the subject-matter I was discussing. [He] felt
> that I should not be talking about the North, or the wilderness,
> or snow, or bears, or cannibalism, or any of that. He felt that
> these were things of the past, and that I would give the English
> the wrong idea about how most Canadians were spending
> their time these days.
>
> Margaret Atwood, *Strange Things:*
> *The Malevolent North in Canadian Literature*[1]

The remarkable expansion of Canadian literary production
during the 1960s and 1970s, together with the growth of cultural
nationalism, led to an intense preoccupation with the question of
what made Canadian literature distinctive. Critics such as
Northrop Frye in *The Bush Garden: Essays on the Canadian
Imagination* (1971), D. G. Jones in *Butterfly on Rock: A Study of
Themes and Images in Canadian Literature* (1970), Margaret
Atwood in *Survival: A Thematic Guide to Canadian Literature*
(1972) and John Moss in *Patterns of Isolation in English–Canadian
Fiction* (1974) constructed their national literary histories around
recurring themes and images. Among them, as Atwood noted
twenty years later in *Strange Things*, were indeed images of the
north, wilderness, snow and so forth. This approach, referred to

as thematic criticism, is now widely considered to be old-fashioned and – in some ways – misleading or reductive. It is certainly problematic in that it tends to presuppose a relatively stable and definable 'Canadian identity', and one which is largely aligned with a White, anglophone perspective. Nevertheless, the texts written by Frye, Atwood, Jones and others have become classics of Canadian literary criticism, and retain considerable influence. In particular, their privileging of wilderness writing has had a significant impact on later critical texts and even – arguably – on creative writing itself.

John Richardson's novel *Wacousta; or, The Prophecy: A Tale of the Canadas* (1832) is perhaps the most influential of Canadian wilderness texts. It is set during the aftermath of France's cession of its Canadian colonies to Britain. Many of the so-called 'Indian' nations had been allied with the French during the preceding conflicts, and following the cession, a confederation among these nations was formed, led by the chief Pontiac (spelled Ponteac in the novel). Its aim was to wipe out the British garrisons which remained along the Western Frontier – that is, along the Great Lakes. The novel concerns the twin attacks on the last two garrisons in 1763; one attack was successful but the other was repelled. This narrative, however, forms only the skeleton of Richardson's story – the rest concerns the intricate relationships among a group of high-born characters, most of whom live in the two forts. *Wacousta* is a lengthy, complicated novel, and the style of some passages is laboured, yet it tells a gripping and dramatic story, and draws on melodrama and Gothic romance to great effect. It is also the source of many images which later came to be seen as central to Canadian literature, and several critics have traced a rich tradition of Gothic writing within the Canadian canon.[2] Wacousta himself, an English gentleman who 'goes native' and fights on the side of Pontiac, is an iconic Canadian figure, embodying hybridity and imposture, and revealing the barbarity within the civilised.

Wacousta epitomises Northrop Frye's highly influential idea of 'the garrison mentality', which is elaborated in his conclusion to the *Literary History of Canada*. The Canadian literary imaginary, Frye contends, is characterised by an impulse to build fortifications both literally, against the encroaching wilderness, and figuratively, against the unknown. *Wacousta* vividly evokes the threatening aspect of the forest surrounding the garrisons, and the view from Michillimackinac fort is described as follows:

> When the eye turned wood-ward, it fell heavily, and without interest, upon a dim and dusky point, known to enter upon savage scenes and unexplored countries; whereas, whenever it reposed upon the lake, it was with an eagerness and energy that embraced the most vivid recollections of the past, and led the imagination buoyantly over every well-remembered scene that had previously been traversed, and which must be traversed again before the land of the European could be pressed once more. The forest, in a word, formed, as it were, the gloomy and impenetrable walls of the prison-house, and the bright lake that lay before it the only portal through which happiness and liberty could again be secured.[3]

The woods are threatening because they are illegible and 'unexplored', and because they are the territory of an unfamiliar and potentially hostile people, who are thought of as 'savage'. As Coral Ann Howells notes: 'Within colonial discourse, wilderness was presented as a space outside civilised social order and Christian moral laws, the place of mysterious and threatening otherness'.[4]

Wacousta places the Canadian forest in opposition to the romantic conception of civilised nature, which is defined by agriculture, cultivation and the picturesque, and which is firmly identified with the remembered scenes of Europe. Michillimackinac 'boasted none of the advantages afforded by culture' and 'failed to produce any thing like a pleasing effect to the eye'.[5] Yet, as Margot Northey points out, the 'gothic terror' of Richardson's novel is 'not associated simply with nature, but with a feeling of menace from within civilized society as well as from without'.[6] Indeed, the terror of *Wacousta* is located primarily in human nature, with all its impulses towards violence and vengeance, rather than in 'nature' in the sense of wild animals, dangerous rivers or dark, disorientating woods. And even though the bloody destruction of Michillimackinac is the work of Pontiac and his confederates, the most moving tragedies of the novel – the deaths of Halloway, Clara, Charles and Valletort, and the madness of Ellen – are precipitated by the deceit, anger and vengefulness of White men.

The various myths of wilderness in Canadian literature may be divided into two main categories. *Wacousta*, together with Susanna Moodie's *Roughing It in the Bush* (1852), the early twentieth-century poems of Robert Service, and many other texts fall into the first group, which represents nature as hostile and treacherous; Margaret Atwood's term for the improbable mortality rates in texts of this kind is 'death by nature'.[7] In the second group the natural environment is the site of authenticity, provides healing, escape and self-knowledge, and may also teach humans about their kinship with animals. The early classics of this genre include the animal tales and wilderness stories published in the late nineteenth and early twentieth centuries by Ernest Thompson Seton, Charles G. D. Roberts and Grey Owl (Archibald Belaney). Many later Canadian texts draw on, and reinvent, this tradition of writing, often from a female point of view: examples include Ethel Wilson's *Swamp Angel* (1954), Margaret Atwood's *Surfacing* (1972) and Marian Engel's *Bear* (1976). In its association with the irrational or Other, on the one hand, and with healing and nurture, on the other hand, the forest can also become a gendered space in Canadian texts, though contemporary authors often write against these metaphors.

In practice, the two categories of wilderness literature I have identified often overlap and blur together: the wilderness tradition has always incorporated contradictions within itself. Indeed, the term 'wilderness' is itself problematic – although primarily associated with forested areas of eastern and western Canada, it can also take on the broader sense of 'the wild', or uncultivated land, and refer to frozen Arctic landscapes or even to the prairies of central Canada. In the first half of the twentieth century, the prairie novel emerged as a genre in the work of Frederick Philip Grove, Robert Stead, Martha Ostenso, W. O. Mitchell and Sinclair Ross, and their depictions of the prairies, as Janice Fiamengo notes, tend towards 'a spare but all-absorbing landscape, an image of bare essentials, expansive and isolating'.[8] The natural environment, in these texts, partakes of both elements of the wilderness tradition: it can be both harsh and regenerative, both inspiring and depressing.

In his discussion of the garrison mentality, Frye acknowledged that urbanisation had led to a kind of inversion of the garrison, so that the wilderness was now within the city, apparently under control but still, in fact, threatening. But this part of his argument is often forgotten; it is his exploration of Canadian literature's fundamental relationship with land, and especially with wild landscapes, which has exerted so much influence over later critics and writers. According to census information for 2001, 80 per cent of Canadians live in cities of more than 10,000 people, and as Justin D. Edwards and Douglas Ivison note in their introduction to *Downtown Canada: Writing Canadian Cities*, 'the sense of discovery and loss' which accompanies the endless repetition of this statistic in the Canadian media '(falsely) suggests that this is a new and radical shift in Canadian demographic patterns'.[9] In fact, the city has long been highly important to Canadian culture, although its significance has been obscured by dominant public mythologies of wilderness and the rural. In contemporary literary and critical discourses, wilderness in all its forms remains central, but writers and critics are now more likely to acknowledge that it is an imaginative or mythical construct, bearing little relation to the daily experience of ordinary Canadians.

One of the difficulties of linking national identity with place in Canada is that the geographies, histories and cultures of the different regions are so very diverse, and that no single image of landscape or society can ever unite the Maritimes with the prairies, the Northwest Territories with Montreal, or the West Coast with the Arctic regions. Although Frye, George Woodcock and other influential critics have always acknowledged the importance of regional diversity,[10] nevertheless until recently there has been a tendency for Ontario writers to dominate the English-Canadian canon, and for literary and artistic images of that province to be taken as representative of the whole of Canada. To counter this tendency, it is important to acknowledge the long traditions of literary production in the other provinces, and accordingly some of the earlier texts considered in this book are by authors from the prairies (*Wild Geese*), British Columbia (*Swamp Angel*), Prince Edward Island (*Anne of Green Gables*) and Newfoundland (*Brébeuf and His Brethren*). In recent Canadian literary criticism, there is a growing emphasis on regionalism and the value of the local, with increasing

analysis of Maritime and western Canadian writing complement-
ing the long-standing attention to prairie literature (see Guide to
Further Reading). As Fiamengo explains: 'Regional has often been
a pejorative label with connotations of limitation and triviality', and
'during periods of heightened nationalism, regionalism has been
regarded as a negative force of fragmentation'. She adds, however,
that in the contemporary era, 'when national and cultural distinctions are threatened by globalization, the insistence on difference
and specificity has acquired a new value in Canada'.[11]

Postmodern theoretical perspectives on space and its representation can be very illuminating when studying the Canadian geographical imagination. Henri Lefebvre, in his influential book *The
Production of Space* (1974), argues that space is the product of particular matrices of economic and social relations, while, in turn,
these collectively produced spaces shape the lives of those who live
within them. Space is therefore a medium through which societies
and economies develop, and not simply a backdrop for them. Many
other scholars, including cultural critics (notably Michel Foucault
and Fredric Jameson) and geographers or planning specialists (for
example, Doreen Massey, David Harvey or Edward W. Soja), have
made important contributions to the theorisation of space, and
there is a growing body of work on relationships between place and
identity (see Guide to Further Reading). In terms of specifically literary analysis, Brian Jarvis, in his book on geography and American
literature, *Postmodern Cartographies* (1998), emphasises the inter-
connections between space and story:

> Given the structural inseparability of space/place/landscape
> and social relations there can be no geographical knowledge
> without historical narrative. In other words, all spaces contain
> stories and must be recognised as the site of an ongoing strug-
> gle over meaning and value.
>
> Space/place/landscape is always represented in relation to
> cultural codes that are embedded in social power structures.
> The three most significant power structures in contemporary
> American society are capitalism, patriarchy and white racial
> hegemony. Accordingly, the subjects of class and capital,
> gender and sexuality, race and ethnicity, . . . are of critical

significance to any study of the workings of the geographical imagination in postmodern culture.[12]

One way to explore these contemporary understandings of space in relation to literary texts is through attention to spatial metaphors. Neil Smith and Cindi Katz argue that:

> The apparent cul-de-sac of a strict identity politics is now quite evident, and has led directly to a softening of the spatial metaphors through which political location is mapped. The discussion of multiple identities, borders and borderlands, margins, and escape from place are all in different ways a response to the political inviability of absolute location.[13]

These critics argue that these new metaphors do not go far enough: the 'border' or 'margin', for example, leaves a central location of power intact. They prefer another set of metaphors, expressing flow and also interplay among people: 'The notions of travel, travelling identities and displacement represent another response to the undue fixity of social identity'.[14] This is because travel defies rigid spatial boundaries, and suggests that social and cultural identities are dynamic and intricate, rather than simple and permanent.

Critical frameworks such as these have informed recent studies of place and Canadian literature in relation to geography, such as W. H. New's *Land Sliding* (1997), Graham Huggan's *Territorial Disputes* (1994), Edwards and Ivison's collection *Writing Canadian Cities*, or the special issue of *Studies in Canadian Literature* entitled *Writing Canadian Space*. These books and essays also take account of the postmodern challenge to the idea that individual or group identities can exist at all, independently of the cultural texts which seek to define them. They question the earlier assumption that a sense of national or personal identity, in countries such as Canada, is fundamentally connected to a sense of place, pointing instead to contemporary writers' emphasis on 'placelessness'[15] and their dislocations of identity. This does not mean that the significance of place has been negated in Canadian writing; rather, literary texts now reveal an increased consciousness of the complex processes by which meanings are inscribed onto – or emptied out of – landscapes.

In recent years, then, a range of modern perspectives on the relationship between geography and writing in Canada has developed. Both critics and imaginative writers now tend to focus on cities and their relationship to natural landscapes; on regional difference; on revisions or displacements of the Canadian wilderness myth; and on ways of conceptualising space in relation to society. Accordingly, this chapter considers classic wilderness narratives, postmodern rewritings of them, novels which effectively turn Canadian cities into protagonists, and novels which evoke various regions of Canada: the Maritimes, Ontario, Manitoba and British Columbia. (Additional regions and cities are represented in texts considered in other chapters.) The texts chosen for close focus here all reflect in depth on landscapes, cities and the ways in which they are invested with meaning. L. M. Montgomery's *Anne of Green Gables* (1908), the most widely read of all Canadian texts, deploys idyllic and pastoral codes in evoking its Prince Edward Island setting, but allows poverty, injustice and pain to remain visible at the margins of the story. Ethel Wilson's *Swamp Angel* (1954), an important novel of the West Coast, directly explores the relationship between place and personal identity, engaging self-consciously with the symbolism of place. *The Republic of Love* (1993), one of Carol Shields's most engaging (but least discussed) novels, maps out the friendships and romances of its characters across the city of Winnipeg, and explores the construction of communities in urban space. Robertson Davies's last book, *The Cunning Man* (1994), examines the evolution of Toronto from a genteel, colonial town to a contemporary metropolis, focusing in particular on the city's mediation of artistic and spiritual tradition. Finally, the short stories 'Wilderness Tips' by Margaret Atwood and 'A Wilderness Station' by Alice Munro explore mythologies of wilderness, relating them to changing ideologies of race and gender, and parodically revisiting earlier Canadian texts.

L. M. MONTGOMERY, *ANNE OF GREEN GABLES* (1908)

In Northrop Frye's famous phrase, Canadian literature is marked by a 'deep terror in regard to nature', or, as Margaret Atwood more flippantly put it in her immensely influential outline of Canadian literature, *Survival*, 'Canadian writers do not trust Nature, they are always suspecting some dirty trick'.[16] Such formulations, however, exclude many highly significant Canadian texts which present a much more alluring vision of landscape. *Anne of Green Gables* is among the numerous important books which were ignored by thematic critics because, as Gabriella Åhmansson explains, its world is one in which:

> winters pass quickly and leave no traces, where survival is taken for granted; a world where the mountains, the bush, the prairie and the transcontinental railway are conspicuously absent. In short, *Anne of Green Gables* is a bad representative of a nation that builds its sense of self on these concepts.[17]

During the middle decades of the twentieth century, Montgomery was written out of Canadian literary history. More recently, though, her fictional and autobiographical texts have been re-evaluated, and are now newly appreciated for many reasons, not least for their pervasive sense of place and evocation of Maritime scenery.

L. M. Montgomery (1874-1942) was brought up in Prince Edward Island by her grandmother, whom she later cared for in old age. During her twenties, she studied at Dalhousie University, taught in schools and worked for a newspaper, going on to establish herself as a writer of short fiction and poetry in the years before *Anne of Green Gables* brought her international fame. On her marriage, in 1911, Montgomery left her beloved island for an Ontario village, where her husband served as Presbyterian minister. Her later novels, most of them directed primarily at adolescent girls but also read by a large adult audience, include seven more 'Anne' books (the last published in 1939) and the '*Emily of New Moon*' trilogy, which appeared in the 1920s.

In *Anne of Green Gables*, brother and sister Matthew and Marilla Cuthbert request a boy from a Nova Scotian orphanage to help with the work of their smallholding, Green Gables, in the village of Avonlea. They are dismayed when a girl, Anne, is sent by mistake, but Matthew is so much charmed by her originality, liveliness and affectionate temper that he persuades Marilla to keep her. The rest

of the novel concerns Anne's friendships and schooling, and it concludes with Matthew's death and Anne's generous decision to give
up the chance of going to college and instead take a teaching post
in Avonlea, in order to stay with Marilla.

Montgomery's portrait of Prince Edward Island is not entirely a
realistic one. While *Wacousta* represents an exaggeratedly hostile,
haunted and terrifying natural environment, *Anne of Green Gables*
portrays an improbably hospitable climate and exceptionally beautiful scenery. Anne's first sight of the view from Green Gables is
described as follows:

> A huge cherry-tree grew outside, so close that its boughs
> tapped against the house, and it was so thick-set with blossoms
> that hardly a leaf was to be seen. On both sides of the house
> was a big orchard, one of apple trees and one of cherry trees,
> also showered over with blossoms; and their grass was all
> sprinkled with dandelions. In the garden below were lilac-
> trees purple with flowers, and their dizzily sweet fragrance
> drifted up to the window on the morning wind.
>
> Below the garden a green field lush with clover sloped down
> to the hollow where the brook ran and where scores of white
> birches grew, upspringing airily out of an undergrowth sug-
> gestive of delightful possibilities in ferns and mosses and
> woodsy things generally. Beyond it was a hill, green and feath-
> ery with spruce and fir; there was a gap in it where the gray
> gable end of the little house she had seen from the other side
> of the Lake of Shining Waters was visible.
>
> Off to the left were the big barns and beyond them, away
> down over green, low-sloping fields, was a sparkling blue
> glimpse of sea.[18]

The description is, to some extent, local and specific – it clearly cor-
responds to aspects of the island's scenery and flora (orchards,
lakes, seashore, fir, birches and so on). But it is also an idealised
landscape, coloured by Anne's imaginative projections and exces-
sive in its fertile luxuriance.

The extended, loving recreation of the scene demonstrates that
the narrator endorses Anne's romantic vision of Prince Edward

Island, yet the idyll is counteracted in several ways. First, the description is preceded by Anne's fear of expulsion from the new-found paradise: 'Wasn't it a lovely place? Suppose she wasn't really going to stay here!' (p. 81). Second, Anne's rapturous response is partly due to her previous confinement among scenes of poverty and ugliness: 'Anne's beauty-loving eyes lingered on it all, taking everything greedily in; she had looked on so many unlovely places in her life, poor child; but this was as lovely as anything she had ever dreamed' (p. 82). Finally, her reverie is interrupted by Marilla, the very person who is threatening to send Anne away. She 'curtly' recalls Anne's attention to the chores, and Marilla's perspective on the view is then juxtaposed with Anne's, foreshadowing her repeated puncturing of the child's bubbles of fancy later in the novel. Anne expresses her wonder at the beauty of the blossom, and Marilla, looking out of the window, merely remarks: 'It's a big tree . . . and it blooms great, but the fruit don't amount to much never – small and wormy' (p. 82). The novel frequently returns to themes of loneliness and poverty (emotional or financial), and continually balances Marilla's resolutely literal, practical outlook on life against Anne's melodramatic and romanticised visions.

Indeed, although popular cultural recreations of Avonlea, such as films, television series, theme parks and the PEI tourist sites, present it as an idyllic pastoral location, this does not entirely accord with Montgomery's texts. The books are not uniformly sunny, and her heroines have to use their imaginations to escape from painful experiences. In *Anne of Green Gables*, Anne tells Matthew:

> This morning when I left the asylum I felt so ashamed because I had to wear this horrid old wincey dress. All the orphans had to wear them, you know . . . When we got on the train I felt as if everybody must be looking at me and pitying me. But I just went to work and imagined that I had on the most beautiful pale blue silk dress . . . and a gold watch, and kid gloves and boots. (p. 66)

In her book *Under Eastern Eyes*, Janice Kulyk Keefer says of a group of Maritime writers, including Montgomery: 'Death, the bloody laws of nature, the tyranny of adults, violence – all poison the sweetness of these writers' Arcadia'. She argues further: 'the idyllic vision is also undercut by what we might call "meta-idylls", realized through the forces of magic, fantasy, mass-cultural cliché, and language itself'.[19] In *Anne of Green Gables*, Anne uses fantasy and play to escape from the experiences of bereavement, injustice, disappointment, poverty and loneliness, and she also finds solace in the beautiful landscapes which surround her. Except in one novel, *The Blue Castle* (1926), Montgomery never wrote about wilderness in the sense of a forest. But like more canonical Canadian narratives of wilderness regeneration, her novels consistently present the natural environment as a place of sanctuary. At the same time, the primary narrative in most of her books is the story of an outsider becoming integrated into a family and community. Her emphasis on the life of a small community is typical of a Canadian sub-genre known as the regional idyll, which includes early twentieth-century authors such as Nellie McClung and Ralph Connor. Small towns and rural communities remain a focus for many later authors, among them Ernest Buckler, Milton Acorn, Alice Munro, Gail Anderson-Dargatz and Alistair MacLeod.

ETHEL WILSON, *SWAMP ANGEL* (1954)

In *Swamp Angel* family and community initially seem to have only minimal significance: Wilson's story concerns a solitary protagonist, who leaves her home and seeks healing and redemption in the sparsely populated British Columbian interior. In *Strange Things*, Margaret Atwood identifies *Swamp Angel* as the earliest example of an emerging pattern in Canadian women's writing:

> Something interesting starts happening to Canadian female protagonists around the middle of the twentieth century. Instead of going off into the woods to be with a man [as the Victorian pioneers did], they start going off into the woods to be by themselves. And sometimes they're even doing it to get *away* from a man.[20]

But although the journey of Ethel Wilson's central character, Maggie Lloyd, initially takes her away from her marriage, house and friends, she is finally reintegrated into an alternative community.

Ethel Wilson (1888–1980) was born in South Africa and taken to England at the age of two, but at ten, she was orphaned and sent to Vancouver to live with her grandmother. She worked as a teacher for fourteen years, before beginning to publish short stories in the 1930s. Her first novel was *Hetty Dorval* (1947), and her literary evocations of Vancouver include *The Innocent Traveller* (1949) and *The Equations of Love* (1952). In Wilson's best-known book, *Swamp Angel*, Maggie loses her first husband in the war and her daughter to polio, and walks out on her detestable second husband. Escaping north from Vancouver, she takes a job as a cook at a fishing lodge near Kamloops. The lodge is owned by Haldar and Vera Gunnarsen, and Maggie brings a Chinese-Canadian boy, Angus, to work there too. The other main character in the novel is Maggie's ageing friend Nell Severance, who lives in Vancouver and stands, to some extent, in the relation of a mother to Maggie, whom she understands better than she does her own daughter, Hilda.

The Swamp Angel of the title is an ambiguous image. A dictionary definition inserted at the start of the novel identifies it as a 200-pound gun mounted in a swamp during the 1863 siege of Charleston, and notes that subsequently an issue of small revolvers was inscribed 'Swamp Angel'. One of these revolvers is cherished by Nell, who juggles with it, but this painfully reminds Hilda of the humiliation she suffered at school because her mother was a juggler. She fears her mother loves the gun more than she loves her daughter. Repeatedly identified as 'a symbol',[21] it is never quite clear what the Angel is a symbol of, though it does seem to be associated with a form of power which Nell, shortly before her death, transmits to Maggie by sending her the gun. Another Vancouver novelist, George Bowering, says that the novel's title signals paradox, explaining:

> Observing that range from primordial slime to divine flight, one might expect a story of triumphant emergence, but I do not think that the angel emerges. I think that no matter how compassionately Maggie acts, even in the Christian terms that the book clearly suggests, the pipefish still swims in her mind.[22]

The pipefish is a 'thin and cruel' thought (p. 40) which Maggie has about her second husband, Edward Vardoe. She is aware of the damage she has inflicted, not so much by leaving him as by marrying him in the first place. But the reader's sympathy is directed entirely towards Maggie; Vardoe is portrayed as repulsive, selfish and weak, whereas Maggie is kind and courageous. She learns from the mistake she made after the death of her first husband and her child, when she 'tried to save herself by an act of compassion and fatal stupidity. She had married Edward Vardoe who had a spaniel's eyes. Now she was to disappear from Edward's eyes' (p. 11).

In order to separate herself from other people's images of her, Maggie initially seeks self-effacement through oneness with the land. After the first stage of her journey north, she settles down to fish: 'she was nothing. No thought, no memories occupied her . . . In the pleasure of casting over the lively stream she forgot . . . her own existence' (p. 40). Travelling onwards on a bus, and annoyed by a talkative woman who claims to be 'crazy about Nature', Maggie turns away to the window: 'She would see each leaf, each stone, each brown trunk of a tree, but she would not listen any more' (p. 70). Her attention to the details of the natural environment is not simply a means of escape, it is her way of uniting herself with that environment. Later, at the lodge, she is released from 'the self-consciousness which she had formerly felt with Edward Vardoe' (p. 133); while swimming, she feels herself 'one with her brothers the seal and the porpoise who tumble and tumble in the salt waves' (p. 126).

There is another stage to Maggie's trajectory, though. She realises that her hours of oneness with the natural world can be only temporary refreshment to her spirits, that:

> she is not really seal or porpoise – that is just a sortie into the past, made by the miracle of water – and in a few minutes she will be brought to earth, brought again to walk the earth where she lives and must stay. (p. 126)

In another passage Maggie thinks that when the last of the summer visitors have left the lake, she will rest: 'Her companions would be the chipmunks and the squirrels . . . the bluejays . . . Perhaps she would, if she stayed long enough, see the sandhill cranes in their flyways' (p. 135). This vision is not fantastic, and Maggie does indeed experience numerous moments of intimate, peaceful companionship with animals and birds. But her period alone with chipmunks and squirrels is clearly identified as 'her holiday' (p. 135); it cannot be the whole of her life.

The restoration provided by her lifestyle at Three Loon Lake enables Maggie to enter into new human relationships and reintegrate herself, not by another marriage but through her commitment to the lodge and the people who work there. Although her relationship with Vera Gunnarsen causes many problems, Maggie eventually forms a bond with Vera. In the novel's last pages, she is out alone on the lake, but the final sentences are these:

> Now she stopped rowing for a moment to get her direction, and looked back toward the lodge. She saw the stocky, comfortable figure of Angus moving from cabin to cabin. Smoke had begun to rise from the stovepipes of the cabins, and smoke flowed up abundantly into the still air from the kitchen chimney. Maggie turned again, took the oars, and rowed hard, straight in the direction of the lodge. (p. 209)

Maggie's 'direction' takes her back to a domestic space, but it is an entirely different one from the kitchen of Vardoe's house, in which she is confined in the opening chapter, performing the 'familiar and almost mechanical' (p. 12) actions of preparing dinner and fending off the ungracious remarks of her husband.

During Maggie's journey away from the city in the early chapters, the narrative, focalised through her attentive eyes, provides a very precise geography of the region, with names of rivers and villages, and details of vegetation, bird-life and the contours of the land. But at one point she imagines herself beyond this particular landscape:

> The very strange beauty of this country through which she passed disturbed Maggie, and projected her vision where her feet could not follow, northward – never southward – but north beyond the Bonaparte, and beyond the Nechako and the Fraser, on and on until she should reach . . . the endless space west of the Mackenzie River, to the Arctic Ocean. (p. 73)

Maggie longs for the imagined North, which is so potent a motif in Canadian literature. The North is suggestive of freedom, space, escape and unspoiled landscapes, but Maggie struggles to attach any precise meaning to it: 'What will it mean, all this country?', she wonders. 'Flowing, melting, rising, obliterating – will it always be the same?' (p. 73). It is possible to read various meanings into Maggie's landscapes, but it would be unwise to attempt to pin down their significance. As Bowering notes, Wilson 'loved the physicality of British Columbia, and used her great sentences to make it brightly visible. If the rivers and lakes are to become allegorical landscape, that will be permitted, but they will live before the imagining eye first'.[23]

Swamp Angel is not a novel in which symbols – be they guns or rivers – have definite moral meanings. It is, though, a novel with moral underpinnings, and there is a sense of the unseen, and of the significant interrelation of particular times, places, people and even animals. In one lovely, almost enchanted scene, Maggie witnesses the meeting of a kitten and a fawn, and delights in the fascinated attention of the fawn and the unconsciousness of the kitten, while in another passage, the narrator observes: 'Meeting partakes in its very essence not only of the persons but of the place of meeting' (p. 95). 'Meeting' and 'place', indeed, are among the central ideas of the novel. In a related scene, Mrs Severance describes coincidence as a 'combination of events which meet at a certain point of time or perhaps place'. She adds: 'the older I grew the more I believed in the fantastic likelihood . . . of coincidence' (pp. 128–9). Though the plot of the novel is very little structured by coincidence, nevertheless chance encounters are always invested with significance, and the characters, narrator and reader make meaning from combinations of events and places, and from 'meetings' of many different kinds.

CAROL SHIELDS, *THE REPUBLIC OF LOVE* (1992)

Carol Shields has always been preoccupied with coincidence. *The Republic of Love* tells the love story of Tom Avery and Fay McLeod, and it transpires that Tom's first wife, Sheila, 'after she stopped being Sheila Avery, married Sammy Sweet, who later married Fritzi Knightly, who was formerly married to Peter Knightly, with whom Fay lived for three years'. From Fay's point of view, 'This Tom-Sheila-Sammy-Fritzi-Peter-Fay merry-go-round dismays her when she stops to think about it, these unspooled connections'.[24] But this disturbing coincidence becomes insignificant when compared with the immense, astonishing coincidence that Fay should fall in love with Tom at the same moment that he falls in love with her. This mutual, simultaneous falling in love, which is taken for granted by so many novels and films, is made strange in *The Republic of Love* – it is marvelled at, and cherished. In the novel, the conventions of love and desire are scrutinised, questioned, taken apart, but finally, triumphantly, reaffirmed.

Carol Shields (1935-2003) was born in Illinois, and moved to Canada on her marriage, in 1957. After giving birth to five children, she returned to university, and then began her writing career. Her first book of poetry appeared in 1972, and her first novel, *Small Ceremonies*, in 1976. Among her eight subsequent novels, the best known is *The Stone Diaries* (1993): it won Canada's most prestigious literary prize, the Governor General's Award, and – by virtue of the author's dual nationality – was also awarded the USA's top prize, the Pulitzer. Shields also published several plays and collections of short stories, as well as further volumes of poetry. She lived for many years in Winnipeg, where *The Republic of Love* is set. Tom, a radio DJ, and Fay, a folklorist, both live in Winnipeg, but do not meet until about halfway through the book; the earlier chapters explore their individual lives and past romances. The narrative begins with Fay's break-up with Peter Knightly, and moves through her engagement to Tom and its temporary dissolution. It concludes, self-consciously gesturing to the romance tradition, with the reuniting of Fay's briefly estranged parents, and the marriage of Tom and Fay.

'Geography is destiny', Fay's friend Iris Jaffe says to her (p. 78), and indeed, the city exerts a determining influence on the friendships, love affairs and professional relationships between the characters. As well as romantic attachment, the novel explores other kinds of love, especially the love which binds people to a place and a community:

The population of Winnipeg is six hundred thousand, a fairly large city, with people who tend to stay put. Families overlap with families, neighborhoods with neighborhoods . . . You were always running into someone you'd gone to school with or someone whose uncle worked with someone else's father. The tentacles of connection were long, complex, and full of the bitter or amusing ironies that characterize blood families.

At the same time. Fay has only a vague idea who the noisy quarreling couple on the floor above her are, and no idea at all who lives in the crumbling triplex next door . . . When her former lover, Nelo Merino, was transferred to Ottawa and wanted her to come with him, she had to ask herself . . . Do I love Nelo more than I love these hundreds, thousands of connections, faces, names, references and cross-references, biographies, scandals, coincidences, these epics, these possibilities? The answer, and it didn't take her long to make up her mind, was no. (pp. 77–8)

Fay's embeddedness in Winnipeg sustains her, even during the periods when she lives alone, but she is occasionally disturbed by her perception that there is 'something tribal and primitive about these human links' (p. 267). She is troubled, in particular, by the realisation that she is slightly acquainted with all of Tom's three ex-wives, and this leads her to harbour fantasies of escaping with him to another city. But this idea is never taken seriously, any more than the possibility of moving to Ottawa with Nelo was, which only emphasises the primary importance of community and place in Fay's life.

Fay's love for Winnipeg and its people leads her to invest even the most ordinary aspects of the city with a certain glamour. She takes pleasure in walks round her neighbourhood, is intrigued by the names of the streets and is even 'able to see more beauty in these small front yards than she used to' (p. 38). Tom, in a parallel episode, walks around an older part of the city, and notes that the generous gardens 'give the houses a touch of dignity, of unassuming definition' (p. 193). *The Republic of Love* celebrates what many writers would reject as distastefully bourgeois: suburbs, repeating patterns and middle-class arrangements, conventions and rituals.

The novel, like much of Shields's work, locates beauty and significance in ordinary lives and places.

But *The Republic of Love* is not simply about ordinariness, but about the emergence of the extraordinary – passion and devotion – in the midst of the everyday. Carol Shields reinvents Winnipeg as a setting for romance, and in a crucial passage the narrator observes:

> It's possible to speak ironically about romance, but no adult with any sense talks about love's richness and transcendence, that it actually happens, that it's happening right now, in the last years of our long, hard, lean, bitter, and promiscuous century. Even *here* it's happening, in this flat, midcontinental city with its half million people and its traffic and weather and asphalt parking lots and languishing flower borders and yellow-leafed trees – right here, the miracle of it. (p. 248)

Winnipeg is inscribed into the text with unusual precision and detail. The characters' trajectories are mapped out across the city: each time someone is introduced, the location of their house is specified, and whenever a character visits or passes a restaurant, house or shop, its street address is given. This creates an effect of familiarity for readers who have visited Winnipeg, and a sense of partial exclusion for those who have not. Yet there is more to this mapping than is immediately evident. As Perry Nodelman points out in his article 'Living in the Republic of Love', Shields has – presumably deliberately – introduced various small discrepancies; the geography of the novel does not quite match the actual street plan of Winnipeg. Some of the street names she mentions are precisely accurate, others are slightly altered – she turns some of the 'Streets' (which run north – south in Winnipeg) into 'Avenues' (which run east – west). Occasionally, she moves a building over a few blocks, or adds an imaginary one. Nodelman remarks that 'the differences are too close to reality to be mere errors'.[25] Shields's highly specified, yet slightly distorted, map of the city creates a Winnipeg which is both a realistic rendering of an actual place, and a landscape of the mind – a place coloured by fantasy and romance.

In one scene Fay leaves Winnipeg for a weekend, to visit her friends' lakeside cottage. She is aware that the function of this place is to provide a contrast to city life; its actual physical characteristics are insignificant:

> That phrase – 'the lake' – makes Fay smile. 'Lake' in this part of the world is used generically, meaning any inland body of water large or small, and the word 'cottage' applies equally to a twelve-room house on the Lake of the Woods and a primitive one-room cabin. (p. 109)

Contrary to the expectations set up by the ritual of visiting the 'lake', and by the Canadian literature of wilderness, the lake in Shields's novel proves not to be a place of regeneration. It briefly appears idyllic, but this is immediately undercut by Fay's awareness that her host's recovery from alcoholism has led him to a form of unconscious cruelty: 'it seems to Fay, lying on the warm pier and listening to the cool sulky slap of lake water . . . that Frank Morris has been blinded by his dramatic renewal and doesn't even see how his wife, Anne, is slipping away' (p. 109). This is not, then, a place where perceptions become clearer and health is restored; later in the novel, Anne proves to have severe kidney problems. Indeed, it is the city, and not the rural location, which possesses restorative powers in *The Republic of Love*. Tom marvels at the trees: their first growth of leaves is always destroyed in June by canker worms, but they are able to grow new foliage, performing 'an additional cycle of regeneration' (p. 101). The leaves, flowers and seed, he feels, 'give comfort and color to this northerly splotch on the map' (p. 101). The natural world, then, is present within the city, and provides more sustenance than an occasional weekend away can do.

Yet Tom's feeling about Winnipeg is ambiguous, and he is wearied by its uglier aspects:

> Tom wonders why he stays here. The climate gets him down, and so does the grid of streets, bridges, shopping centers, traffic lights, and pedestrian crossings – at times the punishing municipal familiarity of these fixtures causes him to lean forward on the steering wheel of his car and whimper. How many hundreds of times has he spun his wheels off the ramp at the St Vital Mall and entered that hard-surfaced glaring

corridor between joyless shoe stores, trust companies, fast-food counters, discount drugs, and the hollow blue interiors of video franchises . . . This is a place with a short, tough history and a pug-faced name. Elsewhere people blink when you say where you're from, and half the time they don't know where it is. (pp. 99–100)

All this suggests that Winnipeg is indistinguishable from other North American cities, but this perception is largely the result of Tom's cheerless state of mind, and is counteracted by other passages insisting on the distinctiveness and individuality of the city. After indulging in these gloomy thoughts, Tom's mood lifts, and he goes on to consider the handsome buildings and wide boulevards in the older parts of the city, and the wonderful regeneration of the trees every June, and eventually concludes: 'He loves this light-filled city . . . in the wordless way he expresses his most passionate and painful moments' (p. 101).

ROBERTSON DAVIES, *THE CUNNING MAN* (1994)

Jonathan Hullah, narrator of *The Cunning Man*, has a feeling for Toronto which is somewhat akin to Tom Avery's for Winnipeg. He remembers that at the age of nine:

I made my first descent upon the city that has enveloped my life and which I hold in great affection. London is romantic and historically splendid; Paris is infinitely beautiful and has an air of louche aristocracy; Vienna has an ambiguity of spirit – a bittersweet savour – which enchants me. But Toronto – flat-footed, hard-breathing, high-aspiring Toronto – has a very special place in my heart, like a love one is somewhat ashamed of but cannot banish.[26]

Robertson Davies (1913–95) was not a native of Toronto, but lived there for many decades. He was educated in the city, before moving to England, where he continued his studies at Oxford and began his career as an actor in London. Having returned to Canada in 1940, he worked for many years as a newspaper editor, and during the 1960s and 1970s taught English literature at the University of Toronto. Davies is the author of plays, literary criticism and essays, as well as novels. His best-known books fall into trilogies (The Salterton Trilogy, The Deptford Trilogy, The Cornish Trilogy), and the two last novels he wrote, *Murther and Walking Spirits* (1991) and *The Cunning Man*, were intended as parts of a final trilogy.

The Cunning Man takes the form of a retrospective of Jonathan Hullah's life, which extends over most of the twentieth century. Jonathan is brought up in Sioux Lookout in remote northwestern Ontario, and later attends boarding school and university in Toronto before establishing his medical practice there. A 'rather special kind of physician' (p. 86), his unusual methods bring him great success as a diagnostician. The novel is greatly concerned with Toronto, which almost becomes the protagonist – an author's note at the start points out: 'The only portrait from life in the book is that of the City of Toronto. All other characters are imaginary' (p. 6). The city is, though, evoked largely through the subjective vision of individual characters. Jonathan says of Toronto: 'It is a city of trees and they are its chief beauty' (p. 32). His focus on the trees, rather than the buildings, the lake, the ravines or any other aspect of Toronto's topography, reveals, perhaps, as much about him as it does about the city; there is a suggestion that he looks for trees because they connect him to his origins. Remembering his childhood 2,000 miles from Toronto, Jonathan writes:

> I learned to know the trees, the white and black spruce, the balsam firs, the jack-pines, the queenly birches growing in stands by themselves, and the trembling aspens that threw such a varied and magical light when the sun shone . . . I will not say that I loved the stillness of the forest, because it was too much a part of my life to be singled out for notice, but that stillness became for me the measure and norm of what life should be and I carry it in my soul still. When I am most in need of rest in the racket and foolish bustle of modern Toronto, I lock my doors and close my curtains and try to recapture the stillness of the forest in which I grew up, and shared with my father. (p. 24)

The gendering of the forest space is interesting here – while the trees are associated with the feminine ('queenly'), the memory of the forest reinforces Jonathan's sense of connection to his father, and this patterning is reminiscent of traditional male-authored texts about Canadian wilderness experience.

Although an opposition between city and forest is apparently established in the passage, it is nevertheless clear that the forest is, in some way, present within Jonathan, and he has imaginative access to it even when he is in Toronto. The motif of the wilderness entering into a person who has lived there subtly connects the novel with a whole tradition of Canadian writing, from John Richardson and Susanna Moodie down to Margaret Atwood and Alice Munro. But whereas writing from, and about, nineteenth-century Canada is largely concerned with the wilderness's invasion of the immigrant body, Jonathan is born in the forest and belongs to it, and so it enters into him in a different way. After leaving school, Jonathan remembers that he 'felt patronizing about Sioux Lookout, as a place that had nothing more to teach me' (p. 118), but from the perspective of maturity, he realises:

> Five years at Colborne had done much to make me superficially a city person and, in my own estimation, a sophisticate. But Sioux Lookout continued to be my Eden, my place of origin in the spirit as well as the flesh. (p. 118)

The novel's third location is an imaginary Ontario town suggestive of Kingston and described as 'the courtly old city of Salterton' (p. 103). The genteel tradition is still alive in 1930s Salterton: the house Jonathan visits has 'an indoor staff of a houseman, an upstairs maid, a cook, and something called "a rough girl"' (p. 98). Jonathan is allured by the atmosphere: 'I assumed that it was indeed the Old World, and at least in part that land of romance', but later realises that it is characterised by 'regret for a past that had never been' (p. 107). As an old man, Jonathan Hullah reflects: 'I see now that Sioux Lookout was the enduring reality of my homeland, and Salterton a retreat into its past' (p. 127). Sioux Lookout comes to stand for relationship to the land and to Native Canadians (who feature significantly in Jonathan's childhood), whereas

Salterton stands for a colonial nostalgia for an imagined European past. This nostalgia is an important subject of Davies's fiction, and is also explored through his depictions of Salterton in his earlier novels, *Tempest-Tost* (1951), *Leaven of Malice* (1954) and *A Mixture of Frailties* (1958). From the vantage point of the 1990s, therefore, the town also represents his own past as a writer, and the lost world which was the subject of his 1950s fiction.

Toronto alters over the course of *The Cunning Man*: Jonathan says he watched it 'change from a colonial outpost of a great Empire to a great city in what looks decidedly like a new empire', and also watched 'the British connection wither . . . and the American connection grow' (p. 468). Yet traces of the beleaguered genteel tradition, with its European-derived ideals of manners and taste, are shown to have endured, not only in the memories of the older characters, but also in the maintenance of certain social rituals by minority groups. One character, Hugh McWearie, points out that in the later twentieth century, the convention of the coming-out party has not quite disappeared: 'The Hungarians still keep it up. A ball every year, where they present their daughters to the Lieutenant-Governor, which is the nearest they can get to royalty' (p. 206).

While *The Cunning Man* does not really lament the passing of 'tribal rituals' (p. 206) such as these, it does regret the erosion of certain other aspects of the European heritage, particularly those associated with art and beauty. In the novel, the church is an important site for the maintenance of cherished traditions, and for the promotion of music and the visual arts. The story is centred on the parish of St Aidan's, based on St Mary Magdalene, Toronto, a well-known Anglo-Catholic church. Several of the characters, including Jonathan and his neighbours Pansy Todhunter and Emily Raven-Hart, attend the services, though uncertain of their faith, for the sake of the excellent music and the ritual – as Pansy puts it, 'this is *beauty* of a very special kind. Beauty and reverence and it is like cool water in the thirsty land' (p. 316). For Jonathan, the peace to be found in the church becomes an analogue for his memory of the 'stillness' in the forest of his childhood.

This peace is, however, shattered by the melodramatic death of Father Ninian Hobbes and the campaign to have him canonised, events which align *The Cunning Man* at least partly with the genre of the detective novel. It is eventually revealed that he was killed by his curate, Charlie Iredale, a school friend of Jonathan's, and Charlie admits many years later that his purpose was to create a saint, so as to 'bring about a revival of deep faith . . . faith that saves a city' (p. 442). The consecration of the sacred sites of Europe by thousands of Catholic saints, whose lives date back over the whole Christian era, cannot of course be replicated in North America, yet Charlie longs for 'one saint', to invest his environment with holiness: 'Toronto . . . what an unlikely place . . . but what pride, what impertinence to think that . . . as if God couldn't declare Himself in Toronto as well as anywhere else . . . Save my city, He said' (p. 442, ellipses in original).

Charlie's preoccupation with Toronto as a possible location for salvation parallels Jonathan's preoccupation with it as a possible location for art. His involvement with artistic, musical and theatrical circles forms a large part of the material for the narrative, and *The Cunning Man* explicitly counters the perception of Toronto – and indeed, the whole of Canada – as a cultural desert. The idea that Canada is culturally barren retains some purchase even now (though it has no longer any foundation), and in the early to mid-twentieth century it was much more prevalent. Pansy voices this assumption, writing in a letter that her lover Emily, in pursuing her career as a sculptor, 'is still *bashing* her head against brick walls in this artistically God-forsaken country' (p. 251). Yet while Pansy considers Emily to be a true artist, it is she herself who is ultimately identified with that role. Her letters themselves are works of art, containing tiny sketches, 'lovely little vignettes', which in Jonathan's view 'gave the letters a brilliance, a beauty, a quality of delightful hilarity' (p. 250). Pansy may be English, but she has lived in Canada for thirty years and become part of the Toronto community, so that her letters, together with the achievements in drama, music and sculpture which Jonathan's narrative documents, provide ample evidence of the flourishing of art in a mid-twentieth-century Canadian city. Although neither Charlie nor Father Hobbes measures up as true saints, several true artists populate the novel, among them Jonathan Hullah himself, who becomes a writer through recording his memoir. The Toronto he creates in his narrative has a rich history and a promising future as a cultural centre, and it is, finally, the object of more love than Jonathan bestows on any of the people he is connected with.

ALICE MUNRO, 'A WILDERNESS STATION', AND MARGARET ATWOOD, 'WILDERNESS TIPS'

Atwood says that her book *Strange Things* departs 'from the position that, although in every culture many stories are told, only some are told and retold, and that these recurrent stories bear examining'.[27] The recurrent stories of backwoods settlements, wilderness explorations and the malevolence, or else the regenerating power, of nature are retold many times in Atwood's own fiction and in that of her contemporary Alice Munro. Between them, they have produced some of the most significant contemporary Canadian wilderness texts. Munro, the best-known Canadian short-fiction writer, sets most of her work in small-town Ontario, exploring the whole period from early Victorian backwoods settlements onwards. 'A Wilderness Station', from her collection *Open Secrets* (1994), is set in the Huron County area of Ontario, and the episodes of the story take place in 1852, 1907 and 1959. Some of Atwood's early texts, notably *The Journals of Susanna Moodie* (1970) and *Surfacing* (1972), are considered classics of Canadian wilderness writing, while some of her critical and creative work of the 1990s revisits the same geographical and imaginative territory, reflecting on and parodying different versions of wilderness mythology. There are three wilderness stories in her collection *Wilderness Tips* (1991), and the title story, set in a lakeside summer cottage, is a particularly intriguing example.

Alice Munro was born in Wingham, Ontario, in 1931. Her first volume of stories, *Dance of the Happy Shades* (1968), won the Governor General's Award, and all her subsequent books are also short story collections, though *Lives of Girls and Women* (1971) is sometimes referred to as a novel since the stories are interlinked. Margaret Atwood was born in Ottawa in 1939, and she, too, won the Governor General's Award for her first book, *The Circle Game* (1966), a collection of poetry. One of the most widely admired living writers worldwide, Atwood is known for her poetry, short fiction, essays, literary criticism, children's writing and above all for her novels. *The Handmaid's Tale* (1984) remains one of her best-known books, and she was awarded the Booker Prize for *The Blind Assassin* (2000), which – like her earlier novels *The Robber Bride* (1993) and *Cat's Eye* (1988) – explores the topography and culture of Toronto.

Munro's story 'A Wilderness Station' was inspired by an incident from Munro's family history,[28] but does not limit itself to historically verifiable material. The story contains several incompatible narratives of the same event, the death of a man named Simon Herron in 1852. These are presented in a brief retrospective memoir by Simon's brother George, and in a series of letters, some written by the ministers in two local parishes and the rest by Annie (McKillop) Herron, an orphan who entered into an arranged marriage with Simon shortly before his death. According to George, his brother was killed by a falling branch. According to Annie's initial narrative, she killed George by throwing a rock at his head, but this story, it transpires, may have been told in order to gain her admittance at a gaol with a reputation for being clean and fairly comfortable. Annie later writes to a close friend, claiming that George killed Simon with an axe, and that she helped him conceal the crime. She further asserts that both brothers were violent, and that her husband beat her.

There is no explicit indication in the story as to which version is true. Ildiko de Papp Carrington contends that Annie is a 'malicious' liar, whose 'confused perception' is the cause of her contradictory accounts,[29] but Isla Duncan rejects this view, arguing that the structure, tone and details of the argument give credence to Annie's account of George's murder of his brother.[30] Certainly, there is much evidence to suggest that this last version is implicitly affirmed, not least because it is written in a more intimate format and a more emotive tone. It may be deduced that George's memoir, published in a local newspaper in 1907, is read by Annie, now an old woman living with a wealthy family for whom she works as a sewing woman. Annie decides to visit George in Carstairs, presumably to remind him of her version of events, and she asks Christena, the daughter of her employer, to take her to see him in her new steam motor car. Christena's recollections of this are set down in 1959 at the request of a university historian, and her letter forms the final narrative of the story. The structure of the text, which is composed entirely of these letters and reports, positions the reader in the role of historian or detective, attempting to piece together what happened.

Atwood's story, while primarily concerned with the myth of wilderness as sanctuary, also inscribes the landscape with violence: one of the characters imagines bringing his axe down on the head of another, and at the very end, a third character contemplates suicide. The story concerns four siblings, Pamela, Prue, Portia and Roland, and a man named George. Formerly Prue's lover, George is now Portia's husband, and by the end of the story has become Pamela's lover also. The five are staying at Wacousta Lodge, a house built by the family's great-grandfather and named after John Richardson's novel. The location of the house is not specified, but is apparently in Ontario's 'cottage country', north of Toronto.

In the first chapter of *Wacousta*, Richardson writes:

> Even at the present day, along that line of remote country we have selected for the theatre of our labours, the garrisons are both few in number and weak in strength, and evidence of cultivation is seldom to be found at any distance in the interior; so that all beyond a certain extent of clearing, continued along the banks of the lakes and rivers, is thick, impervious, rayless forest, the limits of which have never yet been explored, perhaps, by the natives themselves.
>
> Such being the general features of the country even at the present day, it will readily be comprehended how much more wild and desolate was the character they exhibited as far back as the middle of the last century.[31]

The narrator here emphasises the present reality of unexplored wilderness, yet the effect of this passage is to construct wilderness as already partly historical, even from the vantage point of 1832; the phrase 'how much more' suggests the relatively rapid progress of deforestation and cultivation. This perception of wilderness as historical takes on new meaning in an era of anxieties about the effects of human interference with the ecosystem. Munro's story is set in the past, mainly in the nineteenth century, and Atwood's in the present, yet in both the emphasis is on the reconstruction of a wilderness which has disappeared. Writing in 1907, George Herron in 'A Wilderness Station' remarks:

> Now there are gravel roads running north, south, east, and west and a railway not half a mile from my farm. Except for the woodlots, the bush is a thing of the past and I often think of the trees I have cut down and if I had them to cut down today I would be a wealthy man.[32]

On her way to visit him, Annie, who has not been out of the small town of Walley for several decades, says: 'Look at the big fields, where are the stumps gone, where is the bush?' (p. 219). But even in the earlier time frame of 1852, the Walley minister writes to the minister at the new settlement of Carstairs: 'The town has now grown so civilized that we forget the hardship of the hinterlands' (p. 206). The compression of Munro's narrative into the space of a short story intensifies the sense of the wilderness rapidly disappearing from southern Ontario

'Wilderness Tips' similarly creates an effect of layering of time periods, but in a different way. George, a Hungarian immigrant, is fascinated by the cult of wilderness living which was embraced by his wife's great-grandfather, and indicates his respect for the traditions supposedly represented by this ancestor by regularly bowing to his portrait. The great-grandfather, who built the house in the early years of the twentieth century, apparently furnished it according to his mental image of late eighteenth-century colonial wilderness cabins (which were themselves modelled upon English hunting lodges of the sixteenth and seventeenth centuries):

> Pamela is complaining again about the stuffed birds. There are three of them, kept under glass bells in the living room: a duck, a loon, a grouse. These were the bright ideas of the grandfather, meant to go with the generally lodge-like décor: the mangy bearskin rug, complete with claws and head; the miniature birchbark canoe on the mantelpiece; the snowshoes, cracked and drying, crossed above the fireplace; the Hudson's Bay blanket nailed to the wall and beset by moths.[33]

The phraseology in this passage – such as 'bright idea' and 'lodge-like décor' – suggests that the great-grandfather has produced a slightly unconvincing imitation, and he has appropriated functional elements of native Canadian culture and transformed them into aesthetic objects. This was also done by eighteenth-century colonists, as is clear from *Wacousta* in which Clara de Haldimar's apartment is decorated with 'numerous specimens both of the dress and of the equipments of the savages . . . the skins of the beaver, the marten, the otter, and an infinitude of others', as well as 'a model of a bark canoe'.[34]

Atwood's George, even further removed than the great-grandfather from the age of conquerors, colonists and pioneers and from the genuine culture of native peoples, mentally builds what he thinks of as a tradition of wilderness existence, but ends up with a pastiche of styles, artefacts and texts from different periods. George, who simply 'loves traditions' (p. 197), has a tendency to flatten historical time: he does not distinguish between the nineteenth century, when *Wacousta* was written, the eighteenth century, when it is set, and the early twentieth century, when the great-grandfather borrowed its name for his house. Neither does he distinguish between traditional methods of wilderness survival with no protection from starvation or wild beasts and the art of living in a summer cottage with no plumbing.

George, trying to assimilate the literary tradition of Canada alongside its other traditions, reads all the great-grandfather's books, and is intrigued by one published in 1905, called *Wilderness Tips* (Atwood's invention, although it is shelved alongside several real Canadian titles). It takes a boy-scout attitude to the forest, and includes, for example, instructions for lighting fires in rainstorms, 'lyrical passages about the joys of independence and the open air' (p. 206), and 'a lot about the Indians, about how noble they were, how brave, faithful, . . . honourable' (p. 213). As Howells notes, this book purveys 'a white male imperialist fantasy, not unlike the American myth of the Wild West'.[35] Roland shares this fantasy, and it emerges that he cherished the book as a child. Seduced by images of the noble savage generated by White people, Roland wants 'to be an Indian' (p. 212) and to be able to survive by himself in the woods.

As an adult, Roland retains a longing to authenticate himself through identification with the wilderness. He hates his job in finance, and thinks himself a failure because he should be 'out pillaging, not counting the beans'; but he loves chopping wood at Wacousta Lodge, and 'feels alive only up here' (p. 210). He resents George for trying to appropriate the traditions and culture which Roland himself has attempted to appropriate, and regards his brother-in-law as an outsider – a non-Canadian and also a denizen of the corrupt city – who wants to exploit the things which Roland himself holds sacred. Yet George – at least initially – cherishes the same ideals as Roland, and is determined not to 'desecrate' Wacousta Lodge (p. 203). He associates the cottage and lake with the asexual purity of Portia, whom he chose as his wife for precisely this quality, and his attitude evokes the conventional representation of wilderness as feminised, or virgin. Eventually, however, George succumbs and performed an act of desecration after all, by having sex with Pamela. His liaisons with Prue and Pamela undercut the ideal of the purifying return to nature which is present in traditional and modern Canadian wilderness writing.[36]

In a similar manoeuvre, Alice Munro presents the wilderness as a place not of purity, but of sexual exploitation: both Simon and George Herron look at Annie 'in a bad way' (p. 213), and she fears their violence – 'I dreamed nearly every night that one or other of them came and chased me with the axe' (p. 214). She soon escapes from both men, but the fate she avoids is realised in the experience of another inmate of Walley Gaol. The minister writes:

It must be acknowledged that this is truly a hard country for women. Another insane female has been admitted here recently, and her case is more pitiful for she has been driven insane by a rape. Her two attackers have been taken in and are in fact just over the wall from her in the men's section. (p. 206)

In Munro's story, the forest itself contains no menace; there are no hostile Native people or wild animals. The violence which Munro locates in her 'wilderness station' originates entirely with White men, and in this way she writes against traditional depictions of the monstrous wilderness. As women writers, Atwood and Munro reconsider the body of clichéd imagery about the North and the wilderness which has been built up by male authors, and, by continuing to range over this territory, they forge connections with their national literary heritage even as they interrogate its assumptions and offer a fresh perspective on the mythology of wilderness.

CONCLUSION

Owing to Canada's extremely diverse landscapes and immense size, geography and place have always been highly significant dimensions of Canadian literature, but no specific literary images of place or culture can ever be representative of the whole country. Although the mythology of wilderness and the North has been very influential in art and literature, and has long been privileged by critics as central to the national imaginary, nevertheless both early and modern Canadian texts evince an awareness of the constructed, artificial nature of this mythology. Many contemporary authors seek to rewrite or contest the wilderness tradition in various ways, pointing to its contradictions and concealed ideological biases, or deconstructing the binary between city and forest. A range of literary techniques from realism to Gothic have been used to evoke the specific topographies of particular Canadian landscapes and cities, and in more recent writing, as Linda Hutcheon notes: 'The postmodern has also translated the existing Canadian emphasis on regionalism in literature . . . into a concern for the different, the local, the particular – in opposition to the uniform, the universal, the centralized'.[37]

- The wilderness tradition is characterised by contradictions, and a set of incompatible myths of wilderness have developed. The primary opposition is between the myth of the wild North as hostile and potentially fatal, on the one hand, and as pure and regenerative, on the other.
- Postmodern writing and criticism tends to invest the wilderness with more complex meanings, to explore its status as historical or fantastic space, or to dismantle the opposition between urban and rural locations.

- The natural world, in many canonical Canadian texts, is a place of escape and solace, but most fictional protagonists acknowledge the impossibility of complete identification with nature and affirm the importance of human communities.
- The city is very significant to English-Canadian literature. Although Toronto and Vancouver remain the most popular settings, regional capitals in the prairie and Maritime provinces are increasingly being explored by creative writers.
- Particular landscapes do not necessarily determine imaginative responses; rather, places and regions are partly constructed through stories, mythologies and art.

NOTES

1. Margaret Atwood, *Strange Things: The Malevolent North in Canadian Literature* (Oxford: Clarendon Press, 1995), p. 5.
2. See in particular Susanne Becker, *Gothic Forms of Feminine Fictions* (Manchester: Manchester University Press, 1999), and Justin D. Edwards, *Gothic Canada: Reading the Spectre of a National Literature* (Edmonton: University of Alberta Press, 2005).
3. John Richardson, *Wacousta*, ed. John Moss (Ottawa: Tecumseh Press, [1832] 1998), p. 228.
4. Coral Ann Howells, *Margaret Atwood*, 2nd edn (Basingstoke: Palgrave Macmillan, 2005), p. 37.
5. Richardson, *Wacousta*, p. 227.
6. Margot Northey, *The Haunted Wilderness: The Gothic and Grotesque in Canadian Fiction* (Toronto: University of Toronto Press, 1976), p. 24.
7. Margaret Atwood, *Survival: A Thematic Guide to Canadian Literature* (Toronto: Anansi, 1972), p. 54.
8. Janice Fiamengo, 'Regionalism and Urbanism', in *The Cambridge Companion to Canadian Literature*, ed. Eva-Marie Kröller (Cambridge: Cambridge University Press, 2004), pp. 241–62 (p. 249).
9. Justin D. Edwards and Douglas Ivison, 'Introduction' in *Downtown Canada: Writing Canadian Cities*, ed. J. D. Edwards

and D. Ivison (Toronto: University of Toronto Press, 2005), pp. 3–13 (p. 3).

10. See Northrop Frye, 'Conclusion', in *Literary History of Canada*, ed. Carl F. Klinck (Toronto: University of Toronto Press, 1965), pp. 821–49; George Woodcock, *Northern Spring: The Flowering of Canadian Literature* (Vancouver: Douglas and McIntyre, 1987).

11. Fiamengo, 'Regionalism', p. 41.

12. Brian Jarvis, *Postmodern Cartographies: The Geographical Imagination in Contemporary American Literature* (London: Pluto, 1998), p. 7.

13. Neil Smith and Cindi Katz, 'Grounding Metaphor: Towards a Spatialized Politics', in *Place and the Politics of Identity*, ed. Michael Keith and Steve Pile (London: Routledge, 1993), pp. 67–83 (p. 77).

14. Ibid., p. 78.

15. Graham Huggan, *Territorial Disputes: Maps and Mapping Strategies in Contemporary Canadian and Australian Fiction* (Toronto: University of Toronto Press, 1994), p. 56.

16. Northrop Frye, *The Bush Garden: Essays on the Canadian Imagination* (Toronto: Anansi, 1971), p. 225; Atwood, *Survival*, p. 49.

17. Gabriella Åhmansson, *A Life and Its Mirrors: A Feminist Reading of L. M. Montgomery's Fiction* (Uppsala, Sweden: Acta Universatis Upsaliensis, 1991), pp. 51–2.

18. L. M. Montgomery, *Anne of Green Gables*, ed. Cecily Devereux (Peterborough, ON: Broadview, [1908] 2004), pp. 81–2. All subsequent references in the text are to this edition.

19. Janice Kulyk Keefer, *Under Eastern Eyes: A Critical Reading of Maritime Fiction* (Toronto: University of Toronto Press, 1987), p. 188.

20. Atwood, *Strange Things*, p. 101.

21. Wilson, Ethel, *Swamp Angel* (Toronto: McClelland and Stewart, [1954] 1990), p. 100. All subsequent references in the text are to this edition.

22. George Bowering, 'Afterword', in Wilson, *Swamp Angel*, pp. 210–16 (p. 213).

23. Ibid., p. 214.

24. Carol Shields, *The Republic of Love* (London: Flamingo, [1992] 1993), p. 269. All subsequent references in the text are to this edition.

25. Perry Nodelman, 'Living in the Republic of Love: Carol Shields's Winnipeg' (1995), repr. in *Carol Shields: The Arts of a Writing Life*, ed. Neil K. Besner (Winnipeg: Prairie Fire, 2003), pp. 40–55 (p. 49).

26. Robertson Davies, *The Cunning Man* (Harmondsworth: Penguin, [1994] 1995), p. 32. All subsequent references in the text are to this edition.

27. Atwood, *Strange Things*, p. 11.

28. See Christopher E. Gittings, 'Constructing a Scots-Canadian Ground: Family History and Cultural Translation in Alice Munro', *Studies in Short Fiction*, 34: 1 (1997), 27–37.

29. Ildiko de Papp Carrington, *Controlling the Uncontrollable: The Fiction of Alice Munro* (DeKalb, IL: Northern Illinois University Press, 1989), p. 89.

30. See Isla J. Duncan, '"It seems so much the truth it is the truth": Persuasive Testimony in Alice Munro's *A Wilderness Station*', *Studies in Canadian Literature*, 28: 2 (2003), 98–110.

31. Richardson, *Wacousta*, pp. 3–4.

32. Alice Munro, *Open Secrets* (London: Chatto and Windus, 1994), p. 197. All subsequent references in the text are to this edition.

33. Margaret Atwood, *Wilderness Tips* (London: Bloomsbury, [1991] 1995), p. 200. All subsequent references in the text are to this edition.

34. Richardson, *Wacousta*, 233.

35. Howells, *Margaret Atwood*, p. 50.

36. See Faye Hammill, '"Death by Nature": Margaret Atwood's Haunted Forests', *Gothic Studies*, 5: 2 (2003), 47–63.

37. Linda Hutcheon, *The Canadian Postmodern: A Study of Contemporary English-Canadian Fiction* (Toronto: Oxford University Press, 1988), p. 19.

CHAPTER 3

Desire

Above Miner's Pond, geese break out of the sky's
pale shell. They speak non-stop, amazed
they've returned from the stars,
hundreds of miles to describe.

It's not that they're wild, but
their will is the same as desire.
The sky peels back under their blade.
Anne Michaels, 'Miner's Pond'[1]

Miner's Pond in Kingsville, Ontario, belonged to Jack Miner, who
became well known in the early years of the twentieth century for
attracting migrant Canada geese to stop at his home on their way
south. He kept wing-clipped geese in his pond, and these decoyed
hundreds of wild geese, which he was able to study and protect. In
1923 he published a book about his experiences, *Jack Miner and the
Birds*. Anne Michaels's 'Miner's Pond', the title poem of her 1991
collection, takes the geese as its central image, using them to figure
the multiple movements of desire. The geese are associated, firstly,
with migration, which connects desire with place; in a migratory
journey, the longing to be elsewhere is succeeded by an impulse to
return home. The very precise geography of the poem maps the
repeated journeys of the speaker's childhood, and she compares her
family to the geese, returning over and over to the same places: 'Like

them, we carry each year in our bodies / Our blood is time' (p. 64). The reference to time points to a second dimension of desire: the yearning for the past. 'Miner's Pond' is an elegy for a dead child, and in the final stanza, the speaker observes: 'Overhead the geese are a line, / a moving scar' (p. 64). Grief is revealed as another form of longing, a form defined by the absence of the desired object. Lastly, the flight of the geese is 'sexual, one prolonged / reflex' (p. 56); these lines remind us that bird migration patterns are organised around the reproductive season, and suggest that in humans, too, sexuality and migration are instinctual, and intimately connected.

The representation of forms of desire through an image of migrating geese aligns Michaels's poem with many other Canadian texts, among them several which are discussed in this book. In Martha Ostenso's *Wild Geese* (1925), the departure and return of the geese marks the cycle of seasons and the cycle of human sexuality: during the months between their northward and southward journeys, Judith Gare consummates her relationship with her lover and becomes pregnant. E. J. Pratt's *Brébeuf and His Brethren* (1940) introduces an association with religious longing: the birds' determined traversing of the sky becomes a metaphor for the spiritual commitment of the French missionary Jean de Brébeuf, and for the inspiration he finds in the idea of Canada: 'Wild geese drove wedges through the zodiac / The vows were deep he laid upon his soul'.[2] The first image in Ethel Wilson's *Swamp Angel* (1954) is that of migrating birds, evoking Maggie's yearning to escape to a new place, where she can come to terms with the deaths of her husband and child. Similarly, in Margaret Laurence's *The Diviners* (1974), Morag watches 'the Canada geese. Going somewhere. Able to go, at will'.[3] For both Wilson's and Laurence's protagonists, the sight of the geese stimulates an actual journey to unknown places, and indeed, travel, whether across the Atlantic or within Canada, is significant in all the books mentioned. In many literary journeys, the process of travelling is privileged over the destination; arrival does not generally bring the satisfactions which were looked for. Travel is therefore an appropriate figure for desire, which is sustained only by remaining unfulfilled. The recurrent image of wild geese in Canadian literature may be connected with the country's history of immigration and diaspora, and the varied forms of longing which motivate, and result from, such movements. Canada geese, then, take on an iconic value in many literary texts: they might be seen as a distinctively Canadian, yet multivalent, inscription of desire.

In many Canadian texts, the poetics of landscape are intimately bound up with the body and desire, and this chapter examines the interrelationships between place and sexuality through readings of some of Canada's most sensual writing. A long tradition of art and literature has figured the Canadian natural environment erotically; the colonial metaphor of 'virgin land' suggests a landscape which is untouched, ownerless and available for exploration, penetration and exploitation. At once alluring and threatening, the forest in early Canadian writing was often represented in explicitly gendered terms, and this gendering recurs in new, more self-conscious forms in postmodern Canadian texts such as Daphne Marlatt's *Ana Historic* (1988), Margaret Atwood's *Wilderness Tips* (1991) or Alice Munro's *Open Secrets* (1994) (see Chapters 2 and 4). In the early and mid-twentieth century, following the westward expansion of settlement, numerous Canadian texts were set on the prairies, and this landscape, too, was evoked in both sexualised and terrifying terms. Human passions are imaged in landscape in Robert Stead's *Grain* (1926), Sinclair Ross's *As For Me and My House* (1941) and W. O. Mitchell's *Who Has Seen the Wind?* (1947), as well as in Ostenso's *Wild Geese*, chosen for discussion here, in which a particularly striking example of the eroticised prairie environment is to be found. A prize-winning novel set in an agricultural area of Manitoba, it concerns the domination of a family by a cruel patriarch, the sexual awakening of his daughter, and her eroticised relationships with a female friend and a male lover.

In recent Canadian writing, it is often urban rather than natural landscapes which become erotically charged. Another poem from Anne Michaels's *Miner's Pond*, 'Phantom Limbs', exemplifies this:

> So much of the city
> is our bodies. Places in us
> old light still slants through to.
> Places that no longer exist but are full of feeling,
> like phantom limbs.

Even the city carries ruins in its heart.
Longs to be touched in places
only it remembers.   (p. 95)

These lines suggest that human memory and desire can outlast the
temporary structures of the city, but that the city itself is also
capable of longing and remembering. This rhetorical move recalls
the use of the pathetic fallacy in earlier Canadian texts, but
Michaels projects human feelings onto streets and buildings rather
than forests and lakes, and adds further subtlety by inscribing the
city's history onto the bodies of its inhabitants.

Three of the texts discussed in this chapter render the city as the
site of desire. In one of Canada's best-known autobiographies, John
Glassco's *Memoirs of Montparnasse* (1970), the primary eroticised
space is located abroad, in France. Yet Glassco's narrator repeatedly
constructs 1920s Paris in relation to the city he has abandoned,
Montreal, so that Canada retains a distinct presence in this expatriate narrative of a sexual and literary coming of age. Same-sex desire
is an important, if submerged, theme in *Memoirs of Montparnasse*,
while in Leonard Cohen's *Beautiful Losers* (1966) it is an explicit
preoccupation. *Beautiful Losers* is one of Canada's most notorious
novels. Known for its sexual candour and violence, surreal exploration of Quebec's history, and postmodern narrative techniques,
the novel is mainly set in Montreal, but also refers back to the
wilderness which preceded the colonial settlement there. In
Beautiful Losers, sexual experience leads both to transcendence and
destruction, but in Anne Michaels's *Fugitive Pieces* (1996) sexuality is redemptive. Nevertheless she, like Cohen, frequently con-
flates erotic longing with longing for the past. *Fugitive Pieces* is set
partly in Toronto and partly on two Greek islands, places which are
apprehended through all the senses, since the narrative describes
sounds, smells and textures as well as visual qualities. The same is
true of the work of Dionne Brand. Her poems and fictions evoke
geographies of Canada and also her native Trinidad which are both
precise and mythical, bringing the landscape into relation with
diasporic and also woman-centred experience, including lesbian
erotics. In her most admired collection of poems, *Land to Light On*

(1997), the human body becomes a focus for a range of interrelated political and personal themes.

While this chapter will concentrate on ways of reading and writing desire in a specifically Canadian context, it is important to begin by indicating the extensive possibilities for discussing desire in more general theoretical terms. Desire, in its relation to the psychological, economic, medical and political realms, has been theorised by a long series of western philosophers, scientists, cultural critics and anthropologists. Most analyses centre primarily on erotic desire, or at least use sexuality as a model for understanding the motivations and power relations which operate around other kinds of desires. The most prominent theorists of desire may be loosely organised into groups in order to provide a rapid summary of the principal forms of critical analysis which are available. The critical study of desire can be traced back to the sexologists of the late nineteenth and early twentieth centuries (Richard von Krafft-Ebing, Karl Heinrich Ulrichs and Havelock Ellis are among the best known), who attempted to classify sexual behaviours into 'types'. Although sexology has never entirely disappeared, it has been largely superseded by psychoanalysis, pioneered of course by Freud and Lacan, as well as Melanie Klein, Helen Deutsch and others. The later generation of feminists who variously draw on and challenge Freudian and Lacanian paradigms includes Julia Kristeva, Luce Irigaray, Hélène Cixous, Jacqueline Rose and Juliet Mitchell. Other theorists focus on economies of desire, that is, the dialectical forces which make up the libido, and the enmeshing of desire in capitalist systems of expenditure and accumulation (George Bataille, Gilles Deleuze and Félix Guattari, Jean-François Lyotard and Jean Baudrillard). A further group concentrate on desire as a discursive category: Michel Foucault, in his immensely influential *History of Sexuality* (1976–84), examines the way beliefs about sexuality are used to organise power and regulate the social order, and several of the other major philosophers and theorists of the late twentieth century have written on the theatricality of desire, its relationship to language and signifying practices, and the erotic pleasures of reading (Roland Barthes, Jacques Derrida, Catherine Belsey and others). Among the contemporary issues which preoccupy theorists of sexuality is the feminist battle over the censorship of pornography, waged by, for instance, Andrea Dworkin and Catharine A. McKinnon, who argue that porn incites sexual crimes against women, and, on the other side of the question, the collective Feminists Against Censorship, who see porn as the result, rather than the cause, of a sexist society. Another key debate centres on the relationships between categories of sex and gender, and the notion of gender as performative (Judith Butler), and a further, closely related, area of enquiry is now organised under the heading 'queer theory', and pursued by numerous eminent scholars (among them Eve Kosofsky-Sedgwick, Jeffrey Weeks and Gayle Rubin).

Faced with such a wealth of material, it is very difficult to formulate a working definition of desire, and the problem is exacerbated by what Belsey in *Desire: Love Stories in Western Culture* (1994) calls the 'paradoxes of desire', or its 'undecidabilities'. Desire, she writes, is: 'At once shared with a whole culture, but intimate and personal, hopelessly banal and yet unique', and she notes 'the difficulty of fixing, delimiting, delineating a state of mind which is also a state of body, or which perhaps deconstructs the opposition between the two'. Belsey adds: 'Desire eludes final definition, with the result that its character, its nature, its meaning, becomes itself an object of desire for the writer'.[4] Eugene Goodheart, in *Desire and Its Discontents* (1991), points out that modern understandings of the self have radically changed the way in which desire is conceptualised. Philosophers, he explains, traditionally argued that reason should rule desire and passion, but a new philosophy emerged in the later nineteenth century which 'inverts the hierarchy of desire and reason, or alternatively, dissolves the distinction altogether, saying in effect that desire is everything: it generates and consumes all of life'. The illimitability of desire challenges the conventional notion of the bounded, individual self. According to Goodheart:

> In recent years there has been an explosion of talk about desire, drawing on this counter-tradition, that has challenged the values of rationalist discourse, in particular the rationalist model of the self. Coherence, unity, wholeness – the value terms of that discourse – have been transformed into terms of

repression. What is repressed is desire, which has come to stand for freedom or for the thing that needs to be liberated. What is desire?[5]

Rather than attempting a final answer to this question, Belsey and Goodheart each explore the discursive construction of desire and the ways in which it is invested with meaning in literary texts, and their books thus provide a framework for the present discussion.

The relation between desire and the political preoccupies both writers. Goodheart speculates: 'If erotic desire were an emblem of the anarchic self, one might expect eros to be inimical to all forms of tyranny. And indeed, totalitarian societies . . . are notoriously puritanical, because they fear the freedom represented by the erotic life'.[6] But his exploration of particular literary inscriptions of sexual desire reveals 'the despotic violence of physical love', since: 'a character submits to eros in a way that he or she may not always submit even to a totalitarian regime'.[7] Belsey similarly argues that desire can either reinforce or resist existing power structures. She discusses the popular romance, a genre whose repeating structures insistently privilege the cultural ideal of true love, in which sexual desire coincides with a permanent affection: 'Family values, cemented by true love, legitimize oppressive state policies and inadequate social expenditure'. But, she continues: 'At the same time, desire is also the location of resistances to the norms, proprieties and taxonomies of the cultural order'.[8] This potential for resistance is not confined to transgressive sexualities, since: 'desire in all its forms, including heterosexual desire, commonly repudiates legality; at the level of the unconscious its imperatives are absolute; and in consequence it readily overflows . . . the institutions designed to contain it'.[9] The ideal of true love informs some of the texts discussed below; it is reflected on and finally endorsed in *Fugitive Pieces*, and two marriages of love take place at the end of *Wild Geese*. But the heterosexual romances in *Wild Geese*, as well as all the putative 'true love' plots in *Memoirs of Montparnasse* and *Beautiful Losers*, are continually disrupted by alternative sexual forces, including homoeroticism, heterosexual violence, adulterous and premarital sex, pornography and sado-masochism.

These forces also disrupt binary distinctions between mind and body, love and hatred, and especially between homosexuality and heterosexuality. As Joseph Bristow points out in *Sexuality* (1997):

> society has worked hard at dividing sexualities into 'hetero-' and 'homo-' antitheses because there is such a perilous relationship between the two. Since the late Victorian period, we have often assumed that this violent distinction described a natural state of affairs, rather than see how it performed an ideological manoeuvre.[10]

Eve Kosofsky Sedgwick further illuminates the close connections between homosocial and homosexual desire and their collaborative safeguarding of patriarchal power, arguing in *Between Men* (1985) that these processes are concealed by an insistence on the division between homosexuality and heterosexuality.[11] Several of the texts chosen for this chapter challenge this distinction by representing characters who respond erotically to others of both sexes.

In all the Canadian literary examples cited above, wild geese are associated, on the one hand, with the power of the instinct and will, and on the other, with a sense of something missing, something longed for. In conceptualising desire, these two elements may be considered inseparable. Most theorists see desire as predicated on lack; Lacan writes: 'Desire is that which is manifested in the interval that demand hollows within itself', and characterises the Other, desired to complement the subject, as 'the locus of want, or lack',[12] and this argument has informed many later discussions, including Belsey's. But there are other ways of conceptualising desire. Deleuze and Guattari argue in *Anti-Oedipus: Capitalism and Schizophrenia* (1972) that 'Desire does not lack anything', since it is in fact a productive principle, and the objects it produces are real, material objects. Rather than the object, it is the fixed subject which is missing, according to Deleuze and Guattari; they replace the traditional notion of the desiring subject with the 'desiring machine', suggesting an impersonal force which continually adopts unexpected directions and forms new connections and networks.[13] Goodheart, referring to the usage of 'desire' by linguistic theorists such as Kristeva, notes that the word 'does not require a predicate.

Desire moves, floats, negates, shatters, aspires, it is itself a subject', and it refuses 'to be constrained by the satisfactions that would extinguish it'.[14] These are fascinating and influential theories, with considerable purchase in relation to texts such as *Beautiful Losers* or *Land to Light On*, in which the subject is radically destabilised.

The majority of literary texts, though, continue to focus on individual desiring subjects, and critical paradigms which interpret desire in relation to lack or absence may be more useful for reading such texts. 'Absence' refers not only to the literal absence of what is desired by each character, but also to the absence of the real from the world of representation, and the absence of ultimate truths. These things are made particularly explicit in contemporary writing; as Belsey argues: 'Postmodern writing . . . takes for granted that the process of representation can never be the reconstitution of presence; it repudiates the modernist nostalgia for the unpresentable, ineffable truth of things'. Belsey also points out that the language of love, which constructs love itself, is 'inevitably allusive, derivative, citational', that is, that the same phrases, images and stories are repeated over and over.[15] This patterning is most visible in popular cultural texts such as paperback romances and Hollywood films, but is also discernible in narratives ordinarily classified as high culture, which may self-consciously explore or display the citationality of desire. Despite all this, the appeal of literary narrative continues to depend on the reader's desire to discover truths, to know 'what happens' to these particular characters, in this particular story, and what meanings it may have. As Goodheart puts it:

> Desire is the source of narrative. It generates the obstacles it must overcome or circumvent through ruses, deceptions, and displacements. It creates the devious shapes of narrative by aiming for satisfaction, deferring it and discovering its satisfaction as well as agony in deferral.[16]

The citationality and repeating structures of stories of desire do not negate the inventiveness, the 'devious shapes' of individual literary texts, and the sheer diversity of writing on desire means that the critical possibilities for investigating it are endless.

MARTHA OSTENSO, *WILD GEESE* (1925)

Martha Ostenso (1900–63) was born near Bergen in Norway, and her family emigrated to North America in 1902, living in various towns in the Dakotas, Minnesota and Manitoba. After a short period teaching in a school some distance north-west of Winnipeg, Ostenso enrolled at the University of Manitoba. There, she met Professor Douglas Durkin, an older, married man who would become her permanent companion, her literary collaborator and eventually her husband. Her first book was a collection of poems, *A Far Land* (1924). She then submitted *Wild Geese* to a first-novel competition, sponsored by *The Pictorial Review*, the publisher Dodd, Mead, and Company, and the Hollywood studio Famous Players-Lasky. She beat 1,389 competitors, and her prize-winning book became a bestseller. Fifteen more novels, variously set in Canada and the US, were subsequently published under the name of Martha Ostenso, though in fact these were collaborations between Ostenso and Durkin.

Wild Geese is set on an isolated farm in a district of Manitoba populated mainly by Icelanders, though the family at the centre of the novel, the Gares, are of indeterminate ethnicity, and may be Norwegian, or of partly English descent.[17] The farmhouse is ruled by Caleb Gare, a tyrannical, vindictive patriarch. His wife, Amelia, is rendered submissive by her husband's threats to reveal publicly that she has a son, Mark Jordan, born out of wedlock and ignorant of his parentage. Among her legitimate children, Ellen, Charlie and Martin also submit to their father, but Judith rebels. A crisis is precipitated by the arrival of Lind Archer, a teacher from the city, who boards with the Gares and falls in love with Mark Jordan. Lind also encourages Judith's romance with a neighbour, Sven Sandbo, and assists her to defy her father. At the conclusion, Caleb dies and the two couples are married.

Caleb Gare is fanatically possessive about his land: 'The early summer season was to him a terrific, prolonged hour of passion during which he was blind and dumb to everything save the impulse that bound him to the land'.[18] Caleb bestows on his flax the erotic attention which he withholds from his wife: he is shown 'almost furtively running his hand over the rough, fully seeded tops' and 'wad[ing] far into it, touching it now and then, his eyes roving over it hungrily' (p. 264). His passion is reciprocated in a malevolent way when he drowns in a bog: 'something seemed to be tugging at his feet . . . the strength in the earth was irresistible . . . the insidious force in the earth drew him deeper' (pp. 298–9). Numerous critics have interpreted *Wild Geese* purely in terms of the opposition between man and nature, but Daniel Lenoski argues that such readings miss the novel's idealism and vision of hope. He points out that the land is truly hostile only to those characters who seek to exploit and profit from it, whereas Judith enjoys an 'organic' relationship with her surroundings.[19] In one scene, Judith undresses outdoors and lies naked on the ground:

> Oh, how knowing the bare earth was, as if it might have a heart and a mind hidden here in the woods. The fields that Caleb had tilled had no tenderness, she knew. But here was something forbiddenly beautiful, secret as one's own body. (p. 61)

In contrast to her father's failed attempt to dominate the land, which is represented as a perversely erotic quest, Judith finds the natural landscape regenerative and liberating: 'there was something beyond this. She could feel it in the freeness of the air, in the depth of the earth' (p. 61).

Wild Geese is permeated with an intense and often violent eroticism which is rare among Canadian texts of this period. In the novel's most visceral scene, Judith wrestles with Sven:

> Sven crushed the girl's limbs between his own . . . her clothing torn away. Her panting body heaved against his as they lay full length on the ground locked in furious embrace. Judith buried her nails in the flesh over his breast, beat her knees into his loins, set her teeth in the more tender skin over the veins in his wrists . . . Sven's breath fell in hot gusts on Judith's face. Suddenly her hand, that was fastened like steel on his throat, relaxed and fell away . . .
> 'Kiss me – now', she said in a breath. (p. 103)

Judith is a very unconventional heroine for her period. The violence of her desire for Sven, and her fierce insistence on equality with him, are directly contrary to the representation of women as sexually passive, which was still the norm in Canadian writing from this period. Judith also disrupts family values by engaging in a sexual relationship with a man she has been forbidden to see, and by her illegitimate pregnancy. Her most shocking act of all results from her father's attempt to punish her: she retaliates by throwing an axe at his head. While the secondary heroine, Lind, represents a more romanticised, ethereal image of femininity, she is nevertheless complicit in Judith's premarital sex and defiance of her father, and neither woman is finally punished. The moral codes of early twentieth-century publishing demanded that instances of female passion or violence led to either retribution or penitence: Ostenso's text boldly resists these norms, and deprecates Judith's sister Ellen for her submission to male authority. Ellen gives up the chance of marrying the man she loves, Malcolm, because Caleb wishes her to remain on the farm and labour without pay. The reader is encouraged to hope that Ellen will leave with Malcolm, and since he is of partly Native descent, the sympathetic depiction of this putative relationship is a further instance of the transgressive nature of Ostenso's text.

Ostenso's celebration of female autonomy, together with the novel's sexually charged atmosphere and condoning of interracial love, goes some way towards explaining why *Wild Geese* evoked hostility from the very conservative literary establishment in Canada. Another factor was doubtless the homoerotic dimension to the text, which makes it still more unconventional in the context of mainstream interwar Canadian writing. During all the scenes relating to her sexual awakening, Judith thinks of Lind Archer, and the narrator says that Lind's 'delicate fingers had sprung a secret lock in Jude's being. She had opened like a tight bud' (p. 61). The text repeatedly emphasises the physical attraction between them:

Judith came up to Lind in the loft and sat down on the bed, watching the Teacher wash her face and neck and long smooth arms with a fragrant soap. Lind turned and surprised a peculiar look in the girl's eyes. Judith grew red . . .

'It makes my mouth water to watch you do that', she said. 'It's so – oh, I don't know what it is – just as if somebody's stroking my skin.'

'Why don't you use this soap, Judith? . . . Next time you
expect to meet Sven' – Lind lowered her voice and smiled
roguishly at Jude – 'let me fix you all up, will you? Nice
smelling powder and a tiny drop of perfume in your hair. He'll
die of delight . . . '

Judith chuckled and ran her hands over her round breasts .
. . Lind looked at her, stretched full length across the bed.
What a beautiful, challenging body she had! . . .

The Teacher sat down on the floor beside the bed and
Judith loosened the long skeins of bronze hair that fell all
about her shoulders. Judith loved to run her fingers through
it, and to gather it up in a shining coil above the white nape of
Lind's neck. (pp. 196–7)

The erotic tension is only barely contained by Lind's gesture
towards a heterosexual romance plot, in which the 'fixing up' is for
Sven's benefit.

In the small towns of 1920s North America, as Lillian
Faderman points out, 'heterosexuals often never even knew that
homosexuals existed'.[20] In American cities, to be sure, the 1920s
was a period of intense attention to homosexual issues, though it
was by no means a period of tolerance. But in Canada, as Terry
Goldie notes, the development of 'a noteworthy gay culture' and
literature was delayed, and as late as the 1960s homosexuality was
still 'shorthand for sexual perversity'.[21] There is a discernible tradition in English-Canadian fiction of eroticised same-sex relationships, but the novels concerned, including among others John
Richardson's *Wacousta* (1832), F. P. Grove's *Settlers of the Marsh*
(1925) and Ernest Buckler's *The Mountain and the Valley* (1954),
were not read in relation to a queer aesthetic until the 1980s. This
lack of acceptance of same-sex desire may have been one of the
reasons why, as late as the 1960s, John Glassco felt obliged to
rewrite his *Memoirs of Montparnasse*, eliminating references to
homosexual experience and toning down the scenes which
approached pornography.

JOHN GLASSCO, *MEMOIRS OF MONTPARNASSE* (1970)

Memoirs of Montparnasse is set in the same period as *Wild Geese*, though in a location as different as possible from the remote prairie settlement of Ostenso's novel. Glassco's famously hedonistic memoir of his youth belongs both to the 1920s and the 1960s, both to Paris and Montreal. John Glassco (1909–81), known to friends as Buffy, was born in Montreal and studied briefly at McGill University. At nineteen, he left for Paris with his friend Graeme Taylor. He stayed three years, and, after his return to Canada and recovery from tuberculosis, he began writing poetry, erotica, and fiction, as well as translating French texts and editing anthologies. Glassco brought many French-Canadian poets to the attention of anglophone audiences, and was instrumental in establishing translation as an important art in Canada. His own poetry collections include *The Deficit Made Flesh: Poems* (1958), *A Point of Sky* (1964) and *Selected Poems* (1971), which won the Governor General's Award, and his other books include an erotic novel, *The English Governess*, published pseudonymously in 1960, and *The Fatal Women: Three Tales* (1974).

In a preface, Glassco asserts that he began writing *Memoirs of Montparnasse* when he was eighteen, completing it while awaiting an operation in Montreal in 1932–3. To substantiate this, he interpolates into his narrative several asides, reflecting on his Paris experiences from the point of view of a hospital bed. 'I have changed very little of the original', he writes in the preface, admitting only to 'the occasional improvement of a phrase' and the assignment of fictitious names to some of his famous associates.[22] In fact, although an early version of the first chapter of the *Memoirs* was published in Paris in *This Quarter* in 1929, Glassco wrote the rest in 1964. He was probably spurred on by his recent return visits to the city and by the success of two other memoirs of 1920s Left Bank society: fellow Canadian Morley Callaghan's *That Summer in Paris* (1963) and Ernest Hemingway's posthumously published *A Moveable Feast* (1964).

When reading autobiographies it is, of course, important to distinguish the self which writes (the narrator) from the self which is written about (the protagonist), and to distinguish both from the historical author, even though all three share the same name. In this

discussion, therefore, the memoirist is referred to as 'Glassco's narrator', and the younger protagonist as 'Glassco' or 'Buffy' in
inverted commas. In autobiography, both narrator and protagonist
are discursively constructed, and are effectively fictional characters,
and this point is particularly significant in the case of *Memoirs of
Montparnasse* because it is fictionalised to an unusual degree. As
Michael Gnarowski notes, Glassco

> recreated the key 'moments' of his concupiscent coming of
> age in Paris. To them he joined elements and occasions taken
> from the scattered lives of the so-called Lost Generation in an
> imaginative borrowing without much regard for provenance,
> of fact and circumstances.[23]

Glassco described the book as a 'lying chronicle',[24] encapsulating
the tensions between memory and invention which are revealed by
studying the origin and composition of the text. The generic
hybridity of the *Memoirs* is the primary subject of most critics'
analyses of the book, but there is not space here to rehearse these
intriguing arguments; instead, this discussion will focus on the
sensual dimensions of the text, and the dynamic between Canada
and Europe which shapes it.

Memoirs of Montparnasse is, of course, about Paris, but it is also
– though less explicitly – about Canada. Only one chapter is set in
Montreal, but Canada is referred to repeatedly, and partly defines
the narrator's perspective. At the beginning, 'Buffy' and Graeme
are 'united by comradeship, a despisal of everything represented by
the business world, the city of Montreal, and the Canadian scene,
and a desire to get away' (p. 1). Yet the narrator remarks, rather
wistfully, on the beauty of the place they are leaving: 'The loveli-
ness of the late morning was dazzling. The snow, the blue air, the
creaking underfoot of the hard-packed sidewalk – everything is so
hard and gem-like at eleven o'clock in Canada!' (p. 5). In Europe,
the two young men always introduce themselves as Canadians, and
experience moments of pride in their home country and in its
authors. Glassco's narrator recalls many tasty French meals, but he
becomes really lyrical on the subject of food only when describing
Canadian cuisine:

We have a salmon from the Gaspé coast, which when lightly boiled and served with egg-sauce and marinated cucumbers is even superior to the Scotch; we have magnificent oysters and lobsters; we also have two delicious vegetables that for some reason you do not cultivate in Europe, sweet corn and green asparagus. (p. 63)

Here, the narrator employs the precise yet sensuous language which he usually reserves for erotic encounters, and also proclaims Canadian superiority in an area in which France is normally held to excel. In this same episode, the narrator defines himself very clearly in terms of nationality: 'I identified myself as a poet from Canada' (p. 61). (It is interesting to note that, just as Canada shadows Glassco's portrayal of France in *Memoirs of Montparnasse*, so in the poems he wrote in later life – many of which are set in rural Quebec – the ghostly presence of a remembered Europe may frequently be discerned.[25])

Glassco's narrator insists on his nationality only when he is away from Canada; while in Montreal, his primary motivation is a longing to be elsewhere: 'I threw myself into composing surrealist poetry, and [Graeme] continued planning the great Canadian novel. But it was on a dream of Paris that our ideas were vaguely but powerfully concentrated' (p. 1). 'Buffy' and his companion are seduced by the modernist myth of Paris, considering it the heartland of both artistic innovation and sexual liberation. Yet despite their rapturous response to the possibilities for sensual pleasure and literary encounter in Paris, the text cannot conceal the repetitiveness and circularity of their life there. The same people, the same streets, the same cafés recur through the account of their rather circumscribed lives. Admittedly, Paris life is imbued with a certain glamour:

It was one of the first warm days of April. The old women were already selling *muguet* from their barrows, and after buying Stanley a bunch we took a table on the Dôme terrace and drank Chambéry-fraise. Everyone we knew stopped to talk. (p. 126)

Yet the social occasions described, like the numerous love affairs, seem rather indistinguishable and directionless. As Leon Edel noted in his introduction to the first edition of the *Memoirs*: 'There were, as we can now see in this narrative, ruts in Montparnasse as deep as any in that other provincial *Mont* – Montreal. One couldn't escape one's obsessions, and particularly those of Eros'.[26]

Although Glassco's book is usually thought of as an erotic memoir, most of the protagonist's liaisons are abortive, unsatisfying or damaging. The narrator recalls spending 'a good deal of time pursuing casual loves in Montparnasse, where the expense and effort involved . . . were quite incommensurable with the results' (p. 67). He falls in love with an American, Mrs Quayle, who gives him a venereal disease. He sleeps with Emily Pine (Glassco's name for Thelma Wood) but finds her 'quite frigid' (p. 38). Wood, in fact, was primarily lesbian. Indeed, lesbian sexuality continually triumphs over heterosexuality in the text: Buffy's lover Stanley, a Canadian woman, leaves him to move in with Daphne Berners (an alias for Gwen Le Gallienne), and when Buffy himself engages in an affair with Daphne, she stays with him only two weeks before returning to her lover Angela. Buffy's most fulfilling sexual experience is with two prostitutes (it was supposed to be three, but he is 'in no condition to continue' after the second), yet later in the evening, he is stricken with guilt. He encounters Diana Tree (based on Kay Boyle):

> She gripped my knee with compelling force underneath the table and her gaze became melting. She had never looked so beautiful, nor had I ever admired her more: the lovely grey-blue eyes were swimming in ecstasy . . . [S]he put her arms around my neck. 'Darling, let's spend the night together, shall we?' she whispered. 'I am so happy.'
>
> 'But where can we go? We have to consider Bob and Graeme – and – well, the truth is, I'm not feeling very well . . . '.
>
> She wheeled round in her cape and without a word disappeared into the ladies' room . . . The genius of Puritanism, with all its forefixed concatenation of misdeeds and punishments, had served me out properly. (p. 73)

The piling-up of conventional romantic vocabulary in this passage only makes the bathetic ending more ridiculous, and the narrative is momentarily overpowered by the traditional moral framework which 'Buffy' left Canada to escape from.

The many differences between the archived manuscript draft of the *Memoirs* and the published text are detailed by Thomas Tausky, who notes that the manuscript clearly indicates the protagonist's homosexual experiences as well as the homoerotic dimensions of his friendships with Taylor and McAlmon. In the published text, by contrast, there are only 'muted hints' of such things.[27] The manuscript also contains episodes of flagellation, and it endows Mrs Quayle with extreme sexual tastes. Tausky concludes that the protagonist of this earlier version may be distinguished from the character in the published *Memoirs* 'by his eager participation in a wider variety of sexual activities'. He adds:

> The atmosphere of the *Memoirs* is racy enough. The supplementary practices [the manuscript character] engages in nevertheless produce a considerable difference in tone . . .
> The proportion of literary dialogue is somewhat less, and the sexual episodes sometimes have the air of pornography.[28]

The published text is indeed 'racy'; 'Buffy' engages in a three-way relationship with Graeme and Stanley; works as an 'escort' for rich, sexually voracious women; visits a brothel where he shares three women with two friends; and poses for pornographic photographs. But *Memoirs of Montparnasse* is, through the author's revisions and cuts, clearly differentiated from his pseudonymously published pornographic writing; it is not a book which has the potential to shock and disgust, in the way that Cohen's *Beautiful Losers* did.

LEONARD COHEN, *BEAUTIFUL LOSERS* (1966)

Leonard Cohen, poet, novelist, singer, songwriter and film-maker, was born to Jewish parents in Montreal in 1934. His first book of poetry, *Let Us Compare Mythologies* (1956), was followed by three more collections and a first novel, *The Favourite Game* (1963). He began to consolidate a public presence through poetry recitals, some of them accompanied by guitar or jazz music.[29] He was featured in two films, *Six Montreal Poets* (1957) and *Ladies and Gentlemen . . . Mr Leonard Cohen* (1965), and his singing career took off with his signing to CBS Records and the release of his debut album, *The Songs of Leonard Cohen* (1967). During the next decade, Cohen continued with writing and performance, but in the late 1970s he experienced a breakdown. In 1993, some years after resuming his career, he began training at an American Buddhist monastery, and was later ordained as a monk. His most recent album is *Dear Heather* (2004), and his latest poetry collection, *Book of Longing*, appeared in 2006.

Beautiful Losers, Leonard Cohen's best-known book, was initially judged obscene by Canadian critics. Though it was better received in the US, the novel did not begin to sell until after Cohen achieved fame as a performer. It has now sold over 3 million copies, and been translated into twenty languages. The main characters are the unnamed narrator; his wife, Edith, and his friend F., both dead at the point when the narrator is writing; and the seventeenth-century Iroquois martyr, Catherine Tekakwitha, also, of course, dead. The events of the novel, therefore, take place largely in the narrator's imagination and memory, supplemented by 'A Long Letter From F.' A French-Canadian Jewish MP, F. is also a violent revolutionary and supporter of an independent Quebec, but the main emphasis of the narrative is on his more private transgressions. The narrator's and F.'s recollections centre primarily on their homosexual relationship and on their sexual liaisons with Edith, who belonged to a nearly extinct Native tribe, designated the 'A—', on whom the narrator is an authority. Catherine Tekakwitha, whose alterity is likewise fetishised by the male characters, becomes a double for Edith. A convert to Catholicism whose extreme practices of self-mortification led to her early death, Catherine is celebrated in the *Jesuit Relations* (see Chapter 4) and remains a symbol for Native Canadian Catholic spirituality. F. and the narrator, however, are more interested in her pursuit of excess.

Right from its opening paragraph, *Beautiful Losers* breaks taboos by associating the sacred with the sexual:

Catherine Tekakwitha, who are you? . . . Can I love you in my own way? . . . I want to know what goes on under that rosy blanket . . . I fell in love with a religious picture of you. You were standing among birch trees, my favourite trees. God knows how far up your moccasins were laced . . . Do I have any right to come after you with my dusty mind full of the junk of maybe five thousand books? I hardly even get out to the country very often . . . I am so human as to suffer from constipation, the rewards of a sedentary life. Is it any wonder I have sent my heart out into the birch trees?[30]

Confined to an urban location and a purely mental, unhealthy occupation, Cohen's protagonist dreams about natural landscapes and an outdoor life, but these locations by no means offer a redemptive seclusion from corrupt modern life; in fact, trees and forests provide the setting for various perversions of desire. The narrator is fascinated by Catherine's masochistic practices, which included whipping herself in remote forest glades, and sewing hundreds of thorns to the inside of her blanket. He is similarly intrigued by Edith's gang rape at the age of thirteen: 'Edith ran through the woods, thirteen years old, the men after her . . . Edith told me this story . . . and I've been pursuing her little body through the forest ever since, I confess' (p. 57). These fantasies invoke the traditional myth of the virgin forest, available for colonisation, exploitation and penetration by White men; Edith's and Catherine's status as Native women points to the ominous implications of this iconography. Its dangerous modern reinvention, in the context of US neo-imperialism, is also revealed: 'Some part of the Canadian Catholic mind is not certain of the Church's victory over the Medicine Man. No wonder the forests of Quebec are mutilated and sold to America' (p. 58). The final, and most surreal, section of the novel centres on the figure of a hermit, apparently the narrator as a very old man, but with elements of F. too, who lives – significantly – in a tree house, but whose apparent seclusion does not prevent him from molesting small boys.

Beautiful Losers is self-reflexive about pornographic representation, and the potentially pornographic scenes are complicated by the narrator's constant anxiety about whether he and F. have 'any right' to do the things they do to Edith, to one another, and even – in imagination – to Catherine Tekakwitha. The question of 'right' is not limited to the conventional boundaries that they transgress through homosexual and adulterous liaisons, specialised sexual practices and blasphemous or paedophilic fantasy. It points beyond this, to issues of representation, naming, research, authority and the gradients of power which these entail. Initially, it is F. who seems most guilty of exploiting such power differentials in pursuit of his desires. The narrator comments: 'There are, perhaps, ten full-blooded A—s left, four of them teen-age girls. I will add that F. took full advantage of my anthropological status to fuck all four of them' (p. 4). Yet from F.'s point of view, the real guilty party is the narrator, whose concept of fidelity is defined by male sexual ownership of the woman. The narrator resents his friend's deflowering of 'my four teen-age A—s' (p. 9) and is jealous of Edith's erotic encounters with F., but does not consider his own sex with F. to constitute infidelity to his wife. F. finally tells him: 'Surely you know by now that Edith could not belong to you alone' (p. 146).

Following the orgasmic, horrifying scene in which Edith and F. encounter, first, an animated Danish Vibrator, and second, a reincarnation of Hitler, both with an insatiable appetite for human flesh, Edith quotes, in Greek: 'I am Isis. I am all that is, that was, and that will be, and no mortal has lifted my veil' (p. 183).[31] Indeed, despite her remarkably complete physical self-revelation in the preceding scene, Edith remains mysterious and unpossessed, and cannot be fully known by her lovers. Her elusiveness is physically imaged: as F. recalls, 'her bum popped out of my bear hug like a wet watermelon seed, her thighs went by like a missed train' (p. 176). The metaphorical veil worn by Edith/Isis is explicitly connected to the narrator's prurient historical project about the Iroquois Virgin: 'What have I done, what have I not done, to lift your veil, to get under your blanket, Kateri Tekakwitha?' (pp. 98–9).

In his 'pursuit' of Catherine, he is following F.'s reiterated advice to 'fuck a saint' (p. 12), which constitutes, as Northey notes in her discussion of *Beautiful Losers*, a plea to reunite the estranged partnership of body and soul'.[32] F. is convinced that all matter is sacred, yet both he and the narrator are complicit in the commercial exploitation of sexuality. Describing Edith's rape, the narrator writes:

Four men followed Edith. Damn every one of them. I can't blame them . . . O Tongue of the Nation! Why don't you speak for yourself? Can't you see what is behind all this teen-age advertising? . . . Look at all the thirteen-year-old legs on the floor spread in front of the tv screen . . . Dying America wants a thirteen-year-old Abishag to warm its bed. Men who shave want little girls to ravish but sell them high heels instead. (pp. 58–9)

But he adds, as if in extenuation: 'Advertising courts lovely things . . . F. wouldn't want me to hate forever the men who pursued Edith' (p. 59). F. functions, in fact, rather like an advertiser, and understands consumption as a function of desire. As Joseph Bristow notes: 'The notion that the subject expresses desire through the power to consume can be understood in general developments visible in nineteenth- and twentieth-century culture – from purchasing goods in department stores to obtaining an ever-broadening range of sexual commodities, such as pornography'.[33] F., it might be argued, creates Edith as the object of his and his friend's pornographic fantasies, and effectively turns her into a commodity: he claims that he achieved Edith's perfect skin, buttocks and nipples through medical intervention, before she met her husband. At times, F. seems to detach the human body from organic principles and align it with a mass-produced commodity, or indeed with an actual machine, as in the 'telephone dance' scene in which he and Edith put their fingers in each others' ears and, as F. recalls, 'I *became* a telephone. Edith was the electrical conversation that went through me' (p. 33).

The narrator is afraid that he, as well as Edith, is F.'s creation; after his friend's death he feels that 'His voice has got into my ear . . . His style is colonizing me. His will provides me with his room downtown, the factory he bought, his tree house, his soap collection, his papers' (p. 40). The narrator becomes F.'s substitute in the relationship with Edith, and after F. dies of syphilis, his friend becomes a living memorial to him. But despite his relentless didacticism, F. eventually admits in his letter that they were 'each of us the other's teacher' (p. 154) and that his sense of himself depended on the narrator's vision of him: 'Something in your eyes, old lover, described me as the man I wanted to be' (p. 151). This confession, it seems, enables the narrator to emerge from his subjection to F., to respond to his exhortation to 'go beyond my style' (p. 151) and to write the narrative which contains and surrounds F.'s text. Finally, the two men achieve a postmodern version of transcendence: united in the figure of the hermit, they transform into a film image which is projected across the whole sky.

'We've got to learn to stop bravely at the surface. We've got to learn to love appearances', says F. (p. 4). This idea recurs throughout the book, which repeatedly celebrates pleasure, sensation and beauty (including the beauty of what is normally considered ugly or obscene). The injunction to 'love appearances' also comments self-consciously on the process of reading *Beautiful Losers*, mocking the reader's attempt to make meaning from the ludic, surreal text, and inviting him/her to be seduced by its sensual poetry instead. And yet, the novel's rich layering of ideas about philosophy, politics and history issues a simultaneous – and irresistible – invitation to intellectual engagement. The novel's final scene contains the remark: 'Just sit back and enjoy it, I guess' (p. 242), but, as Robert David Stacey remarks: 'If the idea that *Beautiful Losers* is all surface is painful to us, then it is because we haven't learned to sit back, relax, and forget about meaning – knowing all the while that this is not enough'.[34]

ANNE MICHAELS, *FUGITIVE PIECES* (1996)

Fugitive Pieces, like *Beautiful Losers*, is a poetic and visionary novel, structured through the recursive patterns of memory. As in *Beautiful Losers*, the words of one male character are supplemented, after his death, by those of a second man, who becomes his spiritual heir. Jewish experience is explored in both novels, though it is a more central concern in Michaels's book than in Cohen's. Anne Michaels was born in 1958 in Toronto, where she still lives. She studied English at the University of Toronto, and went on to teach creative writing there. *Fugitive Pieces*, her only novel to date, took ten years to write, and was immensely successful, winning several major Canadian, British and Jewish literary prizes. Michaels's 2000 collection *Poems* brings together her three volumes of poetry: *The Weight of Oranges* (1986), which won the Commonwealth Prize for the Americas; *Miner's Pond* (1991), winner of the Canadian Authors Association Award; and *Skin Divers* (1999). Michaels has also composed music for the theatre.

The first two-thirds of *Fugitive Pieces* is narrated by Jakob Beer, a Polish Jew whose family is killed by the Nazis when he is seven. Jakob escapes and is rescued by Athos Roussos, who takes the traumatised child to Zakynthos. After the war, they emigrate to Toronto. Following Athos's death, Jakob marries Alex, but the weight of his sorrow is too much for her, and she leaves. After many years alone, Jakob falls in love with a woman twenty-five years his junior. He takes Michaela to live in Athos's family home on the island of Idhra, and through his new wife's love, he is finally able, in effect, to come out of hiding, finding himself no longer trapped by the past but 'suspended in the present'.[35] The last third of the novel is told by Ben, the child of Holocaust survivors, who is drawn to Jakob and Michaela. Following their accidental death, he visits Idhra, seeking both Jakob's story and a way to understand his own family past.

Fugitive Pieces explores many forms of desire, but the most important ones, which become closely intertwined, are erotic desire and the desire for home. Jakob says, 'We long for place; but place itself longs' (p. 53), and the narrative endows the physical environment with the power not only to affect human lives deeply, but to participate in human emotions. Jakob learns from Athos of 'the astonishing fidelity of minerals magnetized, even after hundreds of millions of years, pointing to the magnetic pole, minerals that have never forgotten magma whose cooling off has left them forever desirous' (p. 53). As a child in Greece, he 'imagined the grief of the hills' and 'felt my own grief expressed there'. Remembering this, he notes: 'It would be almost fifty years and in another country before I would again experience this intense empathy with a landscape' (p. 60). This country is Canada, and Jakob – like the protagonists of many earlier Canadian novels – finds redemption in a journey north, into a forest landscape:

In the spring, we drive further north, past copper mines and paper mills, the abandoned towns born of and rejected by industry. I enter the landscape of her adolescence, which I receive with a bodily tenderness as Michaela relaxes and imperceptibly opens towards it . . . The elegant stone railway station. The gaping mouths of the mines. The faded, forlorn Albion Hotel. All this I saw she loved. I knew then I would show her the landscape of my past as she was showing me hers . . . From Espanola to Sudbury, the quartzite hills absorb the pink evening light like blotting paper, then pale under the moon.

Finally, Michaela takes me to one of the meccas of her childhood, a birch forest growing out of white sand.

This is where I become irrevocably unmoored. The river floods. (pp. 186–8)

This is a very specific, localised landscape, but it takes on larger, almost mythical meanings through the transformative power of Michaela's gaze. Just as her love for the birch forest makes it a sacred space, a 'mecca', so her love for Jakob offers him redemption.

Jakob is 'saved' (p. 183) through erotic experience, which is appropriate for a man who is so intensely involved in the physical world. He writes:

I drift and wake with my mouth on her belly, or on the small of her back, drawn home by the dream into her, her breasts soft loam, hard, sore seeds.

Each night heals gaps between us until we are joined by the scar of dreams. My desolation exhales in the breathing dark. (p. 183)

But it is not only the romantic scenes which are sensual. Some of the most traumatic events in the text, and the most acute experiences of loss, take shape through sensual experience and highly poetic language. Jakob repeatedly recalls the appearance of his dead sister, her 'magnificent hair like black syrup, thick and luxurious' (p. 6), and her 'touch on my back, my shoulders, my hair' (p. 31). He says of prisoners forced to dig up mass graves that 'the dead entered them through their pores', and imagines a man who 'feels a face in his hand, he grasps hair as if in a passion grasp, its matted thickness between his fingers, pulling, his hands full of names. His holy hands move, autonomous' (p. 52). On the basis of passages such as these, Méira Cook argues that:

> Michaels's lush, poetic discourse jars uneasily with the horrors she is narrating and so contributes to our discomfort as readers, at the same time that it provides a way of thinking about metaphor and metonymy as figurative devices that alternatively reveal and conceal the materiality of the event.[36]

In fact, most of the horrifying scenes – the shootings, the ovens, the unbearably cramped hiding places – are recorded in markedly plain, concise language, which contrasts with the lyrical, metaphorical style used elsewhere. Nevertheless, Cook's argument that *Fugitive Pieces* meditates on the relationship between metaphor and the material is illuminating. Jakob writes that 'the German language annihilated metaphor' (p. 143), because the Nazis used words such as 'figuren' or 'stücke' – literally, figures, or dolls, or things – to refer to Jews, in order to justify their extermination by classifying them as non-human (p. 165).

The Jewish experience of diaspora is central to Michaels's exploration of the exile's longing for place or home. In Toronto the Jewish community is just one of many diasporic groups, and Jakob describes his new home as 'a city where almost everyone has come from elsewhere – a market, a caravansary – bringing with them their different ways of dying and marrying, their kitchens and songs' (p. 89). He remembers that when he first found the Jewish market: 'I felt a jolt of grief. Casually, out of the mouths of the cheese-seller and the baker came the ardent tongue of my childhood ... fear and love intertwined' (p. 101). The novel makes no mention, however, of the fact that Prime Minister Mackenzie King severely limited the numbers of Jewish refugees entering Canada; between 1933 and 1945 Canada accepted fewer than 5,000, whereas other countries took far more. In 1939 the SS *St Louis*, carrying 907 German Jews, was turned away by several South American countries and lastly by Canada also. It was forced to return to Europe, where most of its passengers perished. Anne Michaels engages with Jewish history not through well-known, public facts, but through private stories, revealing details and extended images.

Annick Hillger, reading *Fugitive Pieces* in relation to Hebrew tradition, points to the significance of Isaac Luria, a sixteenth-century thinker who wrote of history as 'a state of brokenness, a state of non-redemption'.[37] According to his creation myth, the repeated exiling of the Jews was induced by the Fall, which scattered the holy sparks of the shekinah – a Talmudic concept representing God's dwelling and immanence in the created world. Hillger suggests that the title *Fugitive Pieces* might refer to the Lurianic broken vessel, noting that since the vessel 'has to be restored from all its fragments, the condition of exile is a necessary step on the path to redemption'.[38] The title has multiple valencies, however: as Coral Ann Howells points out in her discussion of Michaels's novel, 'fugue' means 'flight' in French, but it also indicates a musical analogy – 'a fugue is a musical composition structured on two or more themes which recur with variations and are harmonized in counterpoint. This formal patterning has its parallel in the two sequential narratives here'.[39]

'Fugitive Pieces' is also a literary term for lost manuscripts, and a note at the start of Michaels's text explains:

> During the Second World War, countless manuscripts – diaries, memoirs, eyewitness accounts – were lost or destroyed. Some of these narratives were deliberately hidden – buried in back gardens, tucked into walls and under floors – by those who did not live to retrieve them.
>
> Other stories are concealed in memory, neither written nor spoken. Still others are recovered, by circumstance alone. (n.p.)

The rest of the prefatory note summarises Jakob Beer's life, though in fact he is a fictional character, whose story is 'recovered' through Michaels's creative imagination as well as her research. Athos tells Jakob: 'Write to save yourself' (p. 165), and Jakob does so, becoming a poet, and a translator, completing Athos's book on Nazi archaeology, and finally writing his memoirs. His eventual reference to 'Athos's family house – where I now sit and write this' (p. 155) reveals that the text of the novel up to this point is identical to the text of his memoir.

Just as Jakob completes a manuscript begun by Athos, his adoptive father, so his own text is supplemented by Ben's narrative, and Ben, as Hillger notes, 'can in many ways be read as Jakob's son, the son of Israel' (p. 35). He travels to Idhra to search for the notebooks containing the memoir, but finds the place where Jakob lived equally revealing. Once again, Jakob has invested himself in the material realm, and Ben realises: 'A house, more than a diary, is the intimate glimpse' (p. 265). The erotic charge of Jakob's love for Idhra and for Michaela is still palpable: Ben feels 'the power of your place speaking to my body' (p. 266). In this phrase, occurring in the final pages of *Fugitive Pieces*, the novel's emphasis on the intimate connections between desire and geography culminates.

DIONNE BRAND, *LAND TO LIGHT ON* (1997)

The dynamic between body and place also marks the work of Dionne Brand (b. 1953), one of Canada's most high-profile contemporary authors. Her perspectives on exile and diaspora are informed not only by her own migration from the Caribbean to Canada, but also by her ancestors' forced displacement from Africa to the Americas. Born in Trinidad, she emigrated in 1970 to Toronto, where she still lives. As well as being a poet, novelist, short-story writer, essayist and film-maker, Brand is active in both the feminist and Black communities. She has edited and contributed to numerous journals and papers, and engaged extensively in community work and political activism. She published her first book in 1978, and her best-known poetry collections are *No Language is Neutral* (1990) and *Land to Light On*, which received the Governor General's Award. Her novels are *In Another Place, Not Here* (1996), *At the Full and Change of the Moon* (1999) and *What We All Long For* (2005), and her latest book, *Inventory* (2006), is a revisioning of the classic Canadian genre of the long poem.

Land to Light On consists of seven sequences of interlinked, untitled poems. The first, 'I Have Been Losing Roads', concerns an exile coming to terms with an unfamiliar country and reflecting on the corrupt and disastrous international situations reported in newspapers. In the next section, 'All That Has Happened Since', the speaker debates global current affairs, traverses Toronto and contemplates its diverse populations, and imaginatively reconstructs the experience of a woman in Trinidad. The title sequence of the book considers exile and slavery, mapping and national borders, while 'Dialectics' explores the narrator's memories of childhood in Trinidad. In the fifth section, 'Islands Vanish', the narrator, her Ugandan female lover and a Sri Lankan man travel together to Buxton, a Black settlement established in southwestern Ontario in 1849. The next sequence, 'Through My Imperfect Mouth and Life and Way', is addressed to a dead friend, a White woman with a mixed-race daughter. Finally, 'Every Chapter of the World' focuses on the figure of a desolate alcoholic woman living in an impoverished country. The narrating voice and perspective vary among the different sequences, and it is therefore wise to treat the seven speakers as distinct from one another.

In Dionne Brand's poems, emotional and intellectual experience is transmuted into bodily experience, or even literally inscribed on the body through physical responses to stress, pain and desire. Through her images and metaphors, the whole of life is felt through the body, and even absence and loss become physical. She writes, for example, of 'hatreds thinning our mouths and yellowing our fingers'; of 'all the wars we've pried open and run our tongues over like dangerous tin cans'; and of how 'language, politics, frangipani grab the lungs, sweeter than air'.[40] In the opening poem of *Land to Light On*, the speaker copes with an alien, uncomfortable environment by cutting herself off from sensory stimulation. Her strategy is:

> giving up, or misplacing
> surfaces, the seam in grain, so standing
> in a doorway I cannot summon up the yard,
> familiar broken chair or rag of cloth on a blowing line,
> I cannot smell smoke, something burning in a pit,
> or gather air from far off or hear anyone calling.
> The doorway cannot bell a sound, cannot repeat
> what is outside. My eyes is not a mirror. (p. 3)

All the five senses are denied in turn, as the speaker retreats from the 'harm' which the new place may inflict. In the next poem, the harm becomes more tangible, as 'a white man in a red truck on a rural road / jumps out at you, screaming his exact hatred'. The illegible, unpredictable landscape of Canada, where the speaker sees 'nothing recognisable', is paralleled with the incomprehensible violence of the man. As he 'threatens, something about your cunt' (p. 4), the poem draws attention to the literal physical danger to women which underlies the contemptuous use of 'cunt' as an expletive. In this first sequence, language is repeatedly yoked to the body, confining, defining and endangering it:

> and all I have are these hoarse words that still owe
> this life and all I'll be is tied to this century and waiting
> without a knife or courage and still these same words
> strapped to my back. (p. 9)

Brand's vivid imagery reveals the materiality of words and speech. While reading 'the terrifying poetry of newspapers' – particularly stories attesting to the power of multinational capital – the narrator of 'I Have Been Losing Roads' senses the newspaper's words entering her body, and feels her 'coffee turn asphalt', her 'mouth full and tasteless' (p. 13). The 'hoarse' and 'tasteless' words point to the ultimate inadequacy of language to communicate either pain or desire, yet the poems themselves, through their very existence, simultaneously testify to the preciousness of words and the potential of figurative language to reach people, to protest, to celebrate.

Brand's use of dialect is inseparable from her poetic themes, and in *Land to Light On*, Caribbean English is deployed to particular effect in the sequence set in Trinidad:

> I didn't know no dance could be so dark
> and full of serious desire that frighten me
> no arse. A lady and a man not even holding
> tight but some tightness holding them, her
> white low-heeled shoes on the inside of his
> black ones and her shoulders shine shine fire. (p. 58)

This section is titled 'Dialectics', drawing attention not only to the inclusion of 'dialect' forms, but also to the dialectical engagement of new Englishes with the dominant norms of metropolitan English. As Jason Wiens argues in his article on *No Language is Neutral*, Brand's strategic use of dialect constructs 'an enunciative space characterized not so much by a contestational dialogue with a "standard English" as by "standard English" utterances themselves that become submerged, appropriated, and placed in a subordinate position'.[41] The same might be said of *Land to Light On*, in which Brand furthers her exploration of language as a bodily experience by evoking the sonic qualities of Caribbean speech

The focus on words in some of the poems is balanced in others by an emphasis on reading non-verbal signs, including sounds, bodies and landscape. In contrast to the opening poem in the first sequence (quoted above), in which the speaker tries to hear nothing, a later poem shows her straining her ears to catch the meanings of the new place:

> I can hear wood
> breathe and stars crackle on the galvanised
> steel, I can hear smoke turn solid and this
> house is only as safe as flesh . . .
>   I can hear
> the road sigh and the trees shift. I can
> hear them far away from this house late, late
> waiting for what this country is to happen.   (p. 11)

This poem evokes a Canada which offers an uncertain degree of safety, imaged in the 'flesh' which is at once vulnerable, and yet represents the speaker's only permanent home. At the same time, Brand's metaphors render the experience of Canada a sensuous and imaginative one, and the new country becomes a possible space for creativity. This is realised in the writing of the poem itself.

The sense of Canada's potentiality is countered by images of cold which suggest a fear that both creative and sensual activity will be diminished there: 'birds pulling your hair, ice invades / your nostrils in chunks, land fills your throat, you are so busy / with collecting the north, scrambling to the Arctic so wilfully' (p. 43). As well as vividly rendering the immigrant's embodied experience of place, these lines also invoke classic Canadian iconographies of the frozen north. Appropriating and reworking these to represent the journey north from the Caribbean to Canada, Brand also reinscribes earlier authors' depictions of the north as both alluring and potentially fatal:

> and what phrase will now abandon me, what woman
> with a gun and her fingers to her lips draw us to another
> territory further north, further cold, further on,
> into the mouth of the Arctic. (p. 12)

Another poem begins: 'Where is this? Your tongue, gone cold, gone / heavy in this winter light. / On a highway burrowing north don't waste your breath' (p. 14). The 'tongue' here is not only the speaking tongue, whose articulations are inhibited by the landscape which 'cannot hear' (p. 14), but is also part of the eroticised body. The last stanza connects the limits on self-expression with the lack of human warmth and contact. The speaker sees life as 'lit by the heat of touching', but notes wistfully that 'the next house one kilometre away might as well / be ten, it so far from love' (p. 14).

In *Land to Light On*, snow simultaneously figures human coldness and racial prejudice. The section 'Islands Vanish' centres on 'Three Blacks in a car', and the words 'black' and 'dark' recur in counterpoint to 'snow', 'icy' and 'cold'. The three friends encounter prejudice and suspicion as they drive towards Buxton, and the narrator reflects:

> Something there, written as
> wilderness, wood, nickel, water, coal, rock, prairie, erased
> as Athabasca, Algonquin, Salish, Inuit . . . hooded in Buxton
> fugitive, Preston Black Loyalist, railroaded to gold
> mountain. (p. 77, ellipsis in original)

Black Loyalists were slaves who were freed during the American Revolution in the late eighteenth century, on condition that they contributed to the British war effort. When Britain lost the war, the free Blacks were evacuated to Nova Scotia, but they never received their promised land grants, and many lived in conditions little better than the enslavement they had escaped. In connecting the experiences of this group with those of the nineteenth-century Black settlers in Buxton and the First Nations of North America, Brand positions her modern-day characters as inheritors of centuries of discrimination and racially motivated violence. While the items in the list (wilderness, wood and so on) do not at first seem politically charged, the poem emphasises that racial conflict in North America has largely centred on the ownership, use, preservation and even interpretation of these 'natural resources'. Although the speaker in 'Islands Vanish' finishes up asleep with her lover, 'she, legs wrapped around me' (p. 77), in one of the few moments of apparently fulfilled desire in *Land to Light On*, nevertheless she cannot 'lie that we are not harmed' by past and present racism (p. 77) and wonders how they all ended up in 'this white hell' (p. 74).

Space prohibits exploration of the complex politics of Brand's poetry, but several recent articles have engaged with them in depth, taking up a range of positions which reveal the intensity of debate inspired by her work. It is interesting that two of the essays include 'ambivalence' in their titles;[42] as Forster argues, *Land to Light On* 'charts Brand's political ambivalence through the expression of a contradictory political project: the simultaneous construction and subversion of collective identity as a political strategy'.[43] Collective identities, in terms of race, nationality, sexuality, gender, class and so on, form points of reference in Brand's work, but her fictional and poetic characters cannot be wholly defined by such categories, and thus she consistently challenges the essentialising manoeuvres of identity politics. Her focus on the power relationships inherent in the process of naming and labelling others might be seen as part of her larger interest in the materiality of language and its inseparableness from the body.

CONCLUSION

'Desire changes the world!', proclaims the narrator of *Beautiful Losers* (p. 5). This is indeed what happens in the five books considered above. Landscapes, cities, historical narratives and the bodies of others are all transformed by the desiring gaze. The themes explored in the other chapters of this book – geography, history and race – all inform the representations of sexuality and longing in the texts discussed here. Desire is frequently projected onto natural and urban environments or intensified by a sense of connection to place, yet landscape can, equally, be used to figure destructive emotions. Also, the texts analysed here demonstrate that the impulse to explore the country's history may become entwined with the erotic, and that historical trauma can be figured through images of longing and loss, sexual domination or abasement. These texts use politicised representations of sexual relationships, together with metaphors yoking the erotic with the violent, in order to explore the history of marginalised groups, including Jewish, Black and Aboriginal Canadians. These texts evince a critical consciousness of the politics of sexuality, including racial and gendered hierarchies of power, tensions surrounding sexual orientation, and the eroticised logic of capitalism and advertising. They reflect on the relationship between language and the body, simultaneously revealing the limitations of language and celebrating its power to evoke sensory experience.

- Landscapes and cityscapes become eroticised spaces in many Canadian literary texts, and geography and migration impact significantly on the formations of desire.
- In Canadian books which are preoccupied also with history, sexual desire can become conflated with the desire to know and understand the past.
- The emphasis on research and discovery in many Canadian narratives of sensual encounter is related to the way in which desire is used to shape narratives, inviting the reader's curiosity and deferring its satisfaction.
- In the texts chosen for this chapter, descriptions of erotic encounter usually point to meanings beyond the merely sensual. Such episodes may be politically charged in complex ways, relating, for example, to violence, racism, genocide, capitalist exploitation and gendered power relations.
- The materiality of language is often emphasised in postmodern meditations on desire, and for some Canadian writers, poetic language can itself become an erotic experience.

NOTES

1. Anne Michaels, *Poems* (London: Bloomsbury, 2000), p. 56. All subsequent references in the text are to this edition.
2. E. J. Pratt, *Brébeuf and His Brethren* (1940), repr. in *E. J. Pratt: The Complete Poems, Part I*, ed. Sandra Djwa and R. G. Moyles (Toronto: University of Toronto Press, 1989), pp. 46–110 (p. 49).
3. Margaret Laurence, *The Diviners* (Toronto: McClelland and Stewart, [1974] 1988), p. 193.
4. Catherine Belsey, *Desire: Love Stories in Western Culture* (Oxford: Blackwell, 1994), p. 3.
5. Eugene Goodheart, *Desire and Its Discontents* (New York: Columbia University Press, 1991), pp. 1–2.
6. Ibid., p. 14.
7. Ibid., p. 15.
8. Belsey, *Desire*, p. 6.
9. Ibid., p. 7.
10. Joseph Bristow, *Sexuality* (London: Routledge, 1997), p. 205.
11. Eve Kosofsky Sedgwick, *Between Men: English Literature and Male Homosocial Desire* (New York: Columbia University Press, 1985).
12. Jacques Lacan, *Écrits: A Selection*, trans. Alan Sheridan (London: Tavistock, 1977), p. 263.
13. Gilles Deleuze and Félix Guattari, *Anti-Oedipus: Capitalism and Schizophrenia*, trans. Robert Hurley et al. (London: Athlone, 1984), p. 26.
14. Goodheart, *Desire*, pp. 2–3.
15. Belsey, *Desire*, p. 77, p. 81.
16. Goodheart, *Desire*, p. 6.
17. See Robert G. Lawrence, 'The Geography of Martha Ostenso's *Wild Geese*', *Journal of Canadian Fiction*, 16 (1976), 108–14.
18. Martha Ostenso, *Wild Geese* (Toronto: McClelland and Stewart, [1925] 1989), p. 89. All subsequent references in the text are to this edition.
19. Daniel S. Lenoski, 'Martha Ostenso's *Wild Geese*: The Language of Silence', *North Dakota Quarterly*, 52: 3 (1984), 279–96 (pp. 279, 289).
20. Lillian Faderman, *Odd Girls and Twilight Lovers: A History of*

Lesbian Life in Twentieth Century America (London: Penguin, 1992), p. 63.

21. Terry Goldie, *Pink Snow: Homotextual Possibilities in Canadian Fiction* (Peterborough, ON: Broadview, 2003), pp. 238, 107.

22. John Glassco, *Memoirs of Montparnasse*, ed. Michael Gnarowski (Toronto: Oxford University Press, [1970] 1995), p. xxxi. All subsequent references in the text are to this edition.

23. Michael Gnarowski, 'Fiction for the Sake of Art: An Introduction to the Making of *Memoirs of Montparnasse*', in Glassco, *Memoirs of Montparnasse*, pp. x–xxv (p. xiii).

24. Cited in Gnarowski, 'Fiction', p. xxi.

25. See John Glassco, *Selected Poems* (Toronto: Oxford University Press, 1971).

26. Leon Edel, 'Introduction', in Glassco, *Memoirs of Montparnasse*, pp. xxvi–xxix (p. xxviii).

27. Thomas Tausky, '*Memoirs of Montparnasse*: "A Reflection of Myself"', *Canadian Poetry: Studies, Documents, Reviews*, 13 (1983), available at http://www.uwo.ca/english/canadianpoetry/cpjrn/cpjrn/vol13/vol13index.htm

28. Ibid.

29. See David Boucher, *Dylan and Cohen: Poets of Rock and Roll* (New York and London: Continuum, 2004), p. 101.

30. Leonard Cohen, *Beautiful Losers* (London: Black Spring, [1966] 1992), p. 3. All subsequent references in the text are to this edition.

31. On the Hitler figure, see Norman Ravvin, 'Writing around the Holocaust: Uncovering the Ethical Centre of *Beautiful Losers*', *Canadian Poetry: Studies, Documents, Reviews*, 33 (1993).

32. Margot Northey, *The Haunted Wilderness: The Gothic and Grotesque in Canadian Fiction* (Toronto: University of Toronto Press, 1976), p. 103.

33. Bristow, *Sexuality*, p. 58.

34. See Robert David Stacey, 'Pornographic Sublime: *Beautiful Losers* and Narrative Excess', *Essays on Canadian Writing*, 69 (1999), 213–34 (p. 231).

35. Anne Michaels, *Fugitive Pieces* (London: Bloomsbury, [1996] 1998), p. 188. All subsequent references in the text are to this edition.

36. Méira Cook, 'At the Membrane of Language and Silence: Metaphor and Memory in *Fugitive Pieces*', *Canadian Literature*, 164 (2000), 12–33 (p. 16).

37. Annick Hillger, '"Afterbirth of Earth": Messianic Materialism in Anne Michaels's *Fugitive Pieces*', *Canadian Literature*, 160 (1999), 28–45 (p. 33).

38. Ibid., p. 34.

39. Coral Ann Howells, 'Anne Michaels: *Fugitive Pieces*', in *Where Are the Voices Coming From? Canadian Culture and the Legacies of History*, ed. Coral Ann Howells (Amsterdam and New York: Rodopi, 2004), pp. 107–17 (p. 113).

40. Dionne Brand, *Land to Light On* (Toronto: McClelland and Stewart, 1997), pp. 21, 23, 25. All subsequent references in the text are to this edition.

41. Jason Wiens, '"Language Seemed to Split in Two": National Ambivalence(s) and Dionne Brand's *No Language is Neutral*', *Essays on Canadian Writing*, 70 (2000), 81–102 (p. 89).

42. See Wiens, '"Language"'; Sophia Forster, '"Inventory is useless now but just to say": The Politics of Ambivalence in Dionne Brand's *Land to Light On*', *Studies in Canadian Literature*, 27: 2 (2002), 160–82.

43. Forster, 'Inventory', p. 162.

CHAPTER 4

Histories and Stories

but once history's onstage, histrionic as usual (all those wars,
all those historic judgements), the a-historic hasn't a speaking
part. what's imagination next to the weight of the (f)actual?
Daphne Marlatt, Ana Historic[1]

The nature of history, the ways in which it is written, spoken, imagined, researched, even performed, are thematised in Daphne
Marlatt's *Ana Historic* (1988). The novel explores a particular
aspect of Canadian history – the establishment of Vancouver in the
late nineteenth century, and the experiences of women living there
– and at the same time, it reflects self-consciously on ways of
knowing and narrating the past. It may therefore be described as
'historiographic metafiction', a term coined by the influential
Canadian theorist of postmodernity Linda Hutcheon. In her 1988
book *A Poetics of Postmodernism*, Hutcheon writes: 'Historiographic
metafiction shows fiction to be historically conditioned and history
to be discursively structured'.[2] She argues that, in such texts, the
apparently transparent mechanisms of both literary realism and
historical writing are revealed to be selective, contingent and
informed by complex power relations. In *The Canadian Postmodern*,
also published in 1988, Hutcheon emphasises that historiographic
metafiction is not preoccupied simply with its own conventions;
rather, it is 'fiction that is intensely, self-reflexively art, but is also
grounded in historical, social, and political realities', and that it is

'overtly concerned with the acts (and consequences) of the reading and writing of history as well as fiction'.[3] Her book demonstrates that this kind of writing flourished in Canada during the 1970s and 1980s in particular.

A fascination with history is, though, evident in Canadian literature almost from its beginnings. Some of the first novels published in Canada were historical fictions, and the Canadian long poem, a genre which dates back to the late eighteenth century, also frequently takes a historical subject. The sheer number of plays, poems and novels which are set in, or preoccupied with, the past is often considered symptomatic of Canada's need to consolidate its sense of national identity through reference to a shared history. This interpretation is fairly easy to accept when considering texts produced up to the mid-twentieth century, but more recently the impulse to discover the country's past has been paralleled and perhaps exceeded by an impulse to question the possibility of writing national histories. Postmodern writing, in Canada as in other countries, is concerned to interrogate history, and raise questions as to who has the authority to write it, what alternative versions are being suppressed and indeed whether it is possible to access the past at all. As Hutcheon notes, 'the only way we can know the past today is through its traces, its texts'.[4] The impossibility of knowing the past in unmediated forms has led to an intense preoccupation, in contemporary creative writing, with the shaping and distorting role of memory and nostalgia, with the politicisation and ideological charge of narratives of the past, and with the significance of documents, images and research, and the ways in which such evidence is used in reconstructing – or censoring – the past.

Linda Hutcheon focuses her research on recent postmodern novels, but self-consciousness about the relationship between literature and history is not, of course, confined to fiction or to contemporary writing. While it may be especially overt and visible in postmodern Canadian novelists such as (to cite those discussed in this book) Marlatt, Atwood, Laurence, King, Ondaatje, Kogawa and Michaels, it can also be discerned in more subtle forms in earlier texts, and texts in other genres. Consider, for example, the scene of the death of the Jesuit missionary Jean de Brébeuf in 1649, as presented in E. J. Pratt's poem *Brébeuf and His Brethren* (1940):

No doubt in the mind of Brébeuf that this was the last
Journey – three miles over the snow. He knew
That the margins as thin as they were by which he escaped
From death through the eighteen years of his mission toil
Did not belong to this chapter: not by his pen
Would this be told. He knew his place in the line,
For the blaze of the trail that was cut on the bark by Jogues
Shone still. He had heard the story as told by writ
And word of survivors – of how a captive slave
Of the hunters, the skin of his thighs cracked with the frost,
He would steal from the tents to the birches, make a rough
    cross
From two branches, set it in snow and on the peel
Inscribe his vows and dedicate to the Name
In 'litanies of love' what fragments were left
From the wrack of his flesh; . . .
His scarred credentials of faith, the nail-less hands
And withered arms – the signs of the Mohawk fury.[5]

This passage reveals a self-consciousness about the writing of
history because Pratt emphasises Brébeuf's awareness not only that
his own death is unavoidable, but also that it will become part of the
historical record. Pratt's Brébeuf is conscious of 'his place in the
line' of historical development, and of the necessity for him to re-
enact the fate of his fellow missionary Isaac Jogues. These visceral
lines also evoke a sense of history being inscribed both on the body
(Jogues's tortured thighs, hands and arms) and on the landscape
('the blaze of the trail'; the letters cut on the birch bark). This
emphasises the ways in which personal narratives get caught up in
larger historical, political and religious developments: conflicts
between missionaries and Indigenous Canadians are literally
written across Jogues's body, and the religious revivals in this period
determine his fate. The passage also points to the possibility of
'reading' places, images and bodies, as well as written texts, in the
attempt to recover the past.

    This idea informs many later Canadian texts, such as, for
example, Margaret Atwood's *The Journals of Susanna Moodie* (1970),
which recreates a Victorian pioneer author in a sequence of poems

and images. Some of the poems are inspired by Moodie's autobiographical fictions, and others by pictures of her and of the places
where she lived. As a result of her encounter with the Canadian
wilderness, Atwood's Moodie found her 'hands grown stiff, the
fingers / brittle as twigs', while in old age she discovered 'pocked
ravines / cut in my cheeks' (p. 51).[6] The relationships between colonial and postcolonial texts may be explored by reading Susanna
Moodie's *Roughing It in the Bush* (1852) or *Life in the Clearings
versus the Bush* (1853), which enrich our understanding of Atwood's
poems. At the same time, the poems operate retroactively on
Moodie's texts, altering the way they are interpreted by modern
readers. Atwood confronts the somewhat poisonous legacy of
immigrants such as Moodie, for whom England remained an ideal
while Canada was illegible, incomprehensible, hostile. Yet in resur-
recting Moodie, Atwood also reinscribes her colonising vision,
extends her influence and affirms her significance to Canadian
history. In very different ways, all the texts discussed in this chapter
explore relations of colonial dominance and subjugation: it is
crucial to consider how far they actively resist such power structures, and how far they reinforce them.

   That is not to say that the literary value of these books is determined by their level of commitment to decolonising the imagination. But when reading Canadian texts from past decades and
centuries, it is crucial to be aware of the contemporaneous ideologies of race, nation, empire and gender which have shaped them. In
the case of historical writing, the situation becomes more complex,
since the period when the text was produced, as well as the period
when it is set, become significant. As Catherine Belsey observes, 'to
the degree that the present informs our account of the past, we
make history *out of a relation which is always a relation of difference,
between the present and the past*'.[7] Canadian history can by no means
be 'read off' directly from historical poems and novels, yet one of
the pleasures of reading historical fiction and poetry consists in discovering new perspectives on Canada's past and on the ways in
which it has been written and interpreted in different periods.

   History, then, is the most important theme of this book. Several
of the texts discussed in previous chapters engage with Canadian
history: Richardson's *Wacousta* was one of the earliest English-

language Canadian historical novels; Munro's 'A Wilderness Station' is set in nineteenth-century Upper Canada; Kogawa's *Obasan* and Michaels's *Fugitive Pieces* look back to the Second World War, while the historical sweep of Davies's *The Cunning Man* extends from the 1930s to the 1990s. Glassco's *Memoirs of Montparnasse* evokes the 1920s, and *Anne of Green Gables* the 1870s, while Cohen's *Beautiful Losers* engages with the Jesuit missions and the process of writing history. In this final chapter, my discussion of Canadian writers' relationship with history culminates, as writing the past becomes the primary focus. The books chosen for discussion are widely admired, influential texts, set in a variety of periods from the seventeenth century to the mid-twentieth, and in regions including western, eastern and central Canada. Each is pre-occupied with ways of accessing and narrating the past, and together they offer rich material for discussion of the interface between Canadian literature and history. Pratt's *Brébeuf and His Brethren*, Atwood's *Journals of Susanna Moodie* and Marlatt's *Ana Historic* have already been introduced; the other two texts are Margaret Laurence's *The Diviners* (1974) and Michael Ondaatje's *In the Skin of a Lion* (1987). Like Atwood's text, *The Diviners* explores the Canadian pioneer heritage, and it also examines the history of the Métis, and the relationships between mixed-race and White Canadians. *In the Skin of the Lion*, set in the early part of the twentieth century, combines re-imagined historical figures with entirely fictional characters, and focuses on the building of the city of Toronto.

E. J. PRATT, *BRÉBEUF AND HIS BRETHREN* (1940)

E. J. Pratt (1882–1964) was brought up in Newfoundland, at the time still an independent political entity within the British Empire (Newfoundland joined Canada in 1949). He went on to become a professor of English literature at the University of Toronto. An important exponent of the Canadian long poem, Pratt wrote several verse narratives on tragic subjects, such as the sinking of the Titanic and the battle of Dunkirk, and others on Canadian history. *Brébeuf and His Brethren*, one of Pratt's major works, for which he received the Governor General's Award, narrates the endeavours and suffering of Jesuit missionaries to the Huron in the mid-seventeenth century (on the Jesuits and Huron, see Glossary). To a significant extent, Pratt reproduces colonial perspectives on Aboriginal Canadians, but at the same time, his poem might be read as subtly questioning the ideology of mission and conquest. Pratt's attitude to the religious subject matter of his poem is similarly ambivalent: as Angela T. McAuliffe has noted: 'Unbeliever, agnostic, humanist, Christian – the fact that the most vocal critics of E. J. Pratt's poetry have been able to attribute to him such a diversity of religious positions indicates one of the major sources of ambiguity and irony in his work'.[8] Another very interesting aspect of *Brébeuf and His Brethren* is its distinct awareness of the oral nature of Native culture, which existed in tension with the missionaries' preoccupation with the written word.

Jean de Brébeuf (1593–1649) entered the Jesuit novitiate at Rouen in France, and was ordained to the priesthood in 1622. Three years later he made his first trip to Canada and undertook the 800-mile journey by canoe to Huronia. In 1629, just as he was beginning to make converts, he and his fellow missionaries were recalled to France because the English were about to take control of Quebec. The French soon regained their power in New France, and Brébeuf returned in 1633. He was welcomed by his Huron friends, but not all the Huron accepted the Jesuit 'blackrobes', as they were called, and Brébeuf was once condemned to death and once severely beaten. After a respite in Quebec (1641–4), Brébeuf returned to Huronia and experienced much greater success: by 1647 thousands had been converted to Christianity. But the Huron were under constant threat from their enemies, the Iroquois (see Glossary), and did not defend themselves effectively. In 1649 an Iroquois attack overwhelmed the village where Brébeuf was, and he and his companion Gabriel Lalemant were seized, tied to stakes and tortured to death.

The expansionist projects of European states from the sixteenth century onwards were in fact motivated by considerations of profit, space, prestige and political stability, but empire builders frequently appealed to the perceived need to 'civilise' the heathens and spread the word of God. The discourses of crusading, conversion and mission were made compatible with the military rhetoric of heroism. This rhetoric is very evident in the opening lines of Pratt's poem, and prepares for the construction of Jean de Brébeuf as a hero:

> The winds of God were blowing over France,
> Kindling the hearths and altars, changing vows
> Of rote into an alphabet of flame.
> The air was charged with song beyond the range
> Of larks, with wings beyond the stretch of eagles.
> Skylines unknown to maps broke from the mists.   (p. 46)

The reference to 'song' evokes the epic narratives of the past, immortalised in ballads and legends, and this is reinforced in the second stanza: 'The story of the frontier like a saga / Sang through the cells and cloisters of the nation' (p. 47). Already, there is a pre-occupation with telling and retelling, and with the power of story. Also, the vocabulary of New World exploration is deployed in relation to the missionary zeal for expansion into 'unknown' territory, and in the next stanza Canada is described in terms of 'chartless seas and coasts / And the vast blunders of the forest glooms' (p. 48). Such phrases reproduce the colonial construction of Canada as empty, that is, not yet mapped out and written across by European explorers. This, of course, functions to erase Canadian Native peoples; occupying the same textual space as the forest, they effectively become part of the landscape.

If the Aboriginals could be converted to Catholicism, they would – in the eyes of French colonists – become humanised, and this is presented as a heroic cause in the poem:

> So, in the footsteps of their patrons came
> A group of men asking the hardest tasks
> At the new outposts of the Huron bounds.   (p. 48)

Brébeuf's spiritual commitment is presented as entirely sincere: in the third stanza, his vision of Christ on the Via Dolorosa, the way to his death, is described as 'No play upon the fancy', but rather 'the Real Presence to the naked sense' (p. 48). The Real Presence refers to the Catholic belief in transubstantiation: the transformation of the bread and wine of the Eucharist into the actual body of Christ during Communion services. Pratt's line thus emphasises the almost tangible presence of Christ in Brébeuf's life and anticipates the missionaries' Christlike sacrifice of their own bodies.

McAuliffe notes that Brébeuf's vision of the suffering Christ does not appear in any of the secondary materials Pratt consulted, and argues that the poet invented the vision in order to give his protagonist a convincing motive for accepting martyrdom.[9] Yet the poem also hints at other inducements. While still in France, Pratt's Brébeuf is evidently allured by the prospect of excelling in 'the hardest tasks', and also by the exotic images of Canada which he has gleaned:

> Forests and streams and trails thronged through his mind,
> The painted faces of the Iroquois,
> Nomadic bands and smoking bivouacs
> Along the shores of western inland seas,
> With forts and palisades and fiery stakes.
> The stories of Champlain, Brulé, Viel,
> Sagard and Le Caron had reached his town –
> The stories of those northern boundaries
> Where in the winter the white pines could brush
> The Pleiades, and at the equinoxes
> Under the gold and green of the auroras
> Wild geese drove wedges through the zodiac.   (pp. 48–9)

The Canada which the missionaries in the poem encounter has, however, nothing of this imagined romance. They suffer greatly from heat, cold, inhospitable terrain, hunger, mosquitoes and exhaustion; still more from the dirty, noisy living conditions they share with the Huron people; and most of all from the torture imposed by the Iroquois.

The heroism which Pratt attributes to Brébeuf and his 'brethren' – notably Jogues and Gabriel Lalemant – consists in their physical and mental courage in the face of suffering. But this celebration of the missionaries' virtue and bravery is largely contingent on the representation of Native Canadians as villains, a move which recalls the ideologies of colonial texts. It is not simply the practices of torture which construct the Huron and Iroquois as barbaric, but also their rituals of everyday life. European ideals of hygiene, courtesy and orderliness are implicitly evoked when the narrator refers to 'the noise and smoke and vermin of the lodges, / And the insufferable sights and stinks' (p. 57); 'the food from unwashed platters'; the 'squaws and reeking children' who 'violated / The hours of rest' (p. 64).

Pratt's key source for the poem was the *Jesuit Relations and Allied Documents*, an immensely rich and extensive set of records of the New France mission. Brébeuf's detailed letters to his superiors are preserved in volumes 8, 11 and 23 of the *Relations*, and two accounts of his and Lalemant's martyrdom can be found in volume 34 (all available online; see Student Resources). The deaths were witnessed by Christian Huron captives, and the written accounts of Brébeuf's life and death were put together by two fellow missionaries. Sections from these texts are paraphrased in Pratt's poem, together with the vows and pledges of several Jesuits, and to some extent these interpolated texts create a multi-voiced effect, with italics used to distinguish the voices of individual priests from the narrator's voice. The Huron people, however, have barely any voice, and are usually heard only to sing, 'rasp' (p. 64) and 'grunt' (p. 51). While Brébeuf's writing is highly influential, inspires other missionaries and becomes part of the official record – 'this letter was to loom in history' (p. 70) – the perspectives of the Huron and Iroquois are preserved primarily through the Frenchmen's observations of their behaviour, and only occasionally through brief quotation of their words, in translation. These quotations serve merely to emphasise their barbarism: they include the words of the death-song which the Huron force their Iroquois prisoners to sing, and the pronouncement of a brave that he means 'to kill and eat the white flesh of the priests' (p. 80).

Occasionally, a Huron word appears in the poem. Amazed by the Jesuits' clock, the Huron ask what it is saying, and Pratt includes the phrase 'Yo eiouahaoua', translated as 'Time to put on the cauldron' (p. 61). This, according to Brébeuf's 1635 letter in the *Relations*, is what the missionaries claim that their clock says. There is also a reference to an '*oki*' (p. 61), the Huron word for a powerful spirit, which the Aboriginals think must live in the clock. But this passage does not really lend any dignity to their spoken language, and the lines which are supposedly from the Huron point of view reveal them as naive:

> As great a mystery was writing – how
> A Frenchman fifteen miles away could know
> The meaning of black signs the runner brought.   (p. 61)

The mystery of writing is used to build up the converts' faith in the priests' authority; the power of the written word relates directly to the power of the word of God. The narrator, though, evinces a trace of irony, suggesting that the priests' exploitation of Huron credulity is a little cynical.

The whole poem is preoccupied with the tension between orality and literacy: while the Jesuits are intensely concerned with writing and recording, the Aboriginals are associated with spoken language. The stanza at the end of section I describes Brébeuf's effort to learn the Huron language, in order that he can communicate Christian precepts:

> He listened to the sounds and gave them letters,
> Arranged their sequences, caught the inflections
> Extracted nouns from objects, verbs from actions
> And regimented rebel moods and tenses.   (p. 53)

Brébeuf seeks to derive a regularised, written language from Huron speech, and the vocabulary of the passage presents his attempt as a form of conquest, paralleling the disciplinary function of the religious conversion of the First Nations. This passage is saturated with military vocabulary, even referring to 'weapons from the armoury of words' (p. 54), and Brébeuf fears the competing power of 'Huron rhetoric', which he describes as 'sorcery' (p. 53).

Again, it is important to evaluate the text's perspective here: the discourse of battle has long been used to characterise the Christian fight against evil and superstition, but is this discourse being used straightforwardly here, to endorse Brébeuf's courageous efforts, or is there any implicit critique of the attempt to counteract Huron beliefs through mastery of language? This is a difficult point to decide on; what is certain is that the tension between orality and literacy is brought into clear focus, and the skill of the Native orators is fully acknowledged. The classical form of Pratt's poem, which is a Virgilian epic, might suggest a weighting towards the 'literacy' part of the binary. Yet on the other hand, the strong, dramatic central narrative, together with the use of rhythmic and rhetorical tropes with considerable emotional appeal, aligns *Brébeuf and His Brethren* with oral forms, and suggest its amenability to being read aloud. As Djwa and Moyles note, E. J. Pratt was brought up in Maritime seaside villages, and therefore 'comes naturally to his role as a public poet, for the record of Newfoundland's outport life is oral rather than written and the vehicles folk song or folk tale'.[10]

MARGARET ATWOOD, *THE JOURNALS OF SUSANNA MOODIE* (1970)

The relationship between language and power is also a central preoccupation in Margaret Atwood's work, and is very evident in *The Journals of Susanna Moodie*, which explores the transformation of the Moodie character from 'a word / in a foreign language' to one of the 'voices of the land'. Like *Brébeuf and His Brethren*, Atwood's poem sequence centres on a figure from outside Canada who, through a well-documented involvement in the process of colonisation and settlement, has become an iconic character in Canadian history. Atwood has already been introduced (see Chapter 2). Her Victorian predecessor Susanna Strickland Moodie (1803–85) grew up in a decaying mansion in Suffolk, and was obliged to emigrate to Canada because her husband was a half-pay officer with an insufficient income to support a genteel life in England. On arrival in 1832, the Moodies settled in the Upper Canadian backwoods and attempted to farm, with little success. Later they moved to the growing town of Belleville. Susanna Moodie's memoirs of her first twenty years in the colony, *Roughing It in the Bush* (1852) and *Life in the Clearings* (1853), have been canonised as classic pioneer writing, partly through the influence of Atwood's widely read poem sequence.

The Journals of Susanna Moodie consists of twenty-seven poems, together with a prose 'Afterword', which is an integral part of the text although it is sometimes wrongly omitted in editions of Atwood's poetry.[11] In the 'Afterword', Atwood writes:

> These poems were generated by a dream. I dreamt I was watching an opera I had written about Susanna Moodie . . . I had never read her two books about Canada . . . When I did read them, I was disappointed . . . Once I had read the books I forgot about them. The poems occurred later, over a period of a year and a half. (p. 62)

This actually mystifies rather than explains the origin of the poems, suggesting, as Ann Edwards Boutelle notes, 'the non-rational, partly uncontrollable genesis of the work', and so establishing an 'almost mystic connection between Atwood and Moodie'.[12] In this way, Atwood constructs herself as Moodie's literary heir, even though she reads her predecessor's work oppositionally.

But the 'Afterword' also has a broader significance. It suggests that Moodie's profoundly ambivalent response to Canada has been inherited by all Canadians, as a legacy of colonialism. Identifying the 'national mental illness' of Canada as 'paranoid schizophrenia', Atwood notes that Moodie epitomises this: she is 'divided down the middle', since she claims to be a Canadian patriot, but also criticises the country with the detachment of a stranger' (p. 62). The poems in the *Journals* emphasise the gap between the historical Moodie's response to Canada and her articulation of that response in her writing, and they reveal the ideological tensions which gave rise to Moodie's reading of the New World as hostile and sinister. In the 'Afterword', Atwood relates Moodie's mindset to that of later generations of Canadians:

> Perhaps that is the way we still live. We are all immigrants to this place even if we were born here: the country is too big for anyone to inhabit completely, and in the parts unknown to us we move in fear, exiles and invaders. (p. 62)

This is an important passage for students of Canadian literature: it has been so widely quoted that it has been erected into a national myth. Yet this should not blind us to the fact that it is itself, to some extent, a colonialist view. Only White Canadians can be considered 'immigrants', and so the phrase 'we are all immigrants' excludes First Nations people, even though their prior possession of the land is obliquely acknowledged in the word 'invaders'. Atwood's perspective is different in other texts, but the power of this vision of her compatriots as exiles in their own country persists in the Canadian literary imaginary.

As well as the 'Afterword', the first edition of *The Journals of Susanna Moodie* also included a set of collages which Atwood made to illustrate the poems, and these, too, may be considered part of the text. Several of them depict Moodie and her family as cut-out figures, superimposed on a landscape represented in a different visual idiom, and this of course evokes their alienation from the land. Another set of illustrations for the poems had been done by the artist Charles Pachter, but they proved too expensive to reproduce in the 1970 book and were not published until a limited edition appeared in 1980. (The Pachter illustrations were republished in a 1997 luxury edition.) They are highly Gothicised, haunting pictures, suggestive of dream imagery, and the book's sophisticated use of typefaces and text layout effectively integrates the pictures with Atwood's words.

The poems themselves are divided into three sections. 'Journal I 1832–1840' narrates the arrival of Moodie and her husband at Quebec, their journey up the St Lawrence to Upper Canada (which was so named, though it was south of Lower Canada, because it was further upriver), and their settlement in the backwoods, or bush. 'Journal II 1840–1871' takes Moodie to Belleville, but several of the poems in this section recount her disturbing dreams about the bush years, or her recollections of the deaths of several of her children there. 'Journal III Later in Belleville: Career' examines Moodie's old age, death and 'resurrection' as 'the spirit of the land she once hated', as Atwood puts it in the 'Afterword' (p. 64).

The poems examine the distinctions between the real and the imagined, dream and memory, conscious and subconscious. 'Dream 3: Night Bear Which Frightened Cattle', for example, reflects on the processes by which a frightening event is experienced, turned into memory, reduced to anecdote, yet preserved in the subconscious in all its terror. It opens with the narrator remembering, with the 'surface' of her mind, a story about her cattle being frightened by a bear. The bear is at once an imagined beast and a very real threat. The family witnessed only the distress of the cattle, but it is the unseen bear which preys on the mind of Atwood's narrator – she dreams that she is:

> watching the bear I didn't see condense
> itself among the trees, an outline
> tenuous as an echo
>
> but it is real, heavier
> than real   I know
> even by daylight here
> in this visible kitchen
>
> it absorbs all terror.   (pp. 38–9)

Atwood's Moodie is not only menaced by wild animals; she is also haunted by a sense of the active hostility of the land itself. In 'Dream I: The Bush Garden', even vegetables become animate, as the potatoes turn into grubs and the dreamer sees 'radishes thrusting down / their fleshy snouts' (p. 34). In one of the many Gothic images which structure the poem sequence, the strawberries cover her hands with blood when she tries to pick them.

The violence evoked by the bloody strawberries relates to the harshness of the climate, land and living conditions as Susanna Moodie experienced them, but also to the literal violence of warfare. John Moodie took part in the British army's successful suppression of the Rebellions of 1837 against the colonial government (see Glossary), and as a result of this he was made sheriff of Belleville. One of Atwood's poems is titled '1837 War in Retrospect', and its perspective on British imperial expansion contests narratives of the progressive conquest of savagery by rationality. Atwood's Moodie describes history as a list of 'ballooning wishes, flukes, / bent times, plunges and mistakes' (p. 35). In 1837 the historical Susanna Moodie's loyalty to the colonial government meant that she unequivocally endorsed its suppression of the rebellions. But as Atwood herself notes in her 'Afterword', 'ironically, Susanna later admitted that the rebellion was probably a good thing for Canada' (p. 63). Atwood's Moodie notes the difference between the contemporary and the retrospective view; in later years, when the events of the rebellions have lost both clarity and meaning, she views war in terms of a childish game, referring to 'scribble' and a 'crayon diagram of a fort' (p. 35).

The poem sequence traces Moodie's movement from being entirely alien in the New World, where 'the moving water will not show me / my reflection', to being permanently identified with Canada, which becomes her 'kingdom' (p. 60). In one of the last poems, 'Alternate Thoughts From Underground', Atwood's Moodie is dead and buried, but aware of the construction work going on above her in the modern city. She refers to its inhabitants as:

> the invaders of those for whom
> shelter was wood,
> fire was terror and sacred.   (p. 57)

This is an ambiguous passage: it seems to refer to Native Canadians, and yet could equally apply to the pioneers, who lived in log houses and both depended on and feared fire. The terror of fire for the settlers is evoked in 'The Two Fires' and 'Departure from the Bush' in the *Journals*, while the motif of wood also recurs in relation to their lives. In 'The Immigrants', Atwood's narrator watches the new arrivals from Britain who:

> think they will make an order
> like the old one, sow miniature orchards,
> carve children and flocks out of wood.   (p. 32)

But they discover that wood, virtually their only resource in a backwoods life, cannot be transformed into anything permanent: 'wood is for burning' (p. 33).

Nevertheless, the legacy of the pioneers does become permanent in other ways. In 'Alternate Thoughts from Underground', the narrator fears that the building of the modern city will render her 'extinct'. The next poem, however, is titled 'Resurrection', while in the final one, Atwood's Moodie is riding on a bus in 1970s Toronto, and remarks triumphantly that despite being buried under layers of concrete, 'I have / my ways of getting through' (p. 60). The resurrection of Moodie is an image for the continuing alienation of non-First Nations Canadians from their own land:

> Right now, the snow
> is no more familiar
> to you than it was to me:
> this is my doing. (pp. 60–1)

The colonial ways of seeing, inscribed into nineteenth-century literature as well as many later narratives, are the dangerous inheritance which the pioneer past bequeaths to modern Canadians. At the same time, Atwood's text attests to the need for ancestors; it is part of the Canadian movement to discover its own literary and historical origins which gathered pace in the 1960s and 1970s. The pioneer inheritance may be damaging in some ways, but it is also shown to have immense value and interest in terms of an understanding of Canada's history.

MARGARET LAURENCE, *THE DIVINERS* (1974)

The legacy of pioneers is also examined in Margaret Laurence's best-known novel. Catharine Parr Traill (Susanna Moodie's sister) is resurrected in *The Diviners* and influences the protagonist, but she is finally less significant than the alternative Canadian 'ancestors' who feature in the text, including the Métis hero Louis Riel and the mythologised forebears of the modern characters. Like *Brébeuf and His Brethren* and *The Journals of Susanna Moodie*, Laurence's novel is preoccupied with the power and limitations of language, with the dynamic between orality and literacy, and with ways of remembering and writing about the past. *The Diviners* is also concerned with place and landscape, race and ancestry, sexual desire and gender.

Margaret Laurence (1926–87) grew up in Neepawa, Manitoba and began writing fiction while living in Africa, where her husband was working. Having returned to Canada in 1957, she lived in

Vancouver and wrote books set in Ghana. In 1962 she moved alone to England: during a ten-year stay, she wrote her acclaimed novels about the fictional town of Manawaka in Manitoba. They are: *The Stone Angel* (1964), *A Jest of God* (1966), *The Fire-Dwellers* (1979), *A Bird in the House* (1970) and *The Diviners*. Laurence finally settled in Lakefield, Ontario.

The Diviners follows the life story of Morag Gunn, as she reconstructs it in her memory and her writing from the vantage point of her late forties. Morag, a descendant of Scottish emigrants, is orphaned in infancy and informally adopted by Prin Logan and her husband, Christie, a Manawaka garbage collector. One of her school classmates, Jules Tonnerre, a Métis boy, becomes Morag's first lover, but soon afterwards she goes to Winnipeg to study English, and falls in love with her professor, Brooke Skelton. After their marriage, they move to Toronto, but Morag eventually leaves, becomes pregnant by Jules and then relocates to Vancouver. Later, with her daughter, Pique, she moves to London (where she begins a relationship with a Scottish man, Dan McRaith) and finally to a farmstead in the Ontario lake country. The complex geography of the novel is related to the search for home, ancestry and identity. During her girlhood, Morag yearns to escape from Manawaka, and rejoices in her moves to various cities, yet she feels comfortable in none of them; she imagines Toronto as 'paradise',[13] but finds it terrifying. It takes many years for her to acknowledge Manawaka as her own place.

As a child, she is fascinated by Christie's tales of her Scottish ancestors, the Sutherlanders, evicted from their homes during the Highland clearances of the late eighteenth and early nineteenth centuries, and forced to emigrate. Christie celebrates the figure of Piper Gunn, 'a great tall man, a man with the voice of drums and the heart of a child and the gall of a thousand and the strength of conviction' (p. 59), who was said to have led his clan onto the emigration ship, and then on a long march across Canada to the prairies. Morag considers him her ancestor, until, that is, she actually visits Scotland, and realises she does not need to see Sutherland:

> I thought I would have to go. But I guess I don't, after all . . .
> It has to do with Christie. The myths are my reality . . . It's a

deep land, here, all right . . . But it's not mine, except a long
long way back. I always thought it was the land of my ancestors, but it is not. (p. 415)

Morag is here speaking to her Scottish lover, who is married, and
there is a suggestion that she has only borrowed him, just as she
'borrowed' her supposed Scottish heritage. She identifies the true
land of her ancestors as 'Christie's real country. Where I was born'
(p. 415). Recognising that Christie himself is her ancestor, she
begins to mythologise him, paralleling his stories with her own
'Tale of Christie Logan' (p. 390), told to Pique, who has never seen
him.

Morag's attitude to Christie's semi-historical tales of the
Highlanders shifts as she grows up. At first, she listens silently and
trustingly, but she later grows sceptical, and repeatedly challenges
Christie's telling:

Reel and his men started doing a little shooting, do you see,
and killed one or two Englishmen. But the Sutherlanders
didn't trust the goddam English . . . no more than what they
trusted the halfbreeds . . . So they sat on their butts and did
nothing.
(The government Down East sent out the Army from
Ontario and like that, and Riel fled, Christie. He came back to
Saskatchewan in 1885.)
Well, some say that. Others say different. Of course I *know*
the Army and that came out, like, but the truth of the matter
is that them Sutherlanders had *taken back the Fort* before even
the smell of an army got there.
(Oh Christie! They didn't. We took it in History.)
I'm telling you. What happened was this. Piper Gunn says
to his five sons, he says, *What in the fiery freezing hell do all of
you think you're doing, not even making a stab at getting back the
bloody Fort?* (pp. 144–5)

The Diviners repeatedly questions official narratives of history,
offering varying perspectives on the same events ('others say di-
erent'). Passages such as the one just quoted also emphasise the

authority of the teller over his story: Christie's emphatic 'I'm telling you' is privileged, while Morag's pedantic questions are relegated to parentheses. In the sections of the novel in which Morag recalls her childhood, the phrase 'Morag knows' recurs (pp. 42–51); her attempt to lay hold of facts and thus attain some control of her world leads her to underestimate the value of story and dream, but later, as a mature writer, she acknowledges myths as her 'reality'.

The novel emphasises the provisionality and indeterminacy of historical knowledge, draws attention to the investment of the historian in what is being told (denying the possibility of objective accounts) and finally celebrates the power of 'telling', that is, of story and imaginative truth. Morag says of Christie's Highlander tales:

> at first I used to believe every word. Then later I didn't believe a word of them, and thought he'd made them up . . . But later still, I realized they'd been taken from things that happened, and who's to know what really happened? So I started believing in them again, in a different way. (p. 391)

The rhetorical power of Christie's stories associates him, to some extent, with the oral traditions of Aboriginal Canadians, and his outsider's perspective on the Manawaka community is similar to that of the mixed-race Tonnerre family. Jules admires Christie, and this helps Morag to overcome her own shame at Christie's occupation, poor hygiene and eccentricity. Morag also comes to sympathise increasingly with Jules and his family, even though as a schoolgirl she echoed the prejudices of the White community – 'They are dirty and unmentionable' – and denies the similarity she has perceived between herself and Jules: 'He is *not* like her' (p. 79).

Morag's growing allegiance to the Métis prompts her to leave her husband when he refuses to entertain Jules in their apartment. She is furious when he remarks, 'I thought it was supposed to be illegal to give liquor to Indians' (p. 290). Brooke represents imperial power: 'I was born in India. My father was Headmaster of a boys' school not far from Calcutta. Church of England school . . . I was sent to England to boardingschool when I was six' (p. 210). It was 'a military school', in which the boys were given ranks, and Brooke was 'a

Sergeant at the age of eight' (p. 237). Brooke's relations of colonial dominance are played out not only in his racist treatment of Jules but also in his attitude to Morag, which can be read as emblematic of British domination of Canada. She is ashamed to tell him of her upbringing, and he likes her 'mysterious nonexistent past', because 'It's as though you are starting life now, newly' (p. 212). This relates to colonial readings of Canada as an empty space, with no history, a blank sheet on which European ideologies and practices could be freely inscribed. The asymmetry of their relationship is also, of course, gendered: Brooke tends to stroke Morag's breasts or pat her bottom when she says anything challenging, reducing her to her physical being and using her intense desire for him to control her. When she attacks him for calling her 'little one', he says she is 'hysterical' and asks if she is due to menstruate, reading her behaviour simply as a function of her physiology (p. 277).

The figure of Brooke, then, is used to explore patriarchal and colonial ideologies, and these themes also come together in Laurence's representation of Catharine Parr Traill. Traill, as well as Susanna Moodie, lived at one time in Lakefield, Ontario, and Morag buys a farmhouse in a similar location. She enumerates its attractions: 'Land. A river. Log house nearly a century old, built by great pioneering couple, Simon and Sarah Cooper. History. Ancestors' (p. 439). Morag soon revises this view, however. She is oppressed by the pioneers' achievements and endurance, and focuses these feelings through imagined conversations with Traill. Morag hears Traill admonishing: 'I, as you know, managed both to write books, with some modest degree of success, while at the same time cultivating my plot of land and rearing my dear children, of whom I bore nine' (p. 186). Morag envies and yet resists Catharine's colonial mastery over the land, both in terms of her flourishing garden and her botanical endeavours: 'Imagine naming flowers which have never been named before. Like the Garden of Eden. Power!' (p. 186). Similarly, Morag both admires and rejects the pioneer ideal of femininity, which emphasised motherhood, domestic skill and unceasing, selfless effort. She evokes Traill's domestic efficiency with some sarcasm: 'Cleaning the house, baking two hundred loaves of delicious bread, preserving half a ton of plums, pears, cherries, etcetera. All before lunch' (p. 109).

Morag is somewhat shamed by her neighbours A-Okay and Maudie, who grow all their own food and disapprove of her for going to the supermarket by taxi. But the couple embrace the pioneer heritage to a dangerous extent. Maudie is worn out by her labour-intensive methods of housework, even making her dresses 'determinedly herself on a hand-cranker sewing machine' (p. 64), and when Pique goes to live with them, she ends up, as her mother laments, 'working as a cashier in the bloody supermarket all day, and then going home and feeding those squawking chickens and washing dishes and weeding the vegetable gardens' (p. 431). Eventually, Morag rejects Traill as a possible ancestor: 'farewell, sweet saint – henceforth, I summon you not', and decides to stop feeling guilty about not being 'either an old or a new pioneer' (p. 431).

The historical perspectives of the novel, then, embrace several time frames. The recurring image of the river evokes a length of time stretching beyond history: 'Left to itself, the river would probably go on like this, flowing deep, for another million or so years' (p. 12). In terms of human history, the text recreates several pasts: the late eighteenth century, when the Highland clearances began; the early nineteenth century of the Lakefield pioneers; the late nineteenth century of Riel's rebellion; the Depression era of Morag's youth; and the recent past of Pique's childhood. Ways of accessing history, through written record, oral narrative, legend and memory, are thematised in the novel. *The Diviners* explores the past through Morag's recollections ('Memorybank movies'), the lyrics of songs about Jules and his father and grandfather, descriptions of photographs, Christie's tales, and extracts from books, including Traill's *Canadian Settler's Guide* and *The 60th Canadian Field Artillery Battery Book*. Other kinds of texts interpolated into the narrative include letters exchanged by the characters, lists, conversations rendered as dramatic scripts, and excerpts from reviews of Morag's books. This creates a multi-voiced novel, a postmodern collage of narrative forms, which resists singular versions and unitary meanings. At the start of the novel, Morag's friend Royland is introduced: 'A water diviner. Morag always felt she was about to learn something of great significance from him, something which would explain everything. But things remained mysterious, his work, her own, the generations, the river' (p. 12). *The*

Diviners refuses to 'explain everything'. It preserves an element of mystery at its centre, imaged in the figure of the water diviner, who functions as an analogy for the figure of the artist. At the end of the novel, the ageing Royland loses his gift, which passes to A-Okay, the inheritor. Morag, who has just finished the novel she is writing, thinks:

> At least Royland knew he had been a true diviner. There were the wells, proof positive . . . Morag's magic tricks were of a different order. She would never know whether they actually worked or not, or to what extent . . . In a sense, it did not matter. The necessary doing of the thing – that mattered. (p. 477)

The final pages of the novel consist of the words and music for Jules's and Pique's songs: Pique, too, is an inheritor, since her father's gift for songwriting has passed to her following his death.

DAPHNE MARLATT, *ANA HISTORIC* (1988)

The pioneer figure recreated in *Ana Historic* is of quite a different order from Atwood's Moodie or Laurence's Traill. A mysterious and intriguing solitary woman, whose life is attested to only in fragmentary records, Mrs Richards is imagined into being by Annie Torrent, a woman living in modern Vancouver.

Born in 1942, Daphne Marlatt has experience in editing, translation, publishing and university lecturing, as well as creative and critical writing. Much of her work defies classification in terms of genre, and she has also worked collaboratively with photographers, historians and other authors. She was first known for her poetry, much of which is rooted in western Canada, and for her books of oral history, but went on to publish two novels, *Ana Historic* and *Taken* (1996). From the 1980s onwards, she became increasingly identified with feminist and lesbian poetics.

Ana Historic is an experimental fiction which breaks the conventional structure of the sentence, uses capital letters idiosyncratically, and blurs the distinction between the real and the imagined. The novel also thematises language and explores the ways in which history is written. Like Morag in *The Diviners*, Marlatt's character Annie marries one of her professors, a historian, 'known for the diligent research behind his books' (p. 134). Annie helps him with his research, and he says: 'history is built on a groundwork of fact . . . one missing piece can change the shape of the whole picture – you see how important your part in it is?' Annie thinks, 'but i'm no longer doing my part looking for missing pieces. at least not missing facts. not when there are missing persons in all this rubble' (p. 134). The missing persons are the women whose lives have been erased from the historical record. Annie seeks to reinscribe Mrs Richards into the story of Vancouver's development in the late nineteenth century, but is frustrated by the limitations of the available evidence. In terms of official records, she can get at her only through newspaper reports of events such as her appointment as a teacher in 1873, her acquisition of a piano and her marriage.

There is also, unusually, a personal diary, but 'they think her journal suspect at the archives. "inauthentic", fictional possibly, contrived later by a daughter who imagined (how ahistoric) her way into the unspoken world of her mother's girlhood' (p. 30). Annie herself asserts the value of the historical imagination in the recovery of private experience, and rejects the patriarchal construction of history in terms of public events:

> i learned that history is the real story the city fathers tell of the only important events in the world. a tale of their exploits hacked out against a silent backdrop of trees, of wooden masses. so many claims to fame. so many ordinary men turned into heroes. (where are the city mothers?) the city fathers busy building a town out of so many shacks labelled the Western Terminus of the Transcontinental, Gateway to the East – all these capital letters to convince themselves of its, of their, significance. (p. 28)

This statement gives a clue to Marlatt's own use of capital and lower-case letters. Capitals generally indicate the hierarchical and disciplinary structures of the social order. Annie remembers being late for school: 'hear the clock ticking in the Principal's Office. late again. the sound of the word DETENTION, pink slip like a flag in my hands as i opened the door and all those faces slowly turned to eye me' (p. 24). Capitals indicate the authority of the Principal and the form of punishment he can mete out; the word 'detention' evokes prison, as do the surveillance of the eyes and the emphasis on the regulatory function of linear time (the clock ticking). Annie never uses a capital 'I' when referring to herself, a gesture which in this passage seems to indicate her powerlessness and lack of status, but elsewhere could be read as a form of resistance to the self-assertion and self-absorption implied by the upper-case 'I'.

Annie does use 'I' and, indeed, a great many initial capitals, when quoting from Mrs Richards's writing or thinking out what she might say. She reads in her archived diary: 'You would say, Father, they are a Rough Lot and this is no place for a Gentlewoman, and you would be right, perhaps. Still I would rather be here than cooped up there as your handmaiden' (p. 55). In the nineteenth century, initial capitals were used more frequently and with less regularity than they are today, and served to emphasise particular nouns. In the diary extracts, a capital is added to nouns designating fixed social identities, 'Father', 'Gentlewoman', 'Rough Lot', and this draws attention to the limiting and repressive nature of such labels and stereotypes. Annie adopts a similar strategy in describing her own past experiences: 'we went there to be seen, to be certified Teen Angels, Dolls . . . waiting to be Made (passive voice) . . . The Hunks paraded by, eyeing the choice' (p. 82). Again, this system of capitalisation draws attention to the confinement of men and women in particular roles ('Dolls', 'Hunks'), and to the greater activity and power associated with the male roles.

Proper names in *Ana Historic* are consistently given a capital, and yet the text defies the conventional use of names to label and distinguish clearly between individuals. Mrs Richards's name is misleading, since she was never married. The word 'Richards' appears to designate the possession of a man named Richard, which is what Annie feels herself to be in relation to her husband. Annie does not know Mrs Richards's first name, so she calls her Ana, a combination of her own name and that of her mother, Ina. The three women become partially merged, as the subject of Annie's narration slips seamlessly between them, and her feelings about 'Ana' are often projections of emotions relating to her mother and herself. The name Ana is a palindrome, and it is also a prefix whose meaning Annie draws attention to in a passage set out like poetry: 'Ana / that's her name: / back, backward, reversed / again, anew' (p. 43). 'Ana', then, is a symbolic designation, suggesting that Annie has created Mrs Richards 'anew', and that Mrs Richards created herself anew when she came to Canada.

Ina, like Mrs Richards, is an emigrant from England, and Annie's observations on the experience of emigration often apply equally to the two women. Some of them closely parallel ideas offered in *The Journals of Susanna Moodie*. Just as Atwood's Moodie remarks: 'Two voices / took turns using my eyes', so Marlatt's narrator refers to the 'two languages. two allegiances' (p. 23) of the emigrant. Annie says of her mother (but also, implicitly, of Mrs Richards): 'the world you brought with you, transposed, onto a Salish mountainside. and never questioned its terms. "lady." never questioned its values. English gentility in a rain forest?' (pp. 23–4). *Ana Historic* itself is always concerned to question terms and values, and to undo assumptions and expectations. Mrs Richards thinks, 'I am not a Proper Lady perhaps', and Annie notes, 'it is barely sounded, the relationship between proper and property'. She elaborates:

> words, that shifting territory. never one's own. full of deadfalls and hidden claims to a reality others have made.
> lady, for instance. a word that has claimed so much from women trying to maintain it. the well-ironed linen, clean . . . a certain way of walking, of talking. and always that deference. (p. 32)

The novel is intensely preoccupied with the determining influence of words and categories, with what it means to be English, or Canadian, or to be a woman, or a lady, or a wife, and with how those roles are performed under the gaze of others.

Annie says of Ana, 'history married her to Ben Stewart and wrote her off', but Zoe, a woman she meets in the archive, counters: 'wrote her *in* . . . listed her as belonging' (p. 134). The word 'belonging' is deliberately ambiguous here, implying that marrying enables Ana to participate in a community (belong), but also turns her into someone's possession (belonging). Zoe and Annie are attracted to one another, and explore the possibilities of their relationship through reference to Mrs Richards. Zoe suggests that she may have had a lesbian relationship with Birdie Stewart, another woman whose name appears in the records, and concealed it through her marriage to Ben Springer. Annie protests: 'but this is a monstrous leap of imagination', and then wonders, 'whose voice is that?' (p. 135), catching herself mimicking what her husband, the conventional researcher, would say. Finally, Annie imagines out the first erotic encounter between Ana and Birdie, concluding with an admission that the character she has created has exceeded her control:

> Ana, what are you doing? . . . you've moved beyond what i can tell of you, you've taken the leap into this new possibility and i can't imagine what you would say.
>
> which means history wins again?
>
> as if it were a race – one wins, the other has to lose. like the weather lady swinging on her platform, . . . but what if they balance each other (it's one of those half-cloudy, half-sunny days) and we live in history *and* imagination. (p. 139)

Ana Historic affirms the special value of the historical novel: unlike the academic historian, the novelist has the freedom to move beyond her research, to imagine herself into the possible, unrecorded past.

MICHAEL ONDAATJE, *IN THE SKIN OF A LION* (1987)

The dynamic between history and imagination also shapes Michael Ondaatje's novel about Toronto in the early decades of the twentieth century. The plot of *In the Skin of a Lion* is structured around several 'actual' events – notably the building of the Bloor Street Viaduct in the 1910s and of Commissioner R. C. Harris's water purification plant in the 1930s, together with the disappearance of the famous capitalist and theatre magnate Ambrose Small in 1919. These events have an impact on the lives of the small group of fictional and semi-fictional characters whose interrelated stories form the subject of the novel. They are: the Macedonian immigrant Nicholas Temelcoff; the Canadian Patrick Lewis; his lovers Clara Dickens (also the lover of Ambrose) and Alice Gull, both actresses; Alice's daughter Hana; and Caravaggio, an Italian thief. Ondaatje's comment on his later novel *Anil's Ghost* (2000) would also apply to *In the Skin of a Lion*: 'The West is obsessed by celluloid stars and political or military figures. But celebrating the unhistorical is one way to make a moral decision'.[14]

Michael Ondaatje rivals Margaret Atwood in international fame. Born in Sri Lanka in 1943, he moved to Britain at nine, and emigrated to Canada in 1962. He began his writing career as a poet, publishing his first books in the late 1960s, and when he began writing fiction he developed a style with the intensity and lyricism of poetry. Ondaatje's best-known novel is *The English Patient* (1992): it was awarded the Booker Prize, and Anthony Minghella's 1996 film version received nine Academy Awards. Ondaatje's other work includes literary criticism, films and several books which cross the boundaries of genre, combining prose and poetry, photography and collage, history and fiction.

In the Skin of a Lion itself combines history and fiction, and while it does not literally contain pictures, certain real and imagined photographs are significant to the narrative. In particular, Ondaatje draws on photographs of Toronto's civil engineering projects, found in the city archives.[15] The novel is also remarkably visual and sensual in its imagery, and its complex narrative perspectives and intertextual references create a sophisticated structure. One of the epigraphs to *In the Skin of a Lion* is taken from the 4,000-year old *Epic of Gilgamesh*: 'The joyful will stoop with sorrow, and when you have gone to the earth I will let my hair grow long for your sake, I will wander through the wilderness in the skin of a lion'.[16] Gilgamesh, who speaks these words, is a Babylonian king, but after the death of his friend Enkidu, he leaves the city and journeys through darkness and over the waters of death. This pattern recurs in Ondaatje's novel: following Alice's death, Patrick leaves Toronto for Muskoka, where he blows up a luxury hotel and is consequently imprisoned. After his release in 1938, he makes a highly dangerous journey, swimming through a pipe into the water purification plant, intending to confront Commissioner Harris and dynamite the plant. Patrick risks death to avenge Alice, and to protest against the exploitation of the workers (himself included) whose labour made the immense and profitable civil engineering projects of early twentieth-century Toronto possible.

Besides the structural parallels between the two texts, the *Epic of Gilgamesh* is relevant to Ondaatje's novel in other ways, and especially through its self-conscious preoccupation with storytelling. The *Epic* opens with a framing device, a prologue in which a nameless narrator states that he will proclaim to the world the deeds of Gilgamesh. Similarly, *In the Skin of a Lion* sets up a relationship between teller and listener before beginning the story proper: '*This is the story a young girl gathers in a car during the early hours of the morning . . . She listens to the man as he picks up and brings together various corners of the story*' (p. 1). At the end of the novel, we are returned to the frame story, and learn that the travellers in the car are Patrick and Hana. This introductory paragraph anticipates the novel's emphasis on oral telling, but, like *The Epic of Gilgamesh*, Ondaatje's book is also preoccupied with written language. The narrator of the epic tells us that Gilgamesh inscribed the story of his journey on clay tablets, so that what we are reading is a retelling of the hero's written narrative. The prologue seems to guarantee the truth of the story through appeal to Gilgamesh's own recorded words, but at the same time it draws attention to the fact that this is only one of many possible tellings. This doubled gesture is replicated in Ondaatje's text.

In the Skin of a Lion, unlike the *Epic*, does not have a single 'hero'. The role of protagonist shifts between Patrick Lewis, Temelcoff and Caravaggio, and through them we also learn the stories of Alice, Clara, Ambrose and Hana. This structure is self-consciously related to the image of Gilgamesh in the lion's skin, as Patrick recalls:

> Alice had once described a play to him in which several actresses shared the role of the heroine. After half an hour the powerful matriarch removed her large coat from which animal pelts dangled and she passed it, along with her strength, to one of the minor characters. In this way even a silent daughter could put on the cloak and be able to break through her chrysalis into language. Each person had their moment when

they assumed the skins of wild animals, when they took
responsibility for the story. (p. 157)

The silent daughter can be partly identified with Hana, who listens
and is poised to take over the story at the end of *In the Skin of a
Lion*. (Fittingly, *The English Patient* places Hana more centrally,
telling of her experiences during the Second World War.) Just as in
The Diviners Royland's gift of water divining is passed on to A-
Okay, and Jules's gift of songwriting is passed on to Pique, so in
Ondaatje's book there is an emphasis on gifts and stories being
passed on, not only down through the generations, but between
lovers, friends and even prison cellmates.

Patrick, who connects together the stories of the other characters, identifies himself as a 'searcher'. In literal terms, 'searchers'
were people paid by companies to hunt for Ambrose Small, whose
family had offered an $80,000 reward for his discovery. Patrick
becomes one of these, but when he locates Ambrose's mistress,
Clara, the object of his quest changes, and he becomes her lover.
(Ondaatje sometimes bases a character on an actual person, but
signals the fictionalisation. Clara Dickens, for example, is a version
of Clara Smith, the historical Ambrose Small's mistress.) Patrick's
metaphorical role as 'searcher' refers to his attempts to piece
together the stories of the other characters by listening to their
anecdotes, picking up clues, and undertaking research. Similarly,
Temelcoff's role is that of a 'spinner' who 'links everyone' (p. 34);
Patrick eventually discovers that he was the man who saved Alice
Gull's life when, during her time as a nun, she was blown off the
viaduct. Nicholas has never told this story, but once reminded of it
by Patrick, he feels:

> Patrick's gift, that arrow into the past, shows him the wealth in
> himself, how he has been sewn into history. Now he will begin
> to tell stories. He is a tentative man, even with his family. That
> night in bed shyly he tells his wife the story of the nun. (p. 49)

The passing on of stories, the novel suggests, is the only way to
ensure that the histories of ordinary people, those without power,
are 'sewn into history'.

The novel's attitude to power, wealth and labour is complex. Debates about rich and poor, protest and passivity, compassion and justice are staged in Patrick's conversations with Alice, but not resolved. *In the Skin of a Lion* can be read as an affirmation of the value of the worker, and an attempt to recover the hidden stories of the people who built the modern city of Toronto: in the Riverdale Library, Patrick finds articles which 'depicted every detail about the soil, the wood, the weight of concrete, everything but information on those who actually built the bridge' (p. 145). According to Peter Easingwood, the novel 'represents the building of a city as the achievement of the many rather than of the celebrated few. This collective effort is symbolised in the story by the construction of the Bloor Street Viaduct'.[17] But his interpretation is only partially accurate, since in some passages the narrative erases the workers' roles through constructions such as: 'The bridge goes up in a dream' (p. 26). There is also a tendency to romanticise labour, which is particularly problematic because it is not collective effort but the achievements of heroic individuals which are celebrated.

In 1930, during the arduous process of boring a tunnel under Lake Ontario, Patrick works mainly as a digger, but is sometimes required to practise his special skill of dynamiting. At these points, 'Patrick separates himself from the others' (p. 106) to take on a job which only he has courage and ability for, and his shadow, significantly, becomes a 'giant' (p. 107). Temelcoff stands in a similar relation to his co-workers:

> Nicholas Temelcoff is famous on the bridge, a daredevil. He is given all the difficult jobs and he takes them. He descends into the air with no fear. He is a solitary . . . He floats at the three hinges of the crescent-shaped steel arches. These knit the bridge together. The moment of cubism . . . His work is so exceptional and time-saving he earns one dollar an hour while the other bridge workers receive forty cents. There is no jealousy towards him. No one dreams of doing half the things he does. For night work he is paid $1.25, swinging up into the rafters of a trestle holding a flare, free-falling like a dead star. He does not really need to see things, he has charted all that space, knows the pier footings, the width of the cross-walks in

terms of seconds of movement – 281 feet and 6 inches make
up the central span of the bridge . . . He knows his position in
the air as if he is mercury slipping across a map. (pp. 34–5)

The relations between Temelcoff and his underpaid fellow workers
are improbably harmonious, contributing to the effect of fantasy.
While the statistics and precise designations of the bridge's com-
ponents give the impression of an objective, well-researched
account, yet the reference to cubism and the highly literary images
of Temelcoff as a dead star or mercury slipping across a map reveal
that the worker has been transformed into an aesthetic object.[18]
    In another passage the novel seems aware of the dangers of such
transformation. Patrick recalls that at the leather factory where he
once worked, the dyers jumped into the pools of dye to work the
colour into the skins, and so became dyed themselves: 'That is how
Patrick would remember them later. Their bodies standing there
tired, only the heads white. If he were an artist he would have
painted them but that was false celebration' (p. 130). Yet even as
Ondaatje points to the suffering of the dyers, who 'had consumed
the most evil smell in history' (p. 130) and 'would die of consumption' (p. 131), his own narrative succumbs to the aesthetic qualities
of the scene remembered by Patrick: 'in winter this picturesque
yard of colour was even more beautiful, the thin layer of snowfall
between the steaming wells' (p. 131). Passages such as this are
ambiguous in political terms, yet they are characteristic of a narrative which continually finds beauty in unexpected places.

CONCLUSION

Canadian authors have always used the history of their country to
provide colourful subject matter, but they rarely appropriate such
material uncritically, and frequently reflect on the ways in which
historical events are recorded and transmitted. This self-aware
approach is particularly marked in contemporary texts, and historiographic metafiction is an important sub-genre within Canadian
literature. Postcolonial Canadian writing establishes complex relations with the texts and value systems of earlier periods, finding

inspiration in the colonial past but also contesting the grand narratives of empire. The intimate connections between mastery over the land, mastery over colonised peoples and mastery over language are explored in many historically inspired Canadian texts. The books discussed in this chapter examine the historical meanings of the city within the national imaginary, focusing in particular on the city as a sign of the conquest of civilisation over inhospitable wilderness.

Canada's preoccupation with its own history has often been interpreted as symptomatic of the urgency of establishing a sense of national identity in a postcolonial context. In literary texts this preoccupation sometimes emerges in the form of a search for ancestors, and the novels and poems considered in this chapter each 'resurrect' figures from the past. Usually, people who left some kind of written record are chosen for such resurrections, and the creative text has its origins in research. There would seem to be a clear difference between the fictional recreations of famous characters from Canadian history (Susanna Moodie, Catharine Parr Traill, Jean de Brébeuf, Ambrose Small) and the imagined reconstruction of the lives of 'ordinary' Canadians living in past eras (Ana Richards, Patrick Lewis). And yet, the characters of Ana and Patrick, too, were inspired by documentary records: the archived newspapers, photographs and records which Marlatt and Ondaatje explored in Vancouver and Toronto. The narratives surrounding these characters reveal the role of imagination in historical reconstruction, and demonstrate that characters such as Atwood's Moodie or Pratt's Brébeuf are just as much 'fictional' as Ondaatje's Patrick or Marlatt's Ana.

- Many Canadian historical fictions and poems are profoundly ambivalent in political terms, and cannot be read as straightforwardly 'colonial' or 'decolonising'.
- Contemporary historical fiction often self-consciously negotiates between different versions of the same story or the same historical event, drawing attention to the inadequacies and biases of each single account, and to the power relations inherent in the writing and interpretation of history.
- History, in Canadian texts such as those discussed above, is not simply accessed through textual records; it is also inscribed

on both body and landscape. The past is reconstructed partly through the reading of places, photographs and other visual signs.

- The complex narrative structures of Canadian historical novels and poems are often related to their preoccupation with the relationships between, on the one hand, memory and nostalgia and, on the other, record-keeping and research.
- The search for ancestors is a central theme in many fictional narratives of Canadian history, and postmodern literary texts often centre on a recreated, or imagined, figure from the national past.

NOTES

1. Daphne Marlatt, *Ana Historic* (Toronto: Coach House, 1988), p. 139. All subsequent references in the text are to this edition.
2. Linda Hutcheon, *A Poetics of Postmodernism: History, Theory, Fiction* (London: Routledge, 1988), p. 120.
3. Linda Hutcheon, *The Canadian Postmodern: A Study of Contemporary English-Canadian Fiction* (Toronto: Oxford University Press, 1988), pp. 13, 14.
4. Ibid., p. 14.
5. E. J. Pratt, *Brébeuf and His Brethren* (1940), repr. in *E. J. Pratt: The Complete Poems, Part I*, ed. Sandra Djwa and R. G. Moyles (Toronto: University of Toronto Press, 1989), pp. 46–110 (pp. 104–5). All subsequent references in the text are to this edition.
6. Margaret Atwood, *The Journals of Susanna Moodie* (Toronto: Oxford University Press, 1970), pp. 15, 25, 51. All subsequent references in the text are to this edition.
7. Catherine Belsey, 'Reading Cultural History', in *Reading the Past: Literature and History*, ed. Tamsin Spargo (Basingstoke: Palgrave, 2000), p. 112.
8. Angela T. McAuliffe, *Between the Temple and the Cave: The Religious Dimensions of the Poetry of E. J. Pratt* (Montreal and Kingston: McGill-Queen's University Press, 2000), p. 39.
9. Ibid, p. 190.
10. Sandra Djwa and R. G. Moyles, 'Introduction' in *E. J. Pratt: The Complete Poems Part I*, pp. xi–xlviii (p. xiii).

11. Jacqui Smyth, '"Divided Down the Middle": A Cure for *The Journals of Susanna Moodie*', *Essays on Canadian Writing*, 47 (1992), 149–62 (p. 149).

12. Ann Edwards Boutelle, 'Margaret Atwood, Margaret Laurence and Their Nineteenth-Century Forerunners', in *Faith of a (Woman) Writer*, ed. Alice Kessler-Harris and William McBrien (Westport, CT: Greenwood, 1988), pp. 41–7 (p. 42).

13. Margaret Laurence, *The Diviners* (Toronto: McClelland and Stewart, [1974] 1988), p. 219. All subsequent references in the text are to this edition.

14. Michael Ondaatje and Atom Egoyan, 'The Kitchen Table Talks', *Globe and Mail*, 8 April 2000, D6–D7 (p. D6).

15. See http://:www.toronto.ca/archives/photograph.

16. Michael Ondaatje, *In the Skin of a Lion* (London: Picador, [1987] 1988), n.p. All subsequent references in the text are to this edition.

17. Peter Easingwood, 'Michael Ondaatje' (2002), in *The Literary Encyclopedia*. Available at http://www.litencyc.com

18. More specifically, the reference is to John Berger's essay 'The Moment of Cubism', in which he suggests that cubism explores the relationship of humans to material reality, and its transformation by innovations such as steel, electricity, film and radio. See Berger, *The Moment of Cubism and Other Essays* (London: Weidenfeld and Nicolson, 1969), pp. 1–32.

Conclusion

It is often argued that the achieved maturity of Canadian literature is demonstrated by the success of Canadian writers on the international stage. Indeed, numerous authors now have large audiences around the world, and several have won major foreign prizes, notably the Man Booker (formerly Booker) and the Orange Prize. The Canadian Booker winners are Michael Ondaatje, Margaret Atwood and Yann Martel, while Carol Shields, Mordecai Richler, Rohinton Mistry, Robertson Davies and Alice Munro have all been shortlisted at least once. The more recently established Orange Prize for fiction by women has been won by Shields and Anne Michaels; shortlisted writers include Atwood, Jane Urquhart and Ann-Marie Macdonald. This list certainly suggests that Canadian literature is no longer seen as an undeveloped or 'minor' literature according to world standards. Yet the repetition of this litany of names by Canadian critics and journalists anxious to affirm the status of the national literature suggests a continuing desire for foreign approval. Arguably, this recalls the 'colonial cringe' of earlier eras, and it most certainly reveals the conflicted relationship between nationalisms and global literary culture, and the tension between local and international ownership of the literary star.

This conclusion offers some preliminary reflections on issues such as these, examining the impact of shifting patterns of reading, new models of celebrity authorship, and contemporary forms of publicity on Canadian literary culture, as well as commenting on the institutionalisation of Canadian literary studies. These are topics which have inspired some of the most exciting new research in the field. Interdisciplinary approaches to the sociology and economics of reading, authorship and publishing in Canada, together with the related growth area of book history and material culture, have produced numerous innovative books (see Guide to Further Reading), as well as large-scale collaborative projects.[1] Such work takes the study of literature in Canada beyond the academic sphere, engaging with the author as public figure, with the mass media and with the general public as readers.

Several recent books, such as Sarah M. Corse's *Nationalism and Literature: The Politics of Culture in Canada and the United States* (1997) and Graham Huggan's *The Postcolonial Exotic: Marketing the Margins* (2001), consider the politics and economics of Canadian culture in a comparative context. Huggan, in his chapter on the book prize, argues that the award of British-based prizes to writers from Commonwealth countries is by no means a politically innocent manoeuvre:

> The Booker award has tended to favour postcolonial writers – writers either based in countries of the former British Empire . . . or belonging to minority communities (Afro-Caribbean, South/east Asian) in Britain. Is Booker's promotional push the sign of a new transnational era in which writers increasingly demonstrate the global proportions of the English language; or is it rather the strategy of a multinational corporate enterprise that seeks alternative markets in order to expand its own commercial horizons?[2]

Huggan adds that the Booker Prize reveals 'a continuing desire for metropolitan control', which results in part from imperialist nostalgia, and that 'the resistance to such nostalgia that is obviously exercised by many of the writers is effectively recuperated by an "otherness industry" that banks its profits on exotic myths'.[3] Literary prizes operate largely according to a commercial logic: they generate profits both for the companies who sponsor them and for the publishers of shortlisted and winning books. Despite this, as

Corse points out, they do not ultimately function to expose the eco-nomic basis of cultural production; rather:

> The conferral of literary prizes and, *even more importantly*, the public discussions and disagreements about judges' decisions, the charges of evaluative idiocy and favoritism, the prize-bashing . . . ultimately serve to confirm and affirm the exis-tence and value of a cultural hierarchy.[4]

This is because criticisms of prizes, and attacks on supposedly wrong selections, operate on the assumption that it is in fact possi-ble, in some purer, uncontaminated realm, to make unbiased judge-ments about the relative 'greatness' of different books. The whole concept of a literary canon, of course, depends on this assumption.

In recent years, though, the authority of the small group of critics and educators traditionally empowered to select books into the canon has been challenged – at least to some extent – by the reading public. Large-scale reader surveys, in which newspapers, radio stations or television channels publish lists of great books and authors based on audience votes, are becoming very influential across North America, and these surveys are often related to mass reading events, which promote reading as a community or nation-building project. In Canada, the most high profile of these is the CBC's 'Canada Reads', launched in 2002. During an annual series of radio programmes, five celebrity panellists each advocate one work of Canadian fiction which they would like everyone to read. Winners have included Miriam Toews's *A Complicated Kindness* (2004), Guy Vanderhaege's *The Last Crossing* (2001) and Michael Ondaatje's *In the Skin of a Lion* (1987). Audiences are invited to discuss the shortlisted books and vote for their own favourite via a website, yet this voting does not actually influence the outcome. Despite the rhetoric of community and participation implicit in the title 'Canada Reads', the shortlisted books are selected by the celebrities, and the winner is chosen via the broadcast debate. The process of elimination used to select the winning book is often, as Smaro Kamboureli notes, 'whimsical and arbitrary'.[5] Canada Reads, then, is primarily a celebrity spectacle, and in this it contrasts with more localised projects such as 'One Book, One Community'. Each annual OBOC programme is centred on an individual city or region, and supports group reading and discussion of a selected book, together with events such as presentations in local libraries, author appearances or tours of sites mentioned in the story. Danielle Fuller and DeNel Rehberg Sedo point out that these activities rise to the 'challenge of "building community" through an activity that, within Euramerican cultures at least, is frequently conceptualised as a solitary, private activity'.[6]

OBOC projects always choose books by writers who are prepared to spend some time with local readers, and this encourages authors' participation in the promotion of their wares. Indeed, authors are becoming ever more visible in Canada, as the popularity of literary festivals, readings and book signings reveals, and in general terms literary celebrity is increasingly predicated on forms of public performance, whether live appearances, broadcasts or published interviews. In recent years a series of books and articles has immensely improved our understanding of the processes by which celebrity images are constituted and circulated, and the meanings which are invested in them. Most of these concentrate on cinema, music and sport stardom, while literary celebrity is still only a small subsection of this burgeoning field of celebrity studies. Nevertheless, in relation to Canadian literature, it seems likely to attract significant interest in the coming years, as a growing number of Canadian writers achieve international fame, and as the impact of celebrity on patterns of reading and book sales in Canada becomes better understood. Some of the earlier academic studies of celebrity traced a narrative of decline, suggesting that the advent of mass media transformed 'genuine' artistic fame based on achievement into a culture of high-profile yet disposable celebrities, whose renown is founded more on their personality than their work. More recently, other critics have challenged this line of thinking on the basis that is too uniformly hostile to popular culture, and that it dismisses the power of audiences in creating celebrities, as well as underestimating the actual achievements of authors, artists and actors by exaggerating the role of marketing and packaging in producing their fame. Books such as Joe Moran's *Star Authors* (2000) and Lorraine York's *Canadian Literary Celebrity* (2007), which explore authors' strategic negotiations with their own celebrity images and their interventions to shape media representations of them, form a useful corrective to theories which deny any agency to celebrities themselves.

The nature of celebrity is a current obsession in the media as well as the academy, and as Moran writes, celebrity has become 'an unstable, multifaceted phenomenon' and 'a pivotal point of contention in debates about the relationship between cultural authority and exchange value in capitalist societies'. Literary celebrity, he adds, differs from the celebrity produced by commercial mass media in terms of its relation with economics, since the

> encroachment of market values on to literary production . . . forms part of a complicated process in which various legitimating bodies compete for cultural authority and/or commercial success, and regulate the formation of a literary star system and the shifting hierarchy of stars.[7]

Therefore, best-selling and fashionable authors – such as prizewinners and those chosen for communal reading events – often become the focus of debates about literary value and cultural hierarchy. Sales figures are heavily influenced by the meanings attached to the author's celebrity image, as well as by the advocacy of particular books through reader surveys, community reading projects or radio and television book programmes.

The economic basis of cultural production is, then, an important focus in scholarly study of these phenomena, and researchers often draw on the work of French sociologist Pierre Bourdieu. His influential concept of 'the field of cultural production' refers to the network of relations between the producer of art (that is, author, painter, composer and so on) and the agents which determine the reputation and status of the artist and artwork.[8] These agents include reviewers and journalists, critics, educators, publishers, exhibition curators and others who possess the power to award cultural capital and consecrate an artist or work through some form of celebration. Prizes, favourable reviews and invitations to speak, perform or exhibit in a major venue all confer recognition and prestige, but they may also move an artist out of the field of restricted production (directed at a deliberately small, elite audience) and towards the field of large-scale production (directed at mass audiences). As critics including Graham Huggan and Lorraine York have noted, Canadian literary stars such as Margaret Atwood and Michael Ondaatje are unusual in that they have succeeded in straddling these two fields.[9] Achieving sales in the range normally reserved for thriller or romance fiction, they are nevertheless regarded as 'serious' literary writers, and their books are consecrated by means of extensive academic discussion, prizes and inclusion on school or university syllabuses. As a result, authors such as these need to manage their own star images, and negotiate the tensions between art and commerce which interviewers and journalists perpetually comment on. The image of the celebrity becomes itself a text, and readings of those star texts inform some of the most interesting recent research on Canadian literary culture.

In her discussion of Atwood, Carol Shields and literary celebrity, Lisa Hayden writes:

A new kind of hypercelebrity culture has emerged within the last twenty years. The developing sophistication of electronic media, new modes of communication and the globalisation of the Western economic system have significantly increased the visibility and accessibility of celebrity figures. The sheer pervasiveness of celebrity from the 1980s onwards has encouraged the idea that it is a new phenomenon, as opposed to a discursive construct that has a specific historical context and background.[10]

Indeed, all the cultural phenomena I have mentioned above – reading groups, celebrity authorship, book prizes and lists of great authors – have a long history in Canada. In the nineteenth and early twentieth centuries, literary societies proliferated in the more populated areas of the country; they often had a very localised membership, and met to hear readings by guest authors or papers on literary topics. As for celebrity authorship, it emerged in more or less its modern form during the 1920s, when the advent of Hollywood led to an unprecedented public fascination with stars. In Canada this new interest in celebrities intersected with the flowering of cultural nationalism, and famous Canadians who could be co-opted into discourses of nationalist self-definition were vigorously promoted. Newspapers conducted reader surveys in order to compile lists of Great Canadians or Great Canadian Writers, just as they do now. (Interestingly, the 1924 list of the ten greatest Canadians put together by the *Maple Leaf Magazine* consisted entirely of men, while exactly eighty years later, CBC Television launched an identical search, and the 1.2 million audience members who voted came up, once again, with an exclusively male list.)

The interwar years saw the establishment of many of the enduring institutions of Canadian literary culture, notably Canadian Book Week (1921), the Canadian Authors Association (1921) and the Governor General's Award (1936). Famous authors were mobilised in support of these initiatives: for example, during the first Canadian Book Week, L. M. Montgomery gave talks in Toronto schools and bookshops to audiences of up to 1,500.[11] Montgomery is one of the four early twentieth-century stars discussed by Lorraine York in *Canadian Literary Celebrity*: the others are Pauline Johnson, Mazo de la Roche and Stephen Leacock. Their careers reveal, as York demonstrates, that early twentieth-century authors struggled as much as Atwood and Shields with the images of themselves which circulated in the media, and with conflicted discourses of publicity and privacy, the aesthetic and the commercial, prestige and popularity.

Unlike today's writers, though, the generation which flourished in the early decades of the twentieth century did not receive consecration through academic study, or see their books adopted as school texts. In his 1973 retrospect of trends in teaching, Desmond Pacey dates the earliest university course in English-Canadian literature to 1906,[12] but subsequent development was slow. Selected texts began to be included on general survey courses, and a few specialist courses were taught intermittently during the interwar years, but, as Pacey notes, by 1948 there were still only two universities which regularly offered courses focusing solely on Canadian literature. The subject did not begin to be studied or researched more widely until the second half of the century, and although the 1970s and 1980s saw an explosion of interest, Canadian studies continued to be regarded by traditionalists as a field attractive only to mediocre scholars. This attitude reveals the residual power of the imperial educational project, which sought to socialise colonised subjects according to British norms by teaching English literature throughout the empire.

In the face of this ideology, as Margaret Atwood wrote in *Survival* (1972), the teaching of Canadian literature became 'a political act'.[13] Cynthia Sugars reflects:

> Like the institutionalization of English literature in the nine-teenth century, and later of American literature (and, more recently, postcolonial literatures of various regions and nationalities), the institutionalized study of Canadian litera-ture was a topic that provoked fierce resistance and contesta-tion. At the turn of the twenty-first century, when postcolonial revisionings and pedagogical interpretations of the discipline of English literature have become more readily accepted, it is perhaps too easy to forget the radical, anti-colonial roots of the discipline of Canadian literature.[14]

Sugars's essay forms the introduction to her collection *Home-Work: Postcolonialism, Pedagogy and Canadian Literature* (2004), which brings together thirty critics with an interest in reflecting on pedagogy, particularly the impact of postcolonial perspectives on classroom practice. Projects such as this demonstrate that, in the field of Canadian literary studies, teaching and research are increas-ingly conceived as interdependent and mutually sustaining.

Canadian literature was first taught in English departments, sub-verting from within the accepted canon of 'English' literature, and it is most often still taught under that rubric. But the growing pop-ularity of interdisciplinary approaches has influenced the ways in which Canadian literature is read, because the literary context, tra-ditions and norms against which the texts are considered alter according to the disciplinary location of the scholar or student. A critic working within the framework of postcolonial studies will compare Canadian texts with literature from other former colonies, while critics and students based in departments of English or American studies will be more likely to use implicit or explicit com-parisons with the British and American canons. In addition, different theoretical approaches such as those introduced in this book (theories of space and place, of desire and sexuality, or of the relationship between history and literature) will of course lead to varied interpretations of Canadian writing. Particular texts and authors may also be taught across a range of literature syllabuses: Margaret Atwood, for example, features on degree-level courses in women's writing, science fiction, postmodernism and ecocriticism, as well as on Canadian or postcolonial literature modules. Canadian literature in the twenty-first century is a vibrant, heterogeneous and expanding discipline which forges productive connections across academic and reading communities.

This Conclusion is not, in fact, conclusive. It deliberately avoids summing up the argument of the preceding chapters, or reaching some final, coherent position on Canadian literature. In keeping with the purpose of this book, it seeks rather to identify current critical debates and questions, and point to some of the most promising areas of current and future research. It is not even the last section of the book: the remaining pages offer suggestions for further primary and secondary reading, together with sets of questions which may be used for seminar discussion or essay writing. This book, then finishes with a movement outwards, into the literally endless possibilities for reading, talking and thinking about Canadian literature.

NOTES

1. For example, the three-volume *History of the Book in Canada*, a bilingual history with associated electronic resources, or the web-disseminated *Beyond the Book*, which focuses on contemporary mass reading events. See http://www.hbic.library.utoronto.ca/ and http://www.beyondthebookproject.org/.
2. Graham Huggan, *The Postcolonial Exotic: Marketing the Margins* (London: Routledge, 2001), p. xii.
3. Ibid., p. xiii.
4. Sarah Corse, *Nationalism and Literature: The Politics of Culture in Canada and the United States* (Cambridge: Cambridge University Press, 1997), p. 100.
5. Smaro Kamboureli, 'The Culture of Celebrity and National Pedagogy', in *Home-Work: Postcolonialism, Pedagogy and*

Canadian Literature, ed. Cynthia Sugars (Ottawa: University of Ottawa Press, 2004), pp. 35–55 (p. 36).

6. Danielle Fuller and DeNel Rehberg Sedo, 'Mass Reading, New Knowledge? Reading for Community in Contemporary Southern Ontario', presentation delivered at Material Cultures and Creation of Knowledge conference, University of Edinburgh, July 2005, p. 5. Available at http://www.beyondthebookproject.org/.

7. Joe Moran, *Star Authors: Literary Celebrity in America* (London: Pluto, 2000), pp. 3–4.

8. See Pierre Bourdieu, *The Field of Cultural Production: Essays on Art and Literature*, ed. Randal Johnson (Cambridge: Polity, 1993).

9. See Huggan, *Postcolonial Exotic*; Lorraine York, *Canadian Literary Celebrity* (Toronto: University of Toronto Press, 2007).

10. Lisa Hayden, 'The Passage of Fame: Margaret Atwood, Carol Shields and Canadian Literary Celebrity', in *The Politics and Poetics of Passage in Canadian and Australian Culture and Fiction*, ed. Charlotte Sturgess (Nantes: CRINI, 2006), pp. 57–75 (p. 57).

11. See Faye Hammill, '"A new and exceedingly brilliant star": L. M. Montgomery, *Anne of Green Gables* and Early Hollywood', *Modern Language Review*, 101 (2006), 653–71.

12. Desmond Pacey, 'The Study of Canadian Literature', *Journal of Canadian Fiction*, 2: 2 (1973), 67–72 (p. 68).

13. Margaret Atwood, *Survival: A Thematic Guide to Canadian Literature* (Toronto: Anansi, 1972), p. 14.

14. Cynthia Sugars, 'Postcolonial Pedagogy and the Impossibility of Teaching: Outside in the (Canadian Literature) Classroom', in *Home-Work*, ed. Sugars, pp. 1–33 (p. 6).

Student Resources

ELECTRONIC RESOURCES AND REFERENCE SOURCES

Electronic resources in Canadian studies are rich and rapidly developing, which is particularly advantageous for those without access to substantial library collections. Electronic text archives alleviate the problems of obtaining Canadian texts outside Canada, but copyright restrictions mean that most such archives are limited to pre-twentieth-century material. Some Canadian texts are mounted individually on dedicated sites and may be located through a general web search engine, but these are more likely to contain errors than are texts mounted within large-scale digitisation projects.

Electronic texts

Canadian Poetry: An Electronic Resource
http://www.uwo.ca/english/canadianpoetry/
Features four valuable anthologies of pre-twentieth-century writing: Early Writing in Canada (canonical poetry and prose), Early Canadian Long Poems; The Confederation Poets; and Poems in Early Canadian Newspapers.

'Canadian Poetry' in Literature Online
http://collections.chadwyck.co.uk/

A textbase containing more than 19,000 English-Canadian poems dating from the seventeenth to the early twentieth centuries. A small number of contemporary poets are also represented.

Project Gutenberg
http://www.gutenberg.org/
The original repository of free online books, which now includes numerous Canadian texts.

Critical sources and literary reference sites

Canada Reads
http://www.cbc.ca/canadareads/
Website for the popular radio book debate, offering a reader's guide and various feature pages for each book discussed.

Canadian Poetry: An Electronic Resource
http://www.uwo.ca/english/canadianpoetry/
This substantial site contains a full-text archive of the journal *Canadian Poetry: Studies, Documents, Reviews* from 1977 to 2003, a set of articles by the respected critic D. M. R. Bentley, and four anthologies of poetry and prose (see under 'Electronic Texts' above).

Canadian Women Poets
http://www.brocku.ca/canadianwomenpoets/
A useful factual source which covers more than sixty women poets, providing for each a short biography, lists of primary texts and awards, and good bibliographies of secondary material.

Northwest Passages
http://www.nwpassages.com/author.asp
A site sponsored by an online Canadian literature bookstore, which includes detailed profiles of more than twenty modern authors, a guide to literary awards in Canada, and a large set of links.

Postcolonial Web
http://www.postcolonialweb.org/

A well-established resource which includes factual pages, images, short reference articles, critical discussions, and selections from theory and literature. The site is divided by theme (authors, theory, history, politics, religion, gender, diasporas) and by country, and provides a bibliography and numerous links.

History and context

About Canada
http://www.mta.ca/faculty/arts/canadian_studies/english/
    about/
Mount Allison University's Canadian Studies site, offering online publications, detailed study guides and annotated bibliographies on key topics in the field, including Canada's Native peoples, multiculturalism in Canada, Canada's cities and the artistic life of Canada.

Canada in the Making
http://www.canadiana.org/citm/index_e.html
A history project developed from the Early Canadiana Online collection. Contains primary sources, thematic narratives on specific topics, links, images and maps.

The History of Canada
http://www.linksnorth.com/canada-history/
Basic but clear, providing explanation of key topics and events.

The Jesuit Relations and Allied Documents
http://puffin.creighton.edu/jesuit/relations/
The full text of this invaluable historical source, downloadable in scanned sections.
Sections of the *Relations* are also available in a facsimile page format in the open access section of Early Canadiana Online:
http://www.canadiana.org/ECO/mtq

Glossaries

Canadiana Glossary
http://www.canadiana.org/citm/glossaire/glossaire1_e.html

Part of a site developed from the Early Canadiana Online collection, this glossary defines 200 terms relevant to Canadian studies.

The Imperial Archive: Key Concepts in Postcolonial Studies
http://www.qub.ac.uk/schools/SchoolofEnglish/imperial/key-concepts/key-concepts.htm
A useful page offering discursive accounts of central terms, with illustrations and references.

General reference

The Canadian Encyclopedia
http://www.canadianencyclopedia.ca/
The freely accessible online version of an influential print encyclopedia. Ideal for looking up historical events, contemporary terms, authors and individual texts. Up to date and trustworthy.

Dictionary of Canadian Biography Online
http://www.biographi.ca/EN/
Extremely authoritative.

The Atlas of Canada
http://atlas.nrcan.gc.ca/site/english/
Generates maps in response to keyword searches.

Statistics Canada
http://www.statcan.ca/start.html
Offers authoritative summary tables and detailed data on a range of subjects, including populations and community profiles (drawn from census returns), education and literacy, social conditions, theatre performances and attendances, and profits generated in cultural industries.

Library catalogues and archive hubs

Archives Canada
http://www.archivescanada.ca/english/index.html

The official site of the Canadian Archival Information Network provides a fully searchable database of material in over 800 collections in Canada.

Libraries and Archives Canada
http://www.collectionscanada.ca/index-e.html
Offers access to the catalogue of the National Library of Canada, which is the best place to check references for books. See also the Electronic Collection, a virtual library of books and journals:
http://epe.lac-bac.gc.ca/

Print reference sources

Ashcroft, Bill, Griffiths, Gareth and Tiffin, Helen, *Post-Colonial Studies: The Key Concepts* (London: Routledge, 2000). The 1998 edition was titled *Key Concepts in Post-Colonial Studies*.
Benson, Eugene and Toye, William (eds), *The Oxford Companion to Canadian Literature*, 2nd edn (Toronto: Oxford University Press, 1997).
Gough, Barry M., *Historical Dictionary of Canada* (Lanham, MD: Scarecrow, 1999).
Hayes, Derek, *Historical Atlas of Canada: A Thousand Years of Canada's History in Maps* (Vancouver: Douglas and McIntyre, 2002).
New, W. H. (ed.), *Encyclopedia of Literature in Canada* (Toronto: University of Toronto Press, 2002).

QUESTIONS FOR DISCUSSION

Chapter 1: Ethnicity, Race, Colonisation

General

In what ways do Canadian literary texts resist racist stereotyping? What narrative or dramatic strategies do writers use to render the orality of First Nations culture?

How useful is the concept of hybridity in reading colonial and post-colonial texts?
How do categories of gender interact with categories of race and nation in the literature discussed in this chapter?

Brooke, *History of Emily Montague*

How does Brooke's narrative link the sentimental story and the Canadian theme? Can the romances in the novel be understood as political?
Dermot McCarthy argues that 'Brooke's feminist agenda seems to clash at times with the imperial-colonial ideology that otherwise disciplines it'. What (if any) evidence can be found for this contention in the text?
Does Brooke offer multiple perspectives on the racial others she describes, or do her various letter-writers converge on one basic view?
How do the scenes set in England supplement or alter the meanings of the book as a whole?

Tekahionwake/Johnson, *selected poetry*

How does Johnson contest or reinscribe the image of the 'Indian' as picturesque?
What is the significance of naming in her work?
What perspectives on female political power are offered in Johnson's texts?
How does her nature poetry resist or appropriate European literary forms and traditions?

Kogawa, *Obasan*

In what ways is *Obasan* a narrative of feminine experience?
What different methods of recovering the past are explored in the text? What does the novel suggest about the ways in which the past experience of Japanese-Canadians will shape their future?
What is the significance of Naomi's dreams?

What are the effects of Kogawa's inclusion of Japanese words in the text?

Highway, *Rez Sisters*

In what ways do the sisters imitate and/or reject White behaviour?
What significance does Toronto have for the characters on the reservation?
Is this a feminist play? How do the characters transgress the conventional boundaries of gender?
Is Nanabush a benign or a threatening figure?

King, *Green Grass Running Water*

How are colonialist and Christian ideologies interconnected in the text?
Why do the western films in the novel have to be repeatedly 'fixed' by the old Indians?
Is it possible to decide whether Coyote is female or male? Does it matter?
How, and with what effects, does King evoke and parody *Moby-Dick*, *Robinson Crusoe* and *The Last of the Mohicans*?

Chapter 2: Wilderness, Cities, Regions

General

To what extent is wilderness presented as historical by the authors discussed in this chapter?
In Canadian literary texts, does love for the city entail rejection of the wilderness, or vice versa, or can one character identify with both types of environment?
How useful is it to read Canadian texts in relation to the region or province in which they are set, or in which their author grew up?
How are relationships between Native Canadians and natural or urban environments characterised in fiction from different periods?
In what ways does the forest become gendered in Canadian literary texts? Is the city also a gendered space?

Montgomery, *Anne of Green Gables*

How does Anne's romantic imagination influence the novel's depiction of Prince Edward Island?
Should *Anne of Green Gables* be read as adult or children's literature?
How does Anne's community exert a disciplinary influence over her?
How does Anne's reading affect her experience and interpretation of her life?

Wilson, *Swamp Angel*

What symbolic meanings attach to the Swamp Angel revolver?
What do Mrs Severance and/or Mr Cunningham represent for Maggie?
How is Vancouver presented in the novel?
In what ways does Ethel Wilson experiment with narrative form and perspective?

Shields, *Republic of Love*

In what ways does Shields reaffirm and/or subvert the conventions of literary romance in *The Republic of Love*?
What meanings attach to mermaids in the text?
To what extent is the portrait of Winnipeg a realist one?
What perspectives does the narrative offer on the language of love?

Davies, *Cunning Man*

In what ways does Toronto change over the course of Jonathan Hullah's life?
How does Esme, as Jonathan's listener, shape or influence the story he tells?
What clues, if any, hint at Charlie's murder of Father Hobbes in the sections of the narrative which precede his revelation to Jonathan?
Could *The Cunning Man* be considered a religious novel?

Munro, *'Wilderness Station,'* and Atwood, *'Wilderness Tips'*

How does the link between landscape and the female body work in these stories?
How do the stories manipulate narrative perspective, and with what effects?
How does the city function in 'Wilderness Tips'?
Can we be certain as to which is the 'true story' in 'A Wilderness Station'?

Chapter 3: Desire

General

What are the effects of intertwining the erotic and the violent in the books discussed in this chapter?
What relationships between desire and place are explored in these texts?
How do issues surrounding race, ethnic minorities or immigration inflect representations of sexual love in Canadian texts?
In what ways do Canadian writers deconstruct the supposed antithesis between homosexuality and heterosexuality?

Ostenso, Wild Geese

How do questions of ethnicity affect the romantic, familial and community relationships which the book explores? Are ethnic identities occluded or made explicit?
Does the relationship between Lind and Mark have a sensual aspect, or is theirs a purely romantic connection?
In what ways does the prairie environment reflect and/or determine the characters' emotions in *Wild Geese*?
How is the narrative shaped by the dynamic between literary realism and romance or Gothic?

Glassco, Memoirs of Montparnasse

In his journal, Glassco described his book as one-quarter lies. Should we consider his book a novel rather than an autobiography?

How do the references to 'Indians' and 'Eskimos' function in the text?

Is *Memoirs of Montparnasse* about the development of a writer or of a sensualist?

What is Glassco's narrator seeking to escape from, or attain, by migrating to Paris?

Cohen, *Beautiful Losers*

How might Catherine's masochistic practices be connected to Edith's and F.'s self-abasement? What are the implications of this?

Margot Northey comments that *Beautiful Losers* fails in its attempt to express mysticism through the grotesque. Do you agree?

What is the relationship between the organic and the mechanical, or the body and the machine, in *Beautiful Losers*?

To what extent are all the female characters in the book inter-changeable?

Michaels, *Fugitive Pieces*

Méira Cook argues that the love scenes in *Fugitive Pieces* 'fail to move the reader because the elegiac tone in which they are described has already been used to effect in scenes of violence and horror'. Do you agree?

Athos believes 'there's no thing that does not yearn'. What forms of yearning are explored in the text, and how are they interrelated?

How might the chapter titles affect readings of *Fugitive Pieces*? Why are some of them repeated?

What perspectives on Canada are offered in Michaels's novel? Does Toronto become identified with home by the main characters?

Brand, *Land to Light On*

How do Brand's shifts between first-, second- and third-person voices and pronouns influence our readings of the poems? To what extent are the speakers aligned with and/or detached from the pro-tagonists or addressees?

How does *Land to Light On* map the geographies of the Caribbean diaspora?

What are the different meanings of 'land' and 'landing' to emerge from the collection?

How does Brand's technique of listing, or making 'inventories', contribute to her poetic and political projects? How does this compare with Leonard Cohen's listing?

Chapter 4: Histories and Stories

General

How do the books chosen for this chapter negotiate between imagination and research in their reconstructions of the Canadian past?

How do the narrative structures of the texts relate to their preoccupation with memory?

How do the themes of language, translation, and the relationship between word and world emerge in these books? Why should they be particularly important in texts concerned with history?

What is the significance of the pioneer heritage for the authors considered here?

Pratt, Brébeuf and His Brethren

In a postcolonial context, can Jean de Brébeuf still be read as a hero of Canadian history? What are the problems inherent in such a reading?

Does the poem dehumanise the Huron and Iroquois people? Is there any hint that the practices of the Jesuits might also be considered barbaric and/or superstitious?

How many different voices are included in the poem? Do the voices of the various missionaries offer a unified perspective or a series of contrasting visions?

Does the poem finally confirm a Christian concept of sacrifice and redemption?

Atwood, *Journals of Susanna Moodie*

Atwood presents the 'journals' in a modern register, rather than an imitation of Victorian literary style. What is the effect of this? (Compare the poems with extracts from Moodie's own books.)

How is Gothic imagery used to explore the terrifying elements of emigration and the Canadian past in *The Journals of Susanna Moodie*?

Do the poems affirm or question Susanna Moodie's iconic status in Canadian history?

What perspectives on wilderness are offered in the *Journals*?

Laurence, *Diviners*

How many different narrative modes are used in the novel (for example, third-person narrative, song and so on)? What might be the purposes and effects of Laurence's complex narrative technique?

What is the significance of the Highland clearances to the novel? How important is Morag's Scottish heritage to her?

What symbolic meanings are invested in Morag's various sexual relationships?

How does the text negotiate between Christie's, Jules's and Morag's versions of the Riel story?

Marlatt, *Ana Historic*

How do the women in the novel relate to the reproductive functions of their bodies?

How does Marlatt explore the idea of gender as performance in *Ana Historic*?

In what ways does the novel explore imperialism?

Is race a significant preoccupation in this text?

Ondaatje, *In the Skin of a Lion*

What perspectives on immigration and immigrant labour does *In the Skin of a Lion* offer?

What is the significance of the role of 'searcher' in the book?

What forms does Ondaatje's preoccupation with language take in the text?

What meanings are invested in the building of the city in Ondaatje's narrative of Canadian history, and how does his book compare in this respect with Marlatt's?

Questions for reading Canadian literature postcolonially

How do 'standard' English and new 'Englishes' interact in Canadian writing, and to what extent does the use of non-standard forms and non-English words constitute a form of resistance?

In what ways are the mythologies, languages, histories and cultural practices of immigrant or Native ethnic groups erased or made visible, normalised or constructed as 'exotic' in texts produced in Canada?

What kinds of allegories and symbols of colonial/postcolonial power relationships are encoded into Canadian literary texts?

How did White settlers and colonisers from Europe seek to impose their political and imaginative perspectives on the New World through writing, and what forms of resistance did they encounter?

How does Canada's status as both colonial agent and subject inform Canadian texts and complicate the attempt to read them in post-colonial frameworks?

To what extent can the conventional practices of literary education, criticism and canon-making reinforce or challenge the power structures which determine White Canadians' relationship with Native peoples, immigrant groups and Europeans?

In what ways can literary texts exploring Canada's past work to decolonise the imagination (or indeed, the reverse), or to rewrite history from a postcolonial perspective?

How far does the political commitment of postcolonialism conflict with the supposedly apolitical project of the postmodern?

ALTERNATIVE PRIMARY TEXTS FOR CHAPTER TOPICS

Chapter 1: Ethnicity, Race, Colonisation

Campbell, Maria, *Halfbreed* (1973). Influential autobiography of a Métis woman.

Clarke, George Elliott, *Whylah Falls* (1990). Verse novel about an imagined Black community in Nova Scotia.

Joe, Rita, *Poems of Rita Joe* (1978). Poetry concerned with (among other things) Mi'kmaq tradition and experiences of racism and poverty.

Ricci, Nino, *Lives of the Saints* (1990). The first novel in a trilogy, set partly in Italy and partly on a boat carrying immigrants to Canada. A major best-seller.

Sears, Djanet, *Afrika Solo* (1990). Canada's first published stage play by a person of African descent, which explores the African roots of diasporic populations in Canada.

Wah, Fred, *Diamond Grill* (1996). Novel about interracial inheritance, with a protagonist whose parents are a Chinese-Scots-Irishman and a Swedish-born Canadian woman.

Chapter 2: Wilderness, Cities, Regions

Clark, Joan, *Swimming toward the Light* (1990). Linked series of stories about a woman learning to survive alone. Settings include a Nova Scotian beach, New Brunswick and the west coast.

Findley, Timothy, *Headhunter* (1993). Novel in which the characters from *Heart of Darkness* are set free in Toronto, which effectively becomes a jungle.

Grove, F. P., *Settlers of the Marsh* (1925). Novel of prairie pioneering, which shocked contemporaries with its treatment of sexuality.

Gunnars, Kristjana, *Silence of the Country* (2002). Poems about a Scandinavian immigrant writing herself into the physical and psychical landscape of British Columbia.

Majzels, Robert, *City of Forgetting* (1997). Novel which populates contemporary Montreal with historical, mythological and literary figures.

Taylor, Timothy, *Stanley Park* (2001). A novel of modern Vancouver, centring on a young chef, an unsolved murder mystery and the homeless of Stanley Park.

Chapter 3: Desire

Crawford, Isabella Valancy, *Malcolm's Katie: A Love Story* (1884). Much-discussed romantic poem, containing striking erotic and political elements.

Davies, Robertson, *The Rebel Angels* (1981). Novel set in a traditional university, with a rich, allusive storyline concerning scholarly and erotic passions.

Engel, Marian, *Bear* (1976). Novel in which a woman goes to live alone in the wilderness, and has an affair with a bear.

Macdonald, Ann-Marie, *Goodnight Desdemona (Good Morning, Juliet)* (1989). Play which rewrites Shakespeare from a (lesbian) female point of view, exploring issues of authorship.

Symons, Scott, *Combat Journal for Place D'Armes* (1967). Multilayered autobiographical fiction set in Montreal, controversial on publication owing to its intensely homoerotic atmosphere.

Turner, Michael, *The Pornographer's Poem* (1999). Novel exploring the sexual ambiguities of 1970s Vancouver.

Chapter 4: Histories and Stories

Johnston, Wayne, *The Colony of Unrequited Dreams* (1998). Fictional epic set in early twentieth-century Newfoundland, centring on the intertwined stories of a politician and a journalist.

Kroetsch, Robert, *Badlands* (1975). Novel in which a woman travels into the Alberta wilderness, retracing an expedition made by her palaeontologist father in 1916.

Lee, SKY, *Disappearing Moon Café* (1990). Novel exploring the history of a family from Vancouver's Chinatown.

Mojica, Monique, *Princess Pocahontas and the Blue Spots* (1991). Play for two female actresses, examining the history of Indigenous women.

Urquhart, Jane, *Away* (1993). Novel telling the story of three generations of an Irish family whose ancestors emigrated to Canada
in the 1840s.
Wiebe, Rudy, *The Temptations of Big Bear* (1973). Epic novel of the
nineteenth-century Canadian west, centring on a Plains Cree
nation and their heroic leader.

GLOSSARY

Aboriginal

Of Indigenous ancestry - that is, descended from peoples who
inhabited Canada before European contact. This term usually
includes the Métis and Inuit.

Acadia

French colony (now NS, PEI, NB, eastern QC), first settled in 1604
and ceded to Britain in 1713. When conflict with France over colonial possessions escalated in the early 1750s, Governor Charles
Lawrence demanded an oath of loyalty to Britain from the
Acadians. On their refusal, he deported all 12,000. A thousand went
into hiding; the rest left, but many died on journeys to other
colonies. A large group settled in Louisiana (Cajuns).

Assimilation

Absorption of a minority into a dominant group. In the mid-nine-
teenth century, Britain's segregationist colonial policies began to be
replaced by an assimilationist approach, designed to socialise the
Native peoples of its colonies according to White norms. In
Canada, this continued into the twentieth century through educational and social policy.

Band

The designation for Aboriginal clans and families in the Indian Act (1876).

Canada East and Canada West *see* Upper Canada and Lower Canada

Canadian Pacific Railway

Transcontinental railway between Vancouver and Montreal, with several branches. Promised to BC when it entered Confederation, the railway was instrumental in the settlement of western Canada. The CPR was incorporated in 1881 and, despite being mired in political and economic conflicts, the railway was completed in 1885. The CPR diversified into other areas, particularly communications and tourism: it owned hotels and dining halls along the route, and later developed steamships and airlines internationally. Passenger traffic declined after the Second World War, and the railway is now primarily a freight line, though it remains an icon of Canadian nationhood.

Confederation

Union of four of the BNA colonies on 1 July 1867, partly motivated by the American Civil War, which foregrounded controversies over the powers of states in relation to those of the Union. Confederation was planned at the 1864 intercolonial conferences in Charlottetown, Quebec, and London, England; the original project was Maritime union, but the final result was a dominion with four provinces (ON, QC, NB and NS) and Ottawa as capital. New provinces were subsequently created in prairie regions, and the other BNA colonies gradually joined Confederation, the last being NL in 1949. The title 'dominion', meaning a self-governing territory within the British Empire (or, after 1926, within the Commonwealth of Nations), was retained until 1947.

Cree

The largest Aboriginal nation in Canada, with members living from the prairies to Quebec. The name originated with a group living near James Bay, called the Kiristinon by the French.

Diaspora

Derived from the ancient Greek *speiro*, to sow, and *dia*, over, term for migration for purposes of colonisation. It later came to refer to the collective expulsion of ethnic or racial groups, who subsequently maintained some form of community or cultural unity while in exile. Used primarily in relation to the Jews, diaspora is now also applied to other banished and dispersed peoples. In Canada, important diasporic populations include South Asian, Scandinavian, Caribbean, Chinese, Japanese and Ukrainian, among others.

Durham Report *see* Rebellions of 1837 and 1838

Federation

A state comprising a federal government, with responsibility for national and international matters, and a number of second-tier constituent state governments, with responsibility for more localised affairs. In practice, areas of policy responsibility and authority often overlap between the two levels of government. In Canada there are ten provinces, together with three territories that have a limited range of constitutional rights and policy competences.

First Nations

Collective name for those descended from Canada's earliest inhabitants. 'First Nations' replaces the earlier term 'Indian', and excludes the culturally distinct Inuit and Métis. Many Aboriginal groups view themselves as nations, but are not recognised as such by the federal government.

Gothic

In literary terms, a genre of writing which seeks to evoke horror and terror, often through heightened imagery involving entrapment, monstrosity and transformation, together with uncanny effects. In Canada, Gothic has always been an important form: many colonial texts rendered the apparently hostile wilderness using Gothic imagery, and later writers have responded to this tradition, creating new forms of terror in urban or small-town locations.

Historiographic metafiction

Term coined by Linda Hutcheon to describe a form of fiction which flourished in Canada and elsewhere in the later twentieth century. Historiographic metafictions are texts which engage with the past while also reflecting on the possibilities and limits of historical knowledge.

Hudson's Bay Company

Canada's oldest trading company, chartered in 1670 in Britain. It held a monopoly over the fur trade in the vast Hudson's Bay watershed, known as Rupert's Land (including all of present-day Minnesota, most of SK and southern AB, and parts of QC, ON, NWT and NU) until 1870, when the Canadian government annexed the area. The company continues today as a department store.

Huron

A confederacy of five Aboriginal tribes who, during the seventeenth century, lived in villages in what is now Simcoe County, ON, engaging in agriculture and trade. Their enemies, the Iroquois, defeated and scattered them in 1649, and small groups settled in different locations in eastern Canada.

Hybridity

Originally a derogatory term referring to blackening or sullying and used in the context of racial miscegenation, now recuperated as a progressive term. In general usage, it means the mingling of two cultures or identities in a multicultural society; in recent postcolonial theory, hybridity is reconceived in terms of a recognition that struggle between self and 'other' is a condition of all culture, and that minorities are continually challenging dominant cultures.

Inuit

Eight tribal groupings in Alaska, Greenland and the Arctic regions of northern Canada (the territory of Nunavut), who speak related languages. They arrived in Alaska about 2,000 BC, displacing earlier inhabitants, and later resisted Norse invasions. The Inuit were known as Eskimos by European colonists.

Iroquois

A confederacy of Aboriginal peoples who originated in what is now northern New York State. They fought with the French in the seventeenth century, but later signed treaties with both the French and British, aligning themselves with the British in the American Revolution. The Iroquois became known as the Six Nations after an additional tribe joined the original five in the early eighteenth century.

Jesuits

Members of the Company of Jesus, a mendicant order of priests founded by St Ignatius Loyola. When Pope Paul III approved the order in 1540, he Latinised the name to Societas Jesu (Society of Jesus). Its members sought to propagate the Catholic faith in Asia and the Americas, as well as closer to home, and were active in education. They arrived in New France in 1625.

Land claims

A legal process enabled by the federal government which recognises and seeks to resolve Aboriginal rights and land titles under treaties signed by their ancestors. The treaties guaranteed government assistance, reserve land and hunting rights, but in return Aboriginal peoples ceded ownership of large tracts of land.

Lower Canada *see* Upper and Lower Canada

Maritime Provinces

Provinces of the eastern seaboard: Newfoundland and Labrador, Nova Scotia, New Brunswick, and Prince Edward Island.

Métis (also Metis)

In non-Native or non-Canadian usage, a term describing people of mixed Native and European origin. Generally, only those of French and Aboriginal descent refer to themselves as 'Métis'; individuals of other ancestries use their Aboriginal affiliation only, or a term such as 'English-Ojibway', rather than 'Metis'. Mixed-race groups have flourished throughout Canada, and the Métis (in the narrower sense) established a distinct cultural identity along the St Lawrence and also in the western prairies, where they came into conflict with the Canadian government over land rights (*see* Riel rebellions). Their group rights were formally recognised in the Constitution Act (1982). The noun *métissage* refers to the creation of a new identity by the mixing of two cultures.

New France

The area of North America controlled by France between the early sixteenth century and 1763. French explorers claimed territory in what is now Canada in the 1520s and 1530s, and fur trading posts and fishing communities were established in the early seventeenth century, notably at Quebec and Port-Royal. Settlement expanded along the St Lawrence, and French explorers and traders voyaged towards the prairies and also down the Mississippi, establishing the colony of Louisiana at its mouth in the 1680s. Louisiana was later ceded to Spain, while France's other colonies were gradually won by Britain, and after 1763 France retained only the tiny islands of St Pierre and Miquelon, as a fishing base.

Northwest Rebellion *see* Riel rebellions

October Crisis

On 5 and 10 October 1970 the separatist Front de la Libération du Québec kidnapped James Cross, British trade commissioner in Montreal, and Pierre Laporte, Quebec minister of labour and immigration. The provincial government requested army assistance, and, controversially, the federal government proclaimed a state of 'apprehended insurrection' under the War Measures Act. Laporte was found dead on 17 October, and those responsible were later arrested.

Ojibwa (or Ojibway or Chippewa)

Aboriginal nation originating in the Georgian Bay and eastern Lake Superior regions. The Ojibwa sided with the French during the fur-trade competition with the British. Subsequently, they moved west, eventually becoming British allies during the American Revolution and War of 1812.

Postcolonial

Relating to formerly colonised countries, most often used in reference to countries which were part of the British Empire. Broadly speaking, postcolonial literature encompasses writing produced in these countries in the era since the end of empire.

Postmodernism

Famously defined by Jean-François Lyotard as 'an incredulity towards metanarratives'. 'Postmodern' can be applied to all sorts of cultural products, including art, architecture and cinema, and in literary terms it usually indicates a certain kind of experimental or eclectic late twentieth- or twenty-first-century text. Postmodern writing tends to reject or modify the realist techniques, ordered morality and structured forms and genres of earlier literature because they impose an artificial coherence on the chaos and contingency of human experience.

Potlatch

Ceremony practised by Aboriginal peoples in north-western coastal North America. Assembled for purposes of either celebration or mourning, the potlatch centres on the exchange of gifts between members of several villages and tribes. The status of the gift-giver varies according to the generosity of the gifts. The potlatch, together with the sun dance, an annual gathering for thanksgiving and sacrifice, was banned by the Canadian government from 1884 to 1951 as part of a policy of cultural and religious assimilation.

Prairie Provinces

Landlocked provinces of central and western Canada: Alberta, Manitoba and Saskatchewan.

Quiet Revolution

Period of rapid social change in Quebec, under Jean Lesage's Liberal government (1960–6). Conservative values were eroded through modernisation, increased taxation and state intervention, and the consolidation of the welfare state, while a process of secularisation undermined the authority of the Catholic Church. More active Quebec nationalism, and also separatism, developed.

Rebellions of 1837 and 1838

Armed uprisings in Upper and Lower Canada, following the government's failure to respond to residents' demands for more accountable systems of governance. The rebellions were suppressed by forces loyal to the government, but led to Lord Durham's *Report on the Affairs in British North America*, which recommended uniting the Canadas under a self-governing legislature.

Reserve (or reservation)

Land set aside by the federal government for status Indians. Reservations are government-owned but managed by the bands living there.

Riel rebellions

Two protests against Dominion land policies in the prairies, known as the Red River Rebellion (1870) and the Northwest Rebellion (1885). The Métis leader Louis Riel assembled First Nations, Métis and discontented White settlers in a conflict with government and volunteer forces. The first rebellion led to the creation of Manitoba, but in the second Riel was defeated and hanged for treason.

Seven Years' War

Conflict lasting from 1756 to 1763, in which Britain, Hanover and Prussia fought against France, Austria, Sweden, Saxony, Russia and eventually Spain. Europe was the main theatre, but France and Britain also battled for control of North America. The last significant French force was defeated in 1760, and the Treaty of Paris (1763) permanently surrendered France's remaining territories (mainly now QC, PEI, Cape Breton) to Britain.

Status Indians

Those Aboriginal peoples whose legal rights and obligations are defined by the Indian Act (1951). Non-status Indians are of Aboriginal ancestry but have given up their status rights voluntarily or through marriage with someone who is not a status Indian. In 1985 the Act was amended to extend Indian status to all Aboriginal women, their children and Aboriginals who were already enfranchised.

Transculture

A term invented by Fernando Ortiz, a scholar of Afro-Cuban culture. In French-Canadian literary theory, *la transculture* (or transculture, in its increasingly prevalent anglicised form) is an umbrella term for First Nations writing, migrant writing and *métissage* texts. Transcultural writers draw on at least two different cultures, and literary study in this field focuses on mediation and exchange rather than resistance.

Transnationalism

The increased flow of people, capital, goods, ideas and information across national boundaries. Transnationalism results from globalisation, cross-border governance mechanisms, migration, and improved communication and transport technologies. The concepts of multiple locations and of networks - that is, forms of cross-border social, political and economic organisation - are important in understanding transnationalism. In terms of migration, the concept is related to diaspora: while diasporic migration has historically been one-directional and not usually voluntary, in the era of transnationalism, migrations may be part of a chosen lifestyle and result in an ongoing two-way movement and communication between the place of origin and the new location.

Treaty of Paris *see* Seven Years' War

United Empire Loyalists

Migrants to Canada following the American Revolution. About 40,000 loyalists of British, German, Dutch and Iroquois ancestry moved north to the colonies which remained under British control.

Upper Canada and Lower Canada

British provinces created from the colony of Quebec in 1791, and so named because Upper Canada was further up the St Lawrence river. Upper Canada had English law and institutions, and Lower Canada had French forms. The 1841 Act of Union reunited the provinces under one government, renaming them Canada West (now southern Ontario) and Canada East (now southern Quebec).

War of 1812

Conflict lasting from 1812 to 1814 between the USA and Britain, over control of the BNA colonies. Combined British, Canadian and allied 'Indian' forces, though outnumbered, repelled the American invasion. No territory changed hands, but Canada's ties with Britain were strengthened.

GUIDE TO FURTHER READING

Rather than a list of all works cited, this is a guide to key secondary reading for each topic and text.

INTRODUCTION

Canadian literary history and the canon

Blodgett, E. D., *Five-Part Invention: A History of Literary History in Canada* (Toronto: University of Toronto Press, 2003).

Heble, Ajay et al. (eds), *New Contexts of Canadian Criticism* (Peterborough, ON: Broadview, 1997).

Lecker, Robert, *Making it Real: The Canonization of English-Canadian Literature* (Toronto: Anansi, 1995).

Lecker, Robert (ed.), *Canadian Canons: Essays in Literary Value* (Toronto: University of Toronto Press, 1991).

New, W. H., *A History of Canadian Literature*, 2nd edn (Montreal and Kingston: McGill-Queen's University Press, 2003).

Indigenous Canadians

Dickason, Olive, *Canada's First Nations: A History of Founding Peoples from Earliest Times*, 3rd edn (Don Mills, ON: Oxford University Press, 2002).

Edwards, John (ed.), *Language in Canada* (Cambridge: Cambridge University Press, 1998).

Fee, Margery, 'What Use Is Ethnicity to Aboriginal Peoples in Canada?' (1995), repr. in *Unhomely States: Theorizing English-Canadian Postcolonialism*, ed. Cynthia Sugars (Peterborough, ON: Broadview, 2004), pp. 267–76.

Petrone, Penny, *Native Literature in Canada: From the Oral Tradition to the Present* (Toronto: Oxford University Press, 1990).

Van Toorn, Penny, 'Aboriginal Writing', in *The Cambridge Companion to Canadian Literature*, ed. Eva-Marie Kröller (Cambridge: Cambridge University Press, 2004), pp. 22–48.

CHAPTER 1: ETHNICITY, RACE, COLONISATION

Multiculturalism and diaspora

Bannerji, Himani, *The Dark Side of the Nation: Essays on Multiculturalism, Nationalism, and Gender* (Toronto: Canadian Scholars, 2000).

Clifford, James, *Routes: Travel and Translation in the Late Twentieth Century* (Cambridge, MA: Harvard University Press, 1997).

Day, Richard, *Multiculturalism and the History of Canadian Diversity* (Toronto: University of Toronto Press, 2000).

Kamboureli, Smaro, *Scandalous Bodies: Diasporic Literature in English Canada* (Toronto: Oxford University Press, 2000).

Verduyn, Christl (ed.), *Literary Pluralities* (Peterborough, ON: Broadview and *Journal of Canadian Studies*, 1998).

Postcolonial theory and Canadian literature

Brydon, Diana (ed.), *Essays on Canadian Writing*, 56 (1995) [special issue: Testing the Limits: Postcolonial Theories and Canadian Literatures].

Moss, Laura (ed.), *Is Canada Postcolonial? Unsettling Canadian Literature* (Waterloo, ON: Wilfrid Laurier University Press, 2003).

Söderlind, Sylvia, *Margin/Alias: Language and Colonization in Canadian and Quebecois Fiction* (Toronto: University of Toronto Press, 1991).

Sugars, Cynthia (ed.), *Unhomely States: Theorizing English-Canadian Postcolonialism* (Peterborough, ON: Broadview, 2004).

Vautier, Marie, *New World Myth: Postmodernism and Postcolonialism in Canadian Fiction* (Montreal and Kingston: McGill-Queen's University Press, 1998).

Brooke, *History of Emily Montague*

McCarthy, Dermot, 'Sisters under the Mink: The Correspondent Fear in *The History of Emily Montague*', *Essays on Canadian Writing*, 51–52 (1993–4), 340–57.

Moss, Laura, 'Colonialism and Postcolonialism in *The History of Emily Montague*', in *The History of Emily Montague*, ed. Laura Moss (Ottawa: Tecumseh, 2001), pp. 451–9.

Perkins, Pam, 'Imagining Eighteenth-Century Quebec: British Literature and Colonial Rhetoric', in *Is Canada Postcolonial? Unsettling Canadian Literature*, ed. Laura Moss (Waterloo, ON: Wilfrid Laurier University Press, 2003), pp. 151–61.

Tekahionwake/Johnson, selected poetry

Rose, Marilyn J., 'Pauline Johnson: New World Poet', *British Journal of Canadian Studies*, 12: 2 (1997), 298–307.

Strong-Boag, Veronica and Gerson, Carole, *Paddling Her Own Canoe: The Times and Texts of E. Pauline Johnson (Tekahionwake)* (Toronto: University of Toronto Press, 2000).

York, Lorraine, '"Your star": Pauline Johnson and the Tensions of Celebrity Discourse', *Canadian Poetry*, 51 (2002), 8–17.

Kogawa, *Obasan*

Goldman, Marlene, 'A Dangerous Circuit: Loss and the Boundaries of Racialized Subjectivity in Joy Kogawa's *Obasan* and Kerri Sakamoto's *The Electrical Field*', *Modern Fiction Studies*, 48: 2 (2002), 362–88.

Helms, Gabriele, *Challenging Canada: Dialogism and Narrative Techniques in Canadian Novels* (Montreal and Kingston: McGill-Queens University Press, 2003).

Phu, Thy, 'Photographic Memory, Undoing Documentary: Obasan's Selective Sight and the Politics of Visibility', *Essays on Canadian Writing*, 80 (2003), 115–40.

Highway, *Rez Sisters*

Johnston, Denis W., 'Lines and Circles: The "Rez" Plays of Tomson Highway', *Canadian Literature*, 124–5 (1990), 254–64.
Nothof, Anne, 'Cultural Collision and Magical Transformation: The Plays of Tomson Highway', *Studies in Canadian Literature*, 20: 2 (1995), 34–43.
Perkins, Lina, 'Remembering the Trickster in Tomson Highway's *The Rez Sisters*', *Modern Drama*, 45: 2 (2002), 259–69.

King, *Green Grass Running Water*

Davidson, Arnold E., et al., *Border Crossings: Thomas King's Cultural Inversions* (Toronto: University of Toronto Press, 2003).
Kröller, Eva-Marie (ed.), *Canadian Literature*, 161–2 (1999) [special issue: On Thomas King].
Linton, Patricia, '"And Here's How It Happened": Trickster Discourse in Thomas King's *Green Grass, Running Water*', *Modern Fiction Studies*, 45 (1999), 212–34.

CHAPTER 2: WILDERNESS, CITIES, REGIONS

Theorising space and place

Beeler, Karin and Horne, Dee (eds), *Diverse Landscapes: Re-Reading Place across Cultures in Contemporary Canadian Writing* (Prince George: University of Northern British Columbia Press, 1996).
Carter, Erica et al. (eds), *Space and Place: Theories of Identity and Location* (London: Lawrence and Wishart, 1993).
Jarvis, Brian, *Postmodern Cartographies: The Geographical Imagination in Contemporary American Literature* (London: Pluto, 1998).

Jordan, David M., *New World Regionalism: Literature in the Americas* (Toronto: University of Toronto Press, 1994).

Warley, Linda et al. (eds), *Studies in Canadian Literature*, 23: 1 (1998) [special issue: *Writing Canadian Space*].

New perspectives on regionalism and urbanism

Edwards, Justin D. and Douglas Ivison (eds), *Downtown Canada: Writing Canadian Cities* (Toronto: University of Toronto Press, 2005).

Fiamengo, Janice, 'Regionalism and Urbanism', in *The Cambridge Companion to Canadian Literature*, ed. Eva-Marie Kröller (Cambridge: Cambridge University Press, 2004), pp. 241–62.

New, W. H., *Land Sliding: Imagining Space, Presence, and Power in Canadian Writing* (Toronto: University of Toronto Press, 1997).

Riegel, Christian and Wyile, Herb (eds), *A Sense of Place: Re-evaluating Regionalism in Canadian and American Writing* (Edmonton: University of Alberta Press, 1997).

Willmott, Glenn, *Unreal City: Modernity in the Canadian Novel in English* (Montreal and Kingston: McGill-Queen's University Press, 2002).

Studies of individual regions

Atwood, Margaret, *Strange Things: The Malevolent North in Canadian Literature* (Oxford: Clarendon, 1995).

Fuller, Danielle, *Writing the Everyday: Women's Textual Communities in Atlantic Canada* (Montreal and Kingston: McGill-Queen's University Press, 2004).

Keahey, Deborah, *Making It Home: Place in Canadian Prairie Literature* (Winnipeg: University of Manitoba Press, 1998).

Keefer, Janice Kulyk, *Under Eastern Eyes: A Critical Reading of Maritime Fiction* (Toronto: University of Toronto Press, 1987).

Ricou, Laurie, *The Arbutus/Madrone Files: Reading the Pacific Northwest* (Edmonton: NeWest, 2002).

Montgomery, *Anne of Green Gables*

Gammel, Irene (ed.), *Making Avonlea: L. M. Montgomery and Popular Culture* (Toronto: University of Toronto Press, 2002).

Gammel, Irene (ed.), *The Intimate Life of L. M. Montgomery* (Toronto: University of Toronto Press, 2005).

Gammel, Irene and Elizabeth Epperly (eds), *L. M. Montgomery and Canadian Culture* (Toronto: University of Toronto Press, 1999).

Wilson, *Swamp Angel*

Gelfant, Blanche, 'Ethel Wilson's Absent City: A Personal View of Vancouver', *Canadian Literature*, 146 (1995), 9–27.

Holmberg, Merike, 'The Lure of the Wild: Canadian Women's Wilderness Writing and Ethel Wilson's *Swamp Angel*', in *Migration, Preservation and Change*, ed. Jeffrey Kaplan (Helsinki: Renvall Institute, University of Helsinki, 1999), pp. 163–9.

McMullen, Lorraine (ed.), *The Ethel Wilson Symposium* (Ottawa: University of Ottawa Press, 1982).

Shields, *Republic of Love*

Hammill, Faye, '*The Republic of Love* and Popular Romance', in *Carol Shields, Narrative Hunger, and the Possibilities of Fiction*, ed. Ted Eden and Dee Goertz (Toronto: University of Toronto Press, 2003), pp. 61–83.

Nodelman, Perry, 'Living in the Republic of Love: Carol Shields's Winnipeg' (1995), repr. in *Carol Shields: The Arts of a Writing Life*, ed. Neil K. Besner (Winnipeg: Prairie Fire, 2003), pp. 40–55.

Thomas, Clara, 'Carol Shields's *The Republic of Love* and *The Stone Diaries*: "Swerves of Destiny" and "Rings of Light"', in '*Union in Partition': Essays in Honour of Jeanne Delbaere*, ed. Gilbert Debusscher and Marc Maufort (Liege, Belgium: L3-Liege Language and Literature, 1997), pp. 153–60.

Davies, *Cunning Man*

Diamond-Nigh, Lynne, *Robertson Davies: Life, Work, and Criticism* (Toronto: York, 1997).

La Bossière, Camille R. and Morra, Linda M. (eds), *Robertson Davies: A Mingling of Contrarieties* (Ottawa: University of Ottawa Press, 2001).

Sugars, Cynthia, 'The Anatomy of Influence: Robertson Davies's Psychosomatic Medicine', *Mosaic*, 33: 4 (2000), 73–89.

Atwood, 'Wilderness Tips'

Beran, Carol L., 'Strangers within the Gates: Margaret Atwood's *Wilderness Tips*', in *Margaret Atwood's Textual Assassinations: Recent Poetry and Fiction*, ed. Sharon Rose Wilson (Columbus: Ohio State University Press, 2003), pp. 74–87.

Condé, Mary, 'The Male Immigrant in Two Canadian Stories (Alice Munro's "Oranges and Apples" and Margaret Atwood's "Wilderness Tips")', *Kunapipi*, 15: 1 (1993), 103–9.

Howells, Coral Ann, 'Writing Wilderness: Margaret Atwood's "Death by Landscape" and "Wilderness Tips"', in *Borderblur: Essays on Poetry and Poetics in Contemporary Canadian Literature*, ed. Shirley Chew and Lynette Hunter (Edinburgh: Quadriga, 1996), pp. 9–18.

Munro, 'Wilderness Station'

Duncan, Isla J., '"It seems so much the truth it is the truth": Persuasive testimony in Alice Munro's *A Wilderness Station*', *Studies in Canadian Literature*, 28: 2 (2003), 98–110.

Smith, Rowland, 'Rewriting the Frontier: Wilderness and Social Code in the Fiction of Alice Munro', in *Telling Stories: Postcolonial Short Fiction in English*, ed. Jacqueline Bardolph (Amsterdam: Rodopi, 2001), pp. 77–90.

Thacker, Robert (ed.), *The Rest of the Story: Critical Essays on Alice Munro* (Toronto: ECW, 1999).

CHAPTER 3: DESIRE

Theories of desire

Belsey, Catherine, *Desire: Love Stories in Western Culture* (Oxford: Blackwell, 1994).

Bristow, Joseph, *Sexuality* (London: Routledge, 1997).

De Rougement, Denis, *Love in the Western World*, trans. Montgomery Belgion (New York: Schocken, 1990).

Goldie, Terry, *Pink Snow: Homotextual Possibilities in Canadian Fiction* (Peterborough, ON: Broadview, 2003).

Goodheart, Eugene, *Desire and Its Discontents* (New York: Columbia University Press, 1991).

Ostenso, *Wild Geese*

Atherton, Stan, *Martha Ostenso and Her Works* (Toronto: ECW, 1991).

Hammill, Faye, 'The Sensations of the 1920s: Martha Ostenso's *Wild Geese* and Mazo de la Roche's *Jalna*', *Studies in Canadian Literature*, 28: 2 (2003), 66–89.

Johnson, Brian, 'Unsettled Landscapes: Uncanny Discourses of Love in Ostenso's *Wild Geese*', *Wascana Review of Contemporary Poetry and Short Fiction*, 34: 2 (1999), 23–41.

Glassco, *Memoirs of Montparnasse*

Brown, Russell, 'Callaghan, Glassco and the Canadian Lost Generation', *Essays on Canadian Writing*, 51 (1993), 83–112.

Bentley, D. M. R. (ed.), *Canadian Poetry: Studies, Documents, Reviews*, 13 (1983) [special issue: John Glassco].

Kokotailo, Philip, *John Glassco's Richer World: Memoirs of Montparnasse* (Toronto: ECW, 1988).

Cohen, *Beautiful Losers*

Boucher, David, *Dylan and Cohen: Poets of Rock and Roll* (London: Continuum, 2004).

Dyck, E. F. (ed.), *Canadian Poetry: Studies, Documents, Reviews*, 33 (1993) [special issue: Proceedings of the Leonard Cohen Conference].

Scobie, Stephen (ed.), *Essays on Canadian Writing*, 69 (1999) [special issue: The Leonard Cohen Issue]. Also published as a book, *Intricate Preparations: Writing Leonard Cohen* (Toronto: ECW, 2000).

Michaels, *Fugitive Pieces*

Bentley, D. M. R., 'Anne Michaels' *Fugitive Pieces*', *Canadian Poetry: Studies, Documents, Reviews*, 41 (1997), 5–20.

Cook, Méira, 'At the Membrane of Language and Silence: Metaphor and Memory in *Fugitive Pieces*', *Canadian Literature*, 164 (2000), 12–33.

Criglington, Meredith, 'Urban Undressing: Walter Benjamin's "Thinking-in-Images" and Anne Michaels' Erotic Archaeology of Memory, *Canadian Literature*, 188 (2006), 86–102.

Brand, *Land to Light On*

Forster, Sophia, '"Inventory is useless now but just to say": The Politics of Ambivalence in Dionne Brand's *Land to Light On*', *Studies in Canadian Literature*, 27: 2 (2002), 160–82.

Fraser, Kaya, 'Language to Light On: Dionne Brand and the Rebellious Word', *Studies in Canadian Literature*, 30: 1 (2005), 291–308.

Walcott, Rinaldo, 'Rhetorics of Blackness, Rhetorics of Belonging: The Politics of Representation in Black Canadian Expressive Culture', *Canadian Review of American Studies*, 29: 2 (1999), 1–24.

CHAPTER 4: HISTORIES AND STORIES

History, postmodernism and Canadian literature

Adam, Ian and Helen Tiffin (eds), *Past the Last Post: Theorizing Post-Colonialism and Post-Modernism* (Calgary: University of Calgary Press, 1991).

Colavincenzo, Marc, 'Trading Magic for Fact', Fact for Magic: Myth and Mythologizing in Postmodern Canadian Historical Fiction (Amsterdam and New York: Rodopi, 2003).

Howells, Coral Ann (ed.), Where Are the Voices Coming From? Canadian Culture and the Legacies of History (Amsterdam and New York: Rodopi, 2004).

Hutcheon, Linda, The Canadian Postmodern: A Study of Contemporary English-Canadian Fiction (Toronto: Oxford University Press, 1988).

Hutcheon, Linda, A Poetics of Postmodernism: History, Theory, Fiction (London: Routledge, 1988).

Pratt, *Brébeuf and His Brethren*

Guth, Gwendolyn, 'Virtu(e)al History: Interpolation in Pratt's Brébeuf and His Brethren', in *Bolder Flights: Essays on the Canadian Long Poem*, ed. Frank M. Tierney and Angela Robbeson (Ottawa: University of Ottawa Press, 1998), pp. 81–9.

Johnson, James F., '*Brébeuf and His Brethren* and *Towards the Last Spike*: The Two Halves of Pratt's National Epic', *Essays on Canadian Writing*, 29 (1984), 142–51.

McAuliffe, Angela T., *Between the Temple and the Cave: The Religious Dimensions of the Poetry of E. J. Pratt* (Montreal and Kingston: McGill-Queen's University Press, 2000).

Atwood, *Journals of Susanna Moodie*

Johnston, Susan, 'Reconstructing the Wilderness: Margaret Atwood's Reading of Susanna Moodie', *Canadian Poetry: Studies, Documents, Reviews*, 13 (1992), 28–54.

Smyth, Jacqui, '"Divided Down the Middle": A Cure for *The Journals of Susanna Moodie*', *Essays on Canadian Writing*, 47 (1992), 149–62.

Stringer, Kim, 'Shared Experiences: Susanna Moodie Relived in Margaret Atwood's *The Journals of Susanna Moodie*', *British Journal of Canadian Studies*, 15: 1–2 (2002), 170–81.

Laurence, *Diviners*

Beckman-Long, Brenda, 'Genre and Gender: Autobiography and Self-Representation in *The Diviners*', *English Studies in Canada*, 30: 3 (2004), 89–110.

Coger, Greta M. K. McCormick (ed.), *New Perspectives on Margaret Laurence: Poetic Narrative, Multiculturalism, and Feminism* (Westport, CT: Greenwood, 1996).

Macfarlane, Karen E., '"A Place to Stand On": (Post)colonial Identity in *The Diviners* and "The Rain Child"', in *Is Canada Postcolonial? Unsettling Canadian Literature*, ed. Laura Moss (Waterloo, ON: Wilfrid Laurier University Press, 2003), pp. 223–36.

Marlatt, *Ana Historic*

Jones, Manina, *That Art of Difference: 'Documentary Collage' and English-Canadian Writing* (Toronto: University of Toronto Press, 1993).

Knutson, Susan, *Narrative in the Feminine: Daphne Marlatt and Nicole Brossard* (Waterloo, ON: Wilfrid Laurier University Press, 2000).

Zwicker, Heather, 'Daphne Marlatt's *Ana Historic*: Queering the Postcolonial Nation', *ARIEL: A Review of International English Literature*, 30: 2 (1999), 161–75.

Ondaatje, *In the Skin of a Lion*

Criglington, Meredith, 'The City as a Site of Counter-memory in Anne Michaels's *Fugitive Pieces* and Michael Ondaatje's *In the Skin of a Lion*', *Essays on Canadian Writing*, 81 (2004), 129–51.

Heble, Ajay, 'Putting together Another Family: *In the Skin of a Lion*, Affiliation, and the Writing of Canadian (Hi)stories', *Essays on Canadian Writing*, 56 (1995), 236–53.

Spearey, Susan, 'Mapping and Masking: The Migrant Experience in Michael Ondaatje's *In the Skin of a Lion*', *Journal of Commonwealth Literature*, 29: 2 (1994), 45–60.

CONCLUSION

The literary marketplace and the politics of culture in Canada

Coleman, Daniel, *White Civility: The Literary Project of English Canada* (Toronto: University of Toronto Press, 2006).

Corse, Sarah, *Nationalism and Literature: The Politics of Culture in Canada and the United States* (Cambridge: Cambridge University Press, 1997).

Davey, Frank, *Canadian Literary Power* (Edmonton: NeWest, 1994).

Huggan, Graham, *The Postcolonial Exotic: Marketing the Margins* (London: Routledge, 2001).

York, Lorraine, *Canadian Literary Celebrity* (Toronto: University of Toronto Press, 2007).

Authorship, publishing, and sociologies of reading

Gerson, Carole, *A Purer Taste: The Writing and Reading of Fiction in Nineteenth-Century Canada* (Toronto: University of Toronto Press, 1989).

Hammill, Faye, *Literary Culture and Female Authorship in Canada, 1760–2000* (Amsterdam and New York: Rodopi, 2003).

Karr, Clarence, *Authors and Audiences: Popular Canadian Fiction in the Early Twentieth Century* (Toronto: McGill-Queen's University Press, 2000).

MacSkimming. Roy, *The Perilous Trade: Publishing Canada's Authors* (Toronto: McClelland and Stewart, 2003).

Murray, Heather, *Come, Bright Improvement: The Literary Societies of Nineteenth-Century Ontario* (Toronto: University of Toronto Press, 2002).

Pedagogies of Canadian literature

Fee, Margery, 'Canadian Literature and English Studies in the Canadian University', *Essays on Canadian Writing*, 48 (1992–3), 20–40.

Fee, Margery and Monkman, Leslie, 'Teaching Canadian Literature', in *Encyclopedia of Literature in Canada*, ed. W. H. New (Toronto: University of Toronto Press, 2002), pp. 1084–9.

Mackey, Eva, *The House of Difference: Cultural Politics and National Identity in Canada* (Toronto: University of Toronto Press, 2002).

Murray, Heather, *Working in English: History, Institution, Resources* (Toronto: University of Toronto Press, 1996).

Sugars, Cynthia (ed.), *Home-Work: Postcolonialism, Pedagogy and Canadian Literature* (Ottawa: University of Ottawa Press, 2004).

Index